# Bring It Home with CorelDRAW®

## A Guide to In-House Graphic Design

## Roger Wambolt

**Course Technology PTR**

*A part of Cengage Learning*

COURSE TECHNOLOGY
CENGAGE Learning·

Australia, Brazil, Japan, Korea, Mexico, Singapore, Spain, United Kingdom, United States

# COURSE TECHNOLOGY
## CENGAGE Learning®

Bring It Home with CorelDRAW®
A Guide to In-House Graphic Design
Roger Wambolt

**Publisher and General Manager,
Course Technology PTR:**
Stacy L. Hiquet

**Associate Director of Marketing:**
Sarah Panella

**Manager of Editorial Services:**
Heather Talbot

**Marketing Manager:**
Mark Hughes

**Acquisitions Editor:**
Heather Hurley

**Project and Copy Editor:**
Marta Justak

**Technical Reviewer:**
Tony Severenuk

**Interior Layout:**
Jill Flores

**Cover Designer:**
Mike Tanamachi

**Indexer:**
Kelly Talbot Editing Services

**Proofreader:**
Kelly Talbot Editing Services

CorelDRAW® is a registered trademark of Corel Corporation in the United States and/or other countries.

All other trademarks are the property of their respective owners.

All images © Cengage Learning unless otherwise noted.

Library of Congress Control Number: 2012934300

ISBN-13: 978-1-4354-6101-7

ISBN-10: 1-4354-6101-0

**Course Technology, a part of Cengage Learning**
20 Channel Center Street
Boston, MA 02210
USA

Cengage Learning is a leading provider of customized learning solutions with office locations around the globe, including Singapore, the United Kingdom, Australia, Mexico, Brazil, and Japan. Locate your local office at: **international.cengage.com/region.**

Cengage Learning products are represented in Canada by Nelson Education, Ltd.

For your lifelong learning solutions, visit **courseptr.com.**

Visit our corporate Web site at **cengage.com.**

Printed in the United States of America
1 2 3 4 5 6 7 14 13 12

*To my wife Annie, for without her love and support,*
*this would not have happened.*

# Foreword

EVERYTHING THAT WE SEE or that we touch in our daily lives has been designed by someone at some point. Even if we are not designers ourselves, the vast majority of us recognize well-designed products, advertisements, magazines, outdoor signs, and packaging, because something about good design elicits positive emotional feelings. The quality of the design is also an intrinsic element of a brand or business, reflecting its values, its personality, its character, its relationship with its followers, and in many cases, a brand's key differentiator.

Think of Dyson vacuum cleaners, the Nike swoosh, the iPad, the John Deere or Rolls Royce logos, the Rolling Stones' tongue, the Android, or the latest magazine ad that appealed to you, and I'm certain that you immediately have a very accurate image in your mind for each of these brands. If we have made it easier for people to remember our brand or product through design, and it stirs our audiences' positive juices, then we have achieved a great deal. I wholeheartedly endorse Thomas J Watson Jr.'s assertion that "good design is good business," and in today's increasingly competitive markets, I believe that good design is a realizable competitive advantage for businesses of all sizes.

The challenge comes when it is time to translate our good ideas into an actual design. Some people will hire a design agency, but for those who want to express their ideas themselves, or who are on a limited budget, there is a professional grade graphics design software program that also caters to newcomers in the world of design, with automated hints attached to every design tool, and a wealth of tutorials, to help learn and get the job done faster.

Like any new software program, CorelDRAW Graphics Suite can be a little intimidating at first. Roger Wambolt's *Bring It Home with CorelDRAW* is an excellent companion to help you decipher the complexities and walk you through the key elements of design.

Roger has been a key member of Corel's customer support team for many years, and is a tireless evangelist of CorelDRAW, so consequently he is in constant contact with users whether on the phone, at trade shows, or at training events. From experienced graphic designers to screen printers, sublimators and engravers, or individuals working on their first design, he has helped them all! As such, Roger has first-hand experience with the difficulties that users encounter, and his knowledge of this powerful design software suite is second to none. In this practical book, Roger demystifies some of the design terminology, takes us through the design process, and explains the key elements of design and how they are applied in CorelDRAW. The latter chapters deal with topics such as creating your own workspaces that make the most sense to you and the tasks that you want to accomplish. There are examples of typical marketing collaterals that are suitable for any business, and Roger demonstrate how to use the numerous tools that come as part of the suite of programs to help you create these collateral materials. The step-by-step tutorials will help you learn the applications quickly, perfect your techniques, and create designs that you knew you could do but weren't sure how.

With interesting examples and clear graphics throughout the book, Roger takes us beyond the mental image of our idea and allows us to translate and prepare the design for output using CorelDRAW. Both educational and an excellent reference, *Bring It Home with CorelDRAW* will be particularly useful to you if you have acquired CorelDRAW Graphics Suite, helping you to get the most from this powerful design software program.

Design is an intrinsic part of everything around us, and I am continually amazed by the creativity and quality of design produced by CorelDRAW customers around the world. Many images that you encounter daily may have been designed using CorelDRAW. With the aid of this book and your own creativity, you can become the proud originator of tomorrow's memorable design and stir the emotions of a public always ready for something new.

I hope that you enjoy this book as much as I have, and that in conjunction with CorelDRAW Graphics Suite, your design skills will be extended and enhanced.

Graphically yours,

Nick Davies
Senior Vice President and General Manager of Graphics Software at Corel

# Acknowledgments

I HAVE THOUGHT ABOUT writing a dedication throughout the entire process, making a point of remembering those who have assisted along the way, and I realize that I would almost have to publish Corel's entire directory, for it is with the tireless dedication of the engineering department, the tenacity of technical support and customer service, and the achievements of the sales team that we have such a great product to be able to use as a design tool.

To say that this project has been one great learning experience is a huge understatement. Throughout the entire process I have had countless experiences, and there are many people whom I should thank for helping this book become a reality.

To Tony Severenuk, my technical editor—someone who I've admired for his skills, knowledge, and humor for the past 17 years at Corel. It is because of his technical expertise and assistance that this book will be a guide for years to come. I owe him a box of red pens!

To Heather Hurley and her team at Cengage for the assistance and coordination of the project, and to Marta Justak, my project editor for the tremendous guidelines and patience that she has provided on my first project of this sort. And for never letting up! Thank you, Marta.

To the developers who have spent countless hours coding and building such a fantastic product for you and me—and to the entire QA team and in particular, Sharon Potts, for her weekend MSN communications to keep me on track and help shed light on some of the mysteries.

To Mark Kelly, Joe Diaze, and the countless others who have assisted throughout the creation of this manuscript

To Cecile Brosius, CorelDRAW marketing manager, Lori Kerfoot and Ludmila Minkova from documentation, and Suzanne Smith, my counterpart over on the other side of the pond.

A special thank you to Nick Davies for writing the foreword for this book and so eloquently capturing the essence of design.

I have thoroughly enjoyed the experience of being able to share my knowledge and experience throughout the creation of this book.

And finally, but most importantly, to my wife, who has put up with many nights and weekends of me at the keyboard. Annie, I love you so much.

# About the Author

ROGER WAMBOLT is the owner of ADART Graphics, an Ottawa-based graphics training company that supports new and experienced graphic designers. Roger has a gift for explaining the "how to" in a fun and accessible way, whether you're creating a business card for the first time or working on a complex sign project.

Roger's graphics career started 17 years ago in the trenches at Corel, providing graphics support for users, and over the years, building a team and

relationships with graphics professionals at all levels and in a variety of verticals, including print, sublimation, screen printing, sign making, engraving, and embroidery.

A CorelDRAW Graphics Suite expert, Roger is a popular presenter at industry tradeshows. He has developed and conducted classroom training and online sessions throughout North America and has authored articles for key industry magazines, including *SQE Professional.*

# About the Technical Editor

PRIOR TO HIS TENURE AT COREL, Tony was a prepress and software technician. Starting on the front lines at Corel in 1993, Tony spent the next five years working toward the ultimate goal— joining the development team.

Assisting with the development of CorelDRAW 9 and beyond, Tony has been helping to influence the direction of CorelDRAW and teach it to users around the world.

Tony is the foremost authority on CorelDRAW and has been the technical editor on literally dozens of publications over the years.

# Contents

## Chapter 4    Elements of Design—File Formats . . . . . . . . 55

## Chapter 5    Elements of Design—Typography . . . . . . . . 71

## Chapter 6   Elements of Design—Color . . . . . . . . . . . . . 85

## Chapter 7   Elements of Design—Resolution . . . . . . . . 101

## Chapter 8   Create Layouts with Ease . . . . . . . . . . . . . 113

## Chapter 9     Designing Your Business Graphic . . . . . . 145

## Appendix A    Troubleshooting 101 for CorelDRAW  ... 203

# Introduction

So, YOU WORK FOR A SMALL FIRM, and you have been asked to look into getting a brochure created for the sales group. You've had some graphic design experience back in college, and you feel that you can tackle the job yourself rather than sending it to the design firm that the company has used in the past. You want to make sure that you cover all the bases to get the artwork ready for the printer, but where do you start?

This book is a guide for the small business employee who may have some basic design and computer skills to create some of the company's graphic needs in-house. It is for those who want to get their work done faster without spending hours learning an application. Using guidelines as well as tips, tricks, and techniques to produce professional-quality designs, this book will walk you through the steps.

This book was written to provide insight into what is required to be able to produce an effective communication piece or to advertise and promote the company that you work for. Starting with an overview of the design process, the book then explains the various elements of style guides.

Next, the book covers the Welcome screen, and shows you how to use the tools and features to create various projects through simple tutorials and concepts. The book also offers templates so you can jump right into a design and get the work done faster, without having to spend weeks learning how to use the application.

After reviewing the elements of design (file formats, typography, and color), you'll move into the various lessons that will make it possible to use the application more effectively and create designs in fewer steps.

CorelDRAW Graphics Suite can help you meet your company's design needs and produce the high-quality pieces that will ensure that you and your company stand out.

One thing to note is that although the tutorials in this book have been written using CorelDRAW X6, they can also be accomplished with older versions of the Corel Graphics Suite, unless otherwise noted.

You will also find a number of appendices, where you will have access to troubleshooting tips and steps to keep you up and running and to assist in any situation where you may run into problems.

Of course, a publication of this nature would not be complete without a glossary of common and industry terms to help you understand the lingo. Finally, Appendix D (an online appendix) features application-specific and design-related Web links that offer insight into design guidelines and a variety of related topics—clipart, raster images, and fonts that can be accessed online.

My hope is that this guide will be something that you use as a reference while creating your designs and working in CorelDRAW.

I hope that you enjoy this book half as much as I did writing it.

—Roger Wambolt

# Enjoy
# the
# Experience

# The Design Process

**1**

I T DOESN'T REALLY MATTER if you work in a large company, a small firm, or are self-employed. If you want to be able to create your own design pieces and control their appearance, you simply have to follow some guidelines in order for the process to be relatively smooth and successful. Graphic design is not just about throwing some images and text on a page and hoping that it does the intended job. It really is much more—it is an art form all unto itself.

# The Design Process

OBVIOUSLY, THERE ARE CERTAIN guidelines to follow to ensure a successful piece. In this chapter, we will look at the design process. In later chapters, we will cover the elements of design and the various tools required to carry out the tasks.

## What Is Graphic Design?

Merriam-Webster dictionary defines graphic design as: *The art or profession of using design elements (as typography and images) to convey information or an effect; also a product of this art.*

The process for creating graphic material begins with a series of steps that start with the need for a specific piece. This need can stem from an idea, a marketing requirement, a demand by customers, or another design that needs some additional material. Once the need has been identified, the process can be broken down into specific steps. By following these steps, you'll help to ensure a successful outcome.

1. Create an outline or brief for what is required.

2. In the brief, sketch any ideas that you or your client may have or require.

3. Review the ideas for likes, dislikes, and emotions.

4. Create mock-ups for review.

5. Present the concept.

6. Develop and produce the solution.

7. Give the final presentation.

# The Brief Is the Foundation

THE BRIEF IS VITAL to the project because it captures all the details of what is required for the design project. The brief guides the design process by highlighting specific questions that the project must focus on.

The following list of questions assumes that you know the company, the product or service, who the clients are, and who the competition is. If you are new to the company, there is additional research that you will have to conduct before the work can start.

1. What is the goal of the project? Is it to increase sale, increase awareness, or an administrative piece?

2. Who is the target audience?

3. What copy (messaging) or graphic images would be required and what colors are to be used?

4. What are the specifications of the project? These specs could include details such as size, number of pages (if multipage), and where it will be used (printed or Web).

5. What is the budget for the project in terms of time and cost? The cost needs to cover items such as printing and the purchase of stock photos or art, if required.

6. Are there any templates, designs, or previous art to follow as a guideline?

Create a few different concepts that can be presented for approval. The process may involve several iterations, but you will need to narrow down the choices of design before the final presentation. This is where the design brief and the research that was conducted earlier will come into play.

All projects that you undertake should have a similar flow to the actual mechanics of creating a design. There is a definite start and end to the process of creating a piece of collateral or a design. Let's take a look at an example of a logo designed for a business.

# Setting Up a Business

IN THIS EXAMPLE, a small used car dealership is starting up and will be operating from the property of an existing auto repair shop. The existing shop, R&R Auto Limited, is owned by Ricky and Robert, two long-time friends, business partners, and highly qualified mechanics. The owner of the new automotive sales company is Ron. Ron is a former race car driver and performance driving instructor. The name of the new company is 3R Motors Ltd. The goal is to come up with a logo that can be used on letterhead, business cards, building signage, and other materials required to run the day-to-day operation.

The need has been generated: To create a logo for a new company along with a viewpoint. To create the brief, we need to investigate the market, the area, and the personal likes and dislikes of the owner (remember, he's a former race car driver). We'll need to tie into the existing R&R Auto logo by utilizing some of their basic colors and clean lines. After the list of tasks, such as interviewing the owner, determining the exact needs, who the target market is, where the logo will be used, preferred colors, and so on, it's time to formulate some concepts.

Through our research process, we uncovered the following salient points:

- ▶ This is a new business.
- ▶ The owner is new to the automobile sales industry.
- ▶ This business must align with the core values of "honesty and integrity" established and diligently practiced by R&R Auto Limited.

- ▶ The client base is expected to be primarily in the following two categories:
  - ❏ Existing clients of R&R Auto Limited who want to upgrade their current vehicle (quality vehicle that meets the needs and has undergone a thorough safety inspection).
  - ❏ Clients looking for a specific performance/luxury vehicle (where the vehicle is viewed as "more than just transportation").
- ▶ The business can be defined in one sentence: Align with R&R Auto for sales to its clients.
- ▶ Customers already appreciate the quality and customer service the business provides for high-performance, high-end vehicles.
- ▶ The business in a few words is exclusive and what the customer wants.
- ▶ Who is the customer? Someone who appreciates the finer things in life at a reasonable price and who knows quality, as well as someone looking for a good honest deal.

After we completed the design concepts, we met with the owner to hone in on a preferred design. This is the stage where time must be taken to review the logo and consider input from other friends, colleagues, and possibly key clients. At this stage, some designs will go over well and others will be rejected, so you can narrow down what everyone agrees on (see Figure 1.1).

When the final decision for our logo was reached, we made any necessary adjustments and received final approval of the new design from the owner (see Figure 1.2).

**Figure 1.2**
*This design shows the completed logo based on feedback and revisions from the business owner.*

After the approval of the logo, it's time to take the design to the next stage. At this point, you can create the various versions that are required: business cards, work orders, invoices, and so on. The owner in our example also requests a version that can be embroidered on polo shirts, caps, and jackets.

Keeping with the clean lines and the theme of "performance vehicles," the customer asked us to create an image that could be used as a design on his signage, and more importantly, as a decal placed on all vehicles that were sold. This design shown in Figure 1.3 will also be used as part of the masthead on the website.

**Figure 1.1**
*Here you can see a few of the designs that were rejected by 3R Motors. They all work, but at this point it is the owner's decision.*

**Figure 1.3**
*Here is the design that will be used for all vehicles sold, as well as the masthead for the website.*

The bottom line is that care and attention to detail must be taken when working on a design. There is an old idiom that says that the "devil is in the details"—and a graphic designer *could* have coined that phrase. Well, not really, but suffice it to say that a small oversight or error, if not caught in time, can turn into an extra expense at the printer or a publication that might look very unprofessional. And if it's an error in the design, the designer absorbs that expense.

# Working with the Manage Workspace

WHEN DESIGNING, you can minimize the chances of making errors by establishing a style guide that can be used for the design and will also help on proofing the document. The style guide will be your reference that illustrates the correct usage of the organization's logo and covers all the various iterations, such as color, black-and-white line art, and grayscale. It provides guidelines and restrictions. The manual correctly identifies the names (or Pantone numbers in the use of spot colors) of each color used. It also gives exact instructions for how logos should be placed in reference to other graphic elements on a page (their dimensions in terms of size and the percentage of the space to be used) and stipulates other restrictions.

Topics within a style guide might include the following:

> ▶ **Logo:** This information would include restrictions for the logo, which may include colors, positioning white space around the logo, and any objects placed within proximity of the logo (see Figure 1.4).

▶ **Tagline:** The tagline is a phrase that customers will use to remember the company. Make sure that it is used consistently, particularly when used with the logo or on its own in marketing and promotional materials. As an example, the tagline for R&R auto is "Stay Tuned"—a play on words of how people should keep their automobiles, as well as what is to come.

▶ **Colors:** Colors are extremely important in portraying the proper logo. If you want to ensure color consistency across all designs, it would be best to use a spot color. One exception to this is during the creation of Web page elements, where typically RGB color values will be used for the logo. The style guide will list the appropriate spot colors used in the logo and any other content that represents the corporate identity, as well as CMYK and RGB values. We will discuss color models a bit later in Chapter 6, "Elements of Design—Color."

▶ **Size, scaling, and clear space:** When using a logo, it is important to allow for enough clear space or blank area around the logo so that it does not appear cluttered. It's also necessary to ensure that other objects do not obstruct or change the appearance of the logo and that there is a minimum size at which the logo can be viewed.

▶ **Typography:** Just as important as the other design elements, and possibly even more, are the fonts used within the logo (if any) and with the copy text. Using fonts from the same type families is essential to maintain a consistent look and feel. Using different, inconsistent fonts or even too many fonts is one of the fastest ways to ruin a look. You should use the same fonts throughout the design piece. Constantly changing fonts can cause the design to look cluttered. As a rule, you should not use any more that two or three fonts in any one design.

▶ **Suggested Templates:** Templates can be used to ensure a consistent professional image, as well as for speed when creating various repetitive pieces. When a template is used for something like an ad, the content will vary, but the layout or format should be consistent. Samples are shown in Figures 1.5 and 1.6.

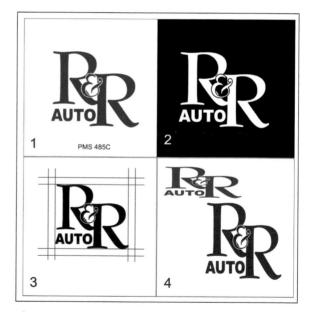

**Figure 1.4**
*Here you can see a short list of items to take into consideration when positioning a logo. 1. Specific color with spot value. 2. Reverse logo. 3. Boundary showing clear space. 4. Image distortion.*

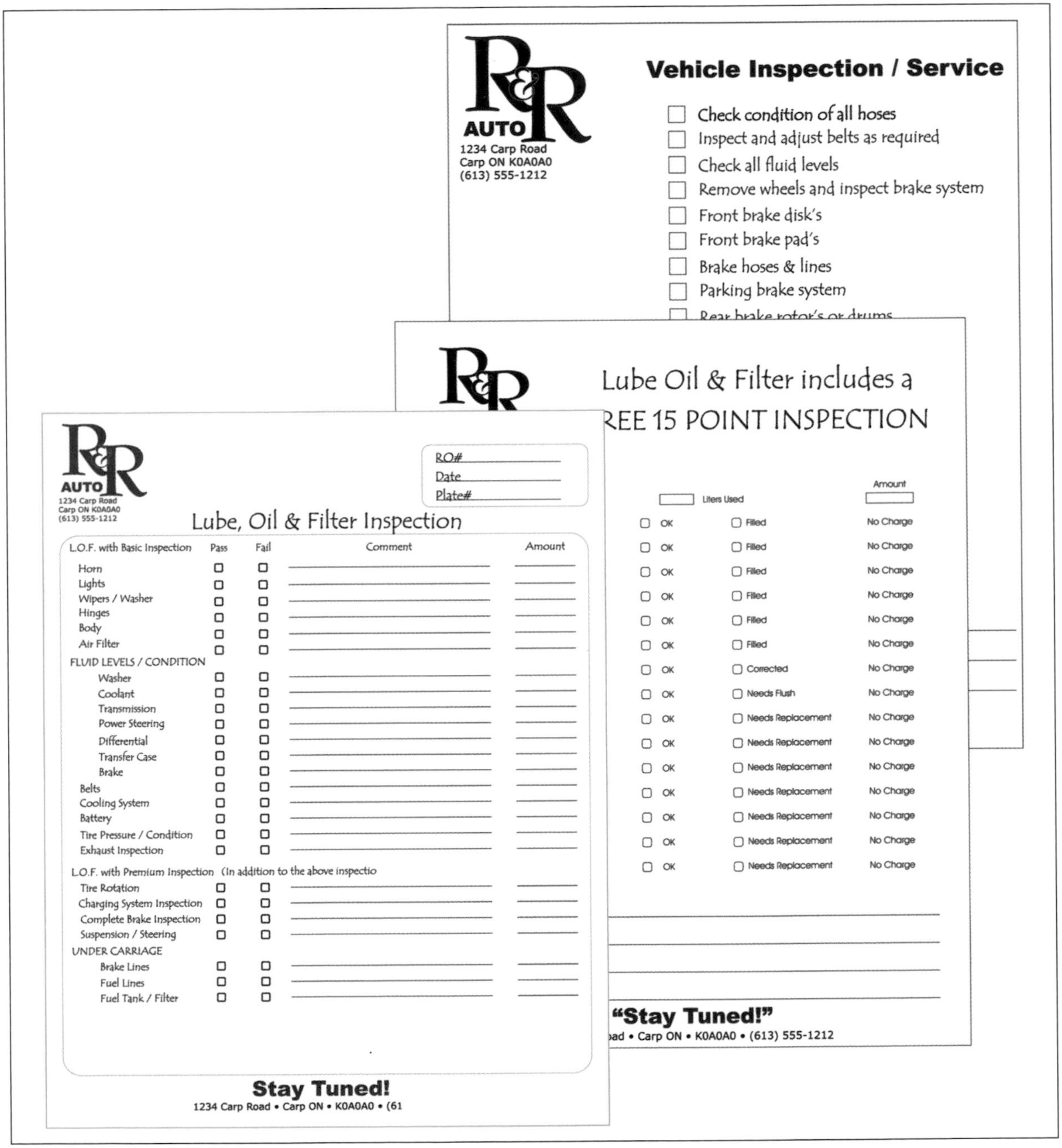

**Figure 1.5**

*Similar to print ads, printed materials must all work together as a family, and the layout must be done in a consistent and professional way. The usage and opportunities for printed materials will change and evolve as marketing and communications needs change.*

**Figure 1.6**
*Pictured here is a sample of an ad that could be used in print media, such as a newspaper or a handbill.*

While it is simple enough to create your own style guide, be sure you cover all the aspects, including the type of collateral required. This would also include, but is certainly not limited to, business cards, letterhead, envelopes, order forms, feature sheets, and even website design guidelines. The primary factor to consider is consistency—this cannot be stressed enough. Once you have the style guide created, the rest is relatively easy for everyone to follow.

When you set out to create a template guide, remember that there are a number of free templates available on the Internet, so take a bit of time and browse around. Find one that suits your needs and make use of it, but feel free to customize it. Years down the road, you will be glad that you did.

After your entire design has been completed, make sure that you review a hard copy as well as soft copy. When you are done, have someone else review it as well, because it is very easy for small details to be overlooked by the creator. You will be amazed how someone else will be able to find some little detail that you missed, which could become a major issue when it goes to press, or worse, is spotted by a customer.

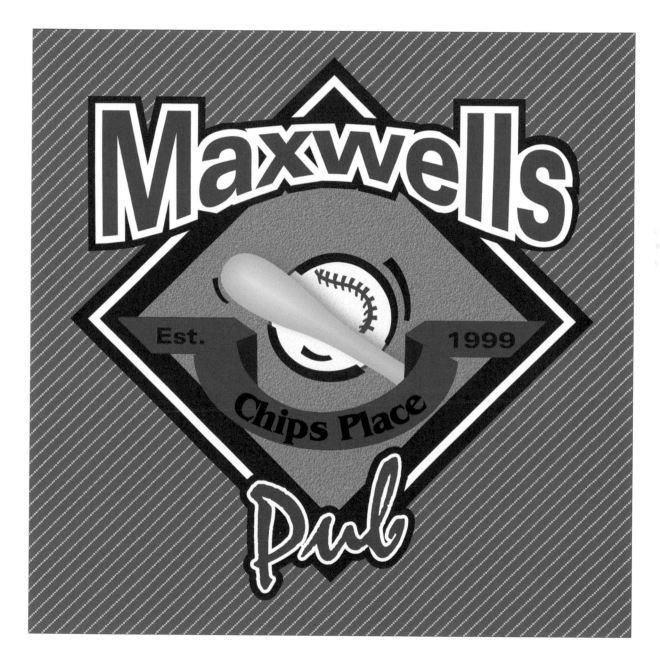

# The History of CorelDRAW

## 2

I N JUNE OF 1985, Corel Corporation was founded by Michael Cowpland to produce a turnkey desktop publishing system. With hardware and software from different manufacturers, Corel had a vehicle for adding utilities that were created in-house and the ability to produce a utility called *Corel Headline*.

Corel Headline was a software package that was created as an add-on to Ventura Publisher. The add-on was a simple program for producing graphic effects on type, as well as creating headlines and other effects in Ventura, which was a program that had very basic graphics capabilities at the time.

# The Ultimate Illustration Package

IN 1987, COREL BEGAN TO DEVOTE additional resources to developing a separately packaged illustration software program. It was to be the "Ventura of draw packages," which meant that it was going to be the first on the market, easy to use, packed with features, and relatively inexpensive, according to Mark Charlseworth, one of the original creators. On January 16, 1989, Corel Corporation shipped the first copy of its product out the door, code-named Waldo (see Figure 2.1).

**Figure 2.1**
*Waldo was the mascot for the release of CorelDRAW 1.0. Waldo was created to "give the product a bit of personality" and was sketched by Mark Charlseworth.*

CorelDRAW was "the ultimate illustration package for all user skill levels working in black and white or color"—with pull-down menus and an icon-based toolbox that worked interactively with a mouse or graphics tablet. Fifty precision fonts were included for LaserJet, PaintJet, and Postscript printers. The result was a true WYSIWYG (*what you see is what you get*) graphics application, which built on the special effects that were available in Corel Headline.

The application was widely well received and outsold all expectations. In April 1989, to accommodate the growing demand by sign makers and others who made use of this basic, yet very powerful program, Corel released version 1.02, which included more than 340 "clip art" images and added 102 different type fonts from 35 font families. To go along with this, a visual guide in the form of a poster to all fonts was also included.

In 1991, the release of CorelDRAW 2 saw a number of new features, including the following:

▶ Print Merge that enabled users to merge text files with graphics files

▶ Envelope tool

▶ Blend tool

▶ Extrusion tool for simulating perspective and volume in objects

▶ Perspective tool

Figure 2.2 shows the splash screen for CorelDRAW 2.0.

**Figure 2.2**
*Corel's new splash screen.*

### A First in the Industry

Although CorelDRAW 3 was the first full retail version to be provided on a CD-ROM, there was actually an earlier release. CorelDRAW 2.01L came on CD, and it was bundled with a DVD drive, Corel LS 2000 SCSI controller, and Corel drivers.

# CorelDRAW 3 and Full Color Design

As of October 1992, with the release of CorelDRAW 3.0, users no longer had to work in black-and-white or wireframe mode. The software program was more robust and easier to design in full color. CorelDRAW 3 had one other thing that made it stand out: It was the first software title to be available on CD-ROM.

In July 1994, color management was added to CorelDRAW 5, allowing users to custom calibrate monitors, printers, and scanners to achieve a more accurate on-screen representation of colors used in documents. This meant that a designer would know what to expect from the design before the file was actually output, which was a huge benefit.

### Easter Egg Hunt

It was around this time period that software manufacturers began putting "Easter Eggs" in the software, which were hidden pictures, messages, or animations. In CorelDRAW 5, if the user was lucky, he could find caricatures of Elvis Presley parachuting from the sky.

# CorelDRAW 6 Improves Printing

ON AUGUST 24, 1995, the release of CorelDRAW 6 had a major impact on the printing industry (see Figure 2.3). Previously, the maximum page size that a designer could create in any Windows application was 36" × 36". With this new release, an impressive 150' × 150' was possible. What this meant was that a designer could create a full-sized billboard or floor plan to scale within CorelDRAW. This addition occurred at the same time that digital printers began printing on adhesive-backed vinyl and that large format prints became available.

**Figure 2.3**
*Here is the splash screen for CorelDRAW 6. CorelDRAW 6 was launched on the same day as Windows 95, August 24, 1995, and it was the first 32-bit design software created for Windows.*

## Additional Releases Add Impressive Features

With the release of each new version, designers were surprised by the tools and features that were added. In 1997, CorelDRAW 7 was released with the context-sensitive Property bar that brought tool parameters to the front so that designers and artists would not have to access submenus or dig into other dialogs. A number of interactive tools, including Interactive Fill, Blend, Transparency, and Envelope, as well as the Find & Replace wizard, were also added.

Various features, such as access to automation for script creation and new writing tools, were added to include an automatic spell checker, thesaurus, and grammar checker.

The addition of still more interactive tools allowed the designer to view the effects as they were being created. Multiple file import was added with the release of CorelDRAW 8, which allowed the designer to import multiple images at a time.

When Corel released CorelDRAW Graphics Suite 9, it included such additions as the ability to have multiple palettes on the screen at the same time, a number of interactive tools including the mesh fill, and the capability to edit color palettes.

Later, a Premium Color Edition of CorelDRAW 9 was released that included professional color management software from Heidelberger Druckmaschinen AG (Heidelberg). This edition gave the ability to color calibrate systems of graphic designers and others who were using high-end digital output, as well as offset printing. At the time, Jim Oran, executive vice president of sales and marketing for Corel Corporation, said, "CorelDRAW 9 Premium Color Edition offers service bureaus, output centers, and professional designers phenomenal control over their color quality." Also added in version 9 was the ability to work with more than one color palette at a time on-screen and to create custom color palettes or edit existing custom palettes with the new Palette Editor.

In the early 2000s, the digital print industry was working on re-engineering hardware and software, including raster image processors (RIP). Other software was also being improved, including CorelDRAW. With the launch of CorelDRAW Graphics Suite 10, a Page Sorter view was added that would enable users to view thumbnails of all the pages in a document and streamline their workflow by specifying trapping and separations parameters in advance, with a full range of In-RIP trapping options for PostScript level 3 output devices and In-RIP separations options. Also included in this release was a completely redesigned user interface (UI) that made color management more intuitive by combining all the essential color management options in one dialog box.

In August 2002, Corel released CorelDRAW Graphics Suite 11, and a year and a half later released CorelDRAW Graphics Suite 12. These versions added features such as a three-point rectangular and ellipse tool, the ability to maintain text formatting when pasting text in from another application, and dynamic guidelines. Dynamic guidelines would allow the user to precisely position, align, and draw objects relative to other objects.

CorelDRAW Graphics Suite X3 introduced a new tracing engine, Corel PowerTRACE, to convert bitmaps into vector graphics, a new Cutout lab in

Corel PHOTO-PAINT, and a new Image Adjustment Lab to quickly improve digital photos. This version also added vector object cropping, previously only possible with bitmaps.

This version introduced a brand new tracing engine called *PowerTRACE* to convert raster images into vector graphics. Also added was the capability to crop vector objects, previously only possible with raster images. This capability would allow designers to easily take a portion of a vector design and repurpose it. Create Boundary was another innovative tool that was added so that screen printers and vinyl cutters could easily create a white base or cut line.

The release of CorelDRAW Graphics Suite X4 in 2008 catered to the user's workflow unlike any previous version, as it included enhanced features such as centerline trace and the ability to merge objects of the same color within PowerTRACE. Other new and enhanced features included interactive tables, additional file format support (including PDF 1.7 and Microsoft Publisher 2007), camera raw support for over 300 cameras, and independent page layers. Online services for collaboration (CorelDRAW ConceptShare) and font identification were also introduced. In keeping with market demand, this version was certified for Windows Vista.

CorelDRAW Graphics Suite X5 sped up the entire design process with significant workflow enhancements. It introduced Corel CONNECT, which included a built-in content finder, a new color management engine for more accurate color control, multicore processing, expanded file compatibility, new drawing features, the option to lock toolbars in place, and new Web capabilities. This version was also optimized for Windows 7 with new touch-screen support.

# And Finally, CorelDRAW X6

THIS NOW BRINGS US TO CorelDRAW X6, released in March of 2012. As always, Corel exceeds itself with each new release. This one is no different. There are a number of enhancements such as new drawing tools, enhanced search capabilities for Corel CONNECT, new typography and styles engines, and a new context sensitive Object Properties docker. By far the biggest impact with this release is the work that has been done with Open Type fonts, the new styles engine, and color harmonies.

As you can see, over the past 20 plus years there have been many, many innovations and milestones that Corel has achieved. From what was originally an add-on to a page-layout program has matured into a robust, easy-to-use application that is packed with features and is relatively inexpensive, exactly what it set out to be in the beginning. It's the perfect tool to enable users to bring their design needs in-house and accomplish the tasks themselves.

# Set Up and Start Smoothly

## 3

**P**ROBABLY THE BEST PLACE TO START, assuming that CorelDRAW is properly installed, is with the Welcome screen. Gone are the days when the Welcome screen was the starting point to create a new document, open an existing document, or start from a template, and little else. Recent versions (and I am referring to CorelDRAW X3 and later) have gone a long way toward providing you with learning tools to make your experience a smooth and educational one.

# The Welcome Screen

UNLIKE OTHER APPLICATIONS, the Welcome Screen within CorelDRAW is now a learning center provided so that you don't have to take a course on how to use the program, as you do with some other graphic applications.

Let's take a look at the CorelDRAW X6 Welcome screen, as shown in Figure 3.1, to see what can be accessed from within each of the tabs.

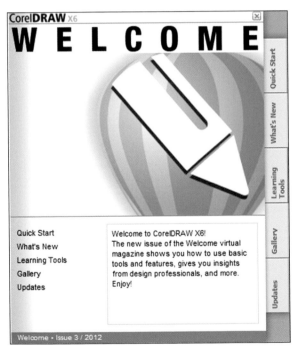

**Figure 3.1**
*The Welcome screen is more like a "virtual magazine" that has five tabs to show you where and how to begin.*

## The Quick Start Tab

The Quick Start tab (see Figure 3.2) shows on the left a preview of one of the previously opened documents that the cursor is currently hovering over just to the right in the Open Recent section. If you have multiple documents listed under Open Recent and scroll through the list, you can see a preview of each of the documents and select the document that you want to open. At the bottom of this area is the option Open other, which will allow you to open a document that may not be included in the list of Open Recent documents.

**Figure 3.2**
*The Quick Start tab is the first page of the Welcome newsletter that appears when you launch CorelDRAW.*

To the right of this area, there are two options: New blank document and New from Template. We will look at each one of these separately.

## New Blank Document

Once you click on the New blank document link on the Welcome screen, it will open the Create a New Document dialog box with the same settings that were used the last time that a new document was created. This is a great time saver in that it quickly allows you to start your next project (see Figure 3.3).

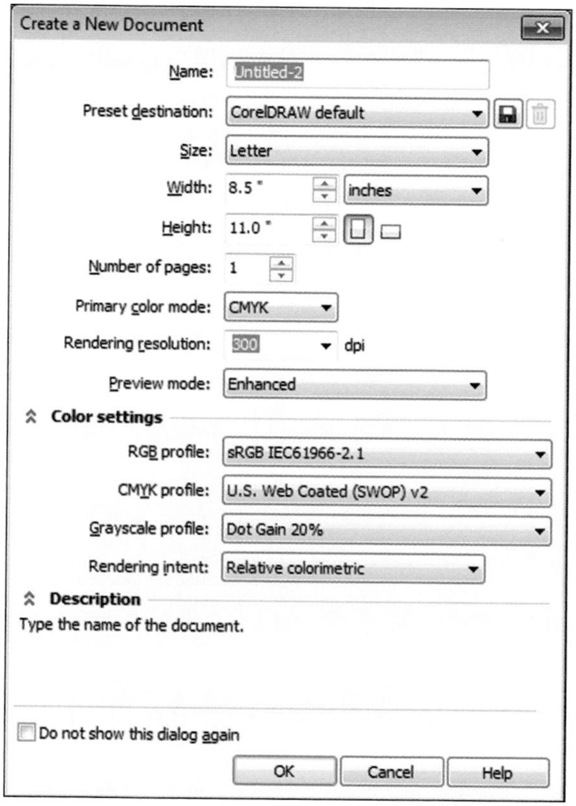

**Figure 3.3**
*The Create a New Document dialog box allows you to select the various settings that will dictate how the new page will be configured.*

There are a number of parameters that can be modified when starting a new document:

▶ **Name:** Allows you to enter the name that you want to give the document. By default, it will simply be called "Untitled" followed by a number.

▶ **Preset Destination:** Includes preset destinations such as CorelDRAW defaults, Default RGB, Web, Default CMYK, and Custom. Selecting any of these settings will determine the other settings within this tab and ultimately the document.

▶ **Size:** Enables the user to select one of 57 different page or document sizes; there is also an option to select a custom page size.

**Did You Know?**

## How Big Can It Be?

Since CorelDRAW 6, the maximum page size for CorelDRAW has been 150 feet $\times$ 150 feet. Try printing that on your desktop printer!

▶ **Width:** Enters a horizontal measurement to the document that you are about to create.

▶ **Height:** Enters a vertical measurement to the document that you are about to create.

▶ **Units:** Selects units from the drop-down next to Width. They include inches, millimeters, pica, points, pixels, ciceros, didots, feet, yards, miles, centimeters, meters, kilometers, and Q and H.

**Did You Know?**

# The Origin of Q and H

Old phototypesetting machines were used to create type on a scroll of photographic film. The "block" or character used was measured in Q and H. This is the gear setting that would pull the film through at a specific speed past a beam of light. Lenses would enlarge or reduce the size of type on the film.

▶ **Number of Pages:** Enables you to select the numbers of pages for a potential document. The maximum number of pages that can be created in a single document is 999; however, more pages in a document means more content and therefore larger file sizes.

▶ **Primary Color Mode:** Allows you to set the default mode for the document. The default color mode affects which color palette is shown, as well as which color model will be the default used when converting color formats and will affect how colors appear. This also determines the colors used when dealing with such things as blends, fills, transparencies, and drop shadows.

▶ **Rendering Resolution:** Sets the default resolution for effects that are created, such as transparencies, drop shadows, and bevel effects. The values selected here are determined by the type of document that is being created.

▶ **Preview Mode:** Changes the way in which a document is displayed on-screen when it is being created. This option can be changed once in the actual document from under the View menu.

▶ **Color Settings:** Allows you to select the color profile that the document will use for RGB, CMYK, and Grayscale, as well as setting the rendering intent.

## New from Template

New from Template is the final option on the Quick Start tab. Selecting this option will open the New from Template dialog box, which will give you access to some creatively designed layouts to use as a starting point for your own designs (see Figure 3.4). The New from Template dialog box has three main areas: the Filter area, Templates, and Designer Notes.

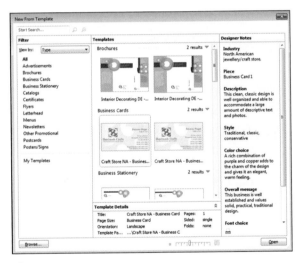

**Figure 3.4**
*The New from Template dialog box is a great place to start if you want to generate a design quickly and have the basic elements already laid out for you.*

### Filter

In the Filter section, you can select templates based on either Type or Industry, and there is also an option to view only custom templates that you may have created.

Viewing by Type will list some of the categories that you would expect to find when creating content for a small business, similar to what we are designing in this book. The categories include items such as Advertisements, Brochures, Business Cards, Business Stationery, Catalogs, Certificates, and so on.

If you are viewing the filters by Industry, it will include such verticals as Community, Education, Hospitality, and Recreation, just to name a few. When creating a custom template, you have the ability to use these categories or create your own.

### *Templates*

Within the Templates panel, you can see a preview of the various templates that are available. Depending on what Type or Industry you have selected under the Filter category, that will determine what thumbnails you will see.

Under the category of Template Details, you can see the specifications of the template that you selected (refer to Figure 3.4). These include Title, Page Size, Orientation, Template Path, Pages, Sides, and Folds.

### *Designer Notes*

The Designer Notes offer insight as to the best uses for the specific template. They can include information such as the type of Industry, Description, Style, Color Choice, and various pieces of information. The type of information can vary depending on the template.

## What's New?

The What's New tab is where you find, well, what's new! This is a listing of some of the key features that have been added to the application since the previous release (see Figure 3.5). As this book is not really version specific, I will not go into detail as to what is under each of the headings of every version, but as an example, the What's New tab for CorelDRAW Graphics Suite X6 reveals that this version has had a number of major features added, as well as improvements to provide better control and performance while creating your design.

**Figure 3.5**
*The What's New tab within the Welcome screen provides information on some of the major enhancements of CorelDRAW X6.*

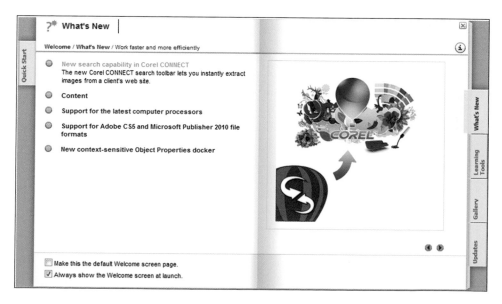

# Learning Tools

Probably the best place to start for anyone using CorelDRAW for the first time would be on the Learning Tools tab within the Welcome screen (see Figure 3.6). Here you will find access to video tutorials, text-based tutorials, and a number of other items that will make the learning process both easy and sometimes fun.

> ▶ **Video Tutorials:** You can watch a series of videos that will take you through the basics of the product. There are typically two full hours of training videos that guide you through learning the more common tasks.

> ▶ **Guidebook:** The guidebook is a link to the downloadable PDF file for CorelDRAW. This book will help you get started with CorelDRAW, and it provides an application overview, tips, techniques, tutorials, and a gallery of artwork. Prior to CorelDRAW Graphics Suite X5, there was a printed manual.

> ▶ **Insights from the Experts:** Here you will find a number of PDF files that are profiles

of professionals who use CorelDRAW on a daily basis to produce exceptional work. These profiles typically take one of the individual's projects and break it down with the objective of teaching how it was built.

> ▶ **Tips & Tricks | History:** This is a link that will provide you with a few tips and tricks that will help speed up your design process. Clicking on History will reveal additional tips for your review. As an example, you can add 10% tint of a color to a selected object by holding down the Ctrl key and clicking on a color swatch in one of the color palettes. For more tips like this, see Appendix C, "Tips, Tricks, and Techniques from the Professionals."

# Gallery

The gallery will provide you with ideas and inspiration, either before you start on a project or possibly when you are in the middle of a design and need to look at it from a different perspective (see Figure 3.7). Clicking on the small triangle in the lower-right corner will allow you to "flip through the pages" of the gallery to view the content.

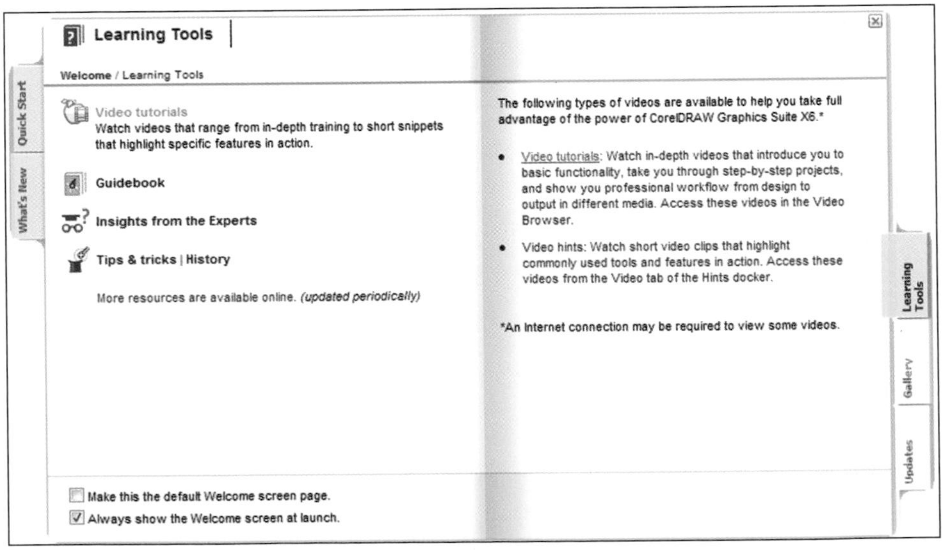

**Figure 3.6**
*The Learning Tools tab provides direct access to tools that will assist those who are new to CorelDRAW or the current version of the application.*

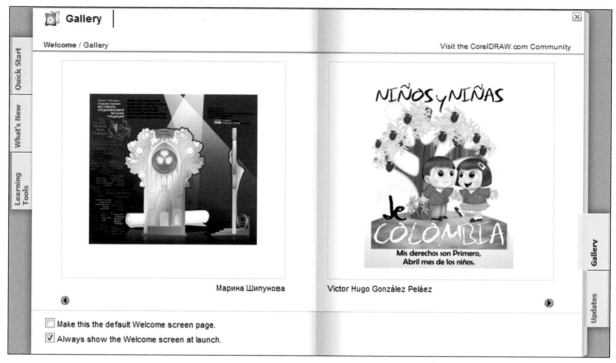

**Figure 3.7**
*Here are a couple of the designs that can be viewed while flipping through the pages of the Gallery.*

## Updates

Updates is the final tab of the Welcome screen, and it gives you the periodic updates that are released for your current version of CorelDRAW. If when turning to this page, you see nothing listed, this is a good indication that you are already running the most current service pack.

Also on the Updates tab is a link for the CorelDRAW community at www.coreldraw.com.

# Hints and Highlight What's New

HINTS AND HIGHLIGHT WHAT'S NEW are two features that, when used in conjunction with each other, help to reveal and explain the new tools and features, particularly when used together. Let's go ahead and start a new document by clicking on the Quick Start tab and selecting New blank document, and you will see what they are all about. For the purpose of this next section, just click the OK button at the bottom of the Create a New Document dialog, and this will select all the defaults.

## Hints

On the right-hand side of the screen are dialogs that are referred to as dockers. A docker is a window or palette that can be, well, docked anywhere on the screen. By default, these are on the right. To access these and many other dockers, go to the Window menu and scroll down to Dockers (see Figure 3.8).

The Hints docker is visible or "on" by default and can be seen in Figure 3.9. The Hints docker is a place where you can learn about the tool that is currently selected, and it will update as you work on your drawing.

A new feature within CorelDRAW Graphics Suite X6 is the Videos tab. These small videos also provide assistance with some of the tools.

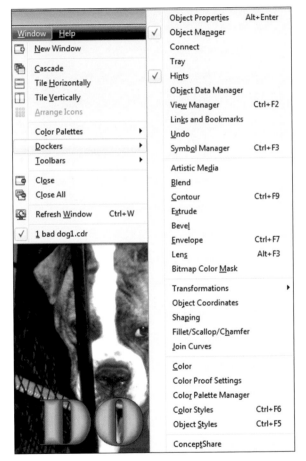

**Figure 3.8**
*These are just a few of the dockers that are available within CorelDRAW. Dockers that have a checkmark to the left of the name are those that are currently open and are visible on the screen.*

In Figure 3.9, I have the Blend tool selected, and you can see that the docker is providing hints for the Blend tool. If for some reason, there is not enough information here, simply click on the small icon of the book in the upper-right corner of the docker, and you will navigate to the information on the Blend tool in the Help file.

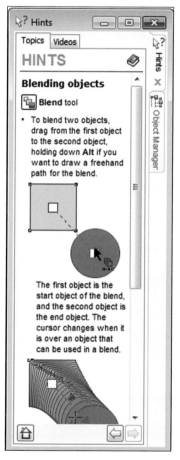

**Figure 3.9**
*The Hints docker is a great way to get a better understanding of exactly how the tool works.*

# Highlights

Corel wants to make it as easy as possible if you upgrade from a previous version. With the release of CorelDRAW X3, a feature called Highlight What's New was introduced. This gives you the ability to have the application highlight the tools or features that have been added or enhanced over a previous version (see Figure 3.10). This is a great way to identify what has changed, and in conjunction with the Hints docker, learn how to use the new feature.

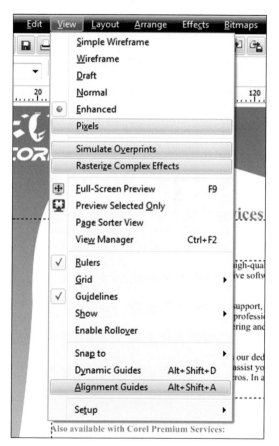

**Figure 3.10**
*Here, you can see the View menu from CorelDRAW X6 with Highlight What's New. Version X3 is selected.*

# Workspace

I HAVE BEEN USING CORELDRAW for almost 20 years now, and it never ceases to amaze me how I can always learn something new in the application or learn a faster technique to help me complete a task.

CorelDRAW has literally hundreds of tools that can be used to assist in the gathering of assets, design creation, and output of your artwork, but if you ask me, by far the most powerful tool in the entire application is the ability to customize the interface (or Workspace) and speed up the way in which you work.

By default, after the installation of CorelDRAW, there are tools, features, and options available in a variety of locations around the screen and within menus. This is referred to as the *Workspace*, and in CorelDRAW, it is completely customizable.

Rather than memorizing shortcut keys that someone else has assigned to a feature, being able to create your own shortcut keys or have access to features where you want them will go a long way toward increasing your productivity and allowing you to work the way that you want.

As an example, if I needed to use the Convert to Bitmap feature, I would simply go to the Bitmap menu and then to Convert to Bitmap. Imagine if you needed to do this two dozen times while laying out a product catalog. Alternatively, I simply tap the letter "F" on the keyboard. That's it, and it's so easy to set up. Think of the time saved.

We are going to start by creating keyboard shortcuts, and then we will take a look at customizing toolbars and menu items. Figure 3.11 shows the Options dialog box with the Shortcut Keys tab selected where some of the customizing takes place.

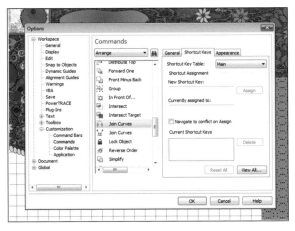

**Figure 3.11**
*Accessing the Customization options can be done by going to the Tools menu and then selecting Customization.*

## Creating Keyboard Shortcuts

For the most part, when I'm designing layouts and logos in CorelDRAW, there are certain features that I use repeatedly. Some of the common views that I use are Wireframe, Enhanced, and Page Sorter to help me navigate through my drawing. In addition, I use Grouping and Ungrouping and Convert to Bitmap.

Now let's look at a brief description of some shortcuts, and then we'll customize them.

▶ **Wireframe** (no default shortcut key): An outline view of a drawing that hides fills but displays extrusions, contour lines, and intermediate blend shapes. Bitmaps are displayed in monochrome.

▶ **Enhanced** (no default shortcut key): The standard view that CorelDRAW defaults to when launched. It displays a drawing with PostScript fills, high-resolution bitmaps, and anti-aliased vector graphics.

▶ **Page Sorter** (no default shortcut key): You can use the Page Sorter View to manage pages while viewing the page contents. This view also lets you change the order of pages, as well as copy, add, rename, and delete pages.

▶ **Grouping** (Ctrl+G): This view allows you to treat two or more objects as a single unit but retain their individual attributes. Grouping lets you apply the same formatting, properties, and other changes to all the objects within the group at the same time.

▶ **Ungrouping** (Ctrl+U): If you want to be able to edit objects in a group, you must first ungroup the objects.

▶ **Fit Text to Frame** (no default shortcut key): This option will adjust the point size of text so that it will fit better within a text frame.

**To customize shortcut keys:**

1. To assign a keyboard shortcut to a command, select Tools > Customization.

2. In the Options Dialog box, select Commands on the left-hand side; this will open up two areas to the right.

3. Under Commands, where you see the word File, click to open the drop-down and select View. Within the View menu, you will typically find Wireframe and Enhanced.

4. Scroll through the entries, locate Wireframe, and select it.

## Printing Shortcuts

To view all shortcut keys that have been assigned to the various commands, go to Tools > Customization, select Commands, and then select the Shortcut Keys tab. On the bottom lower-right corner, click the View All button. This will allow you to View, Print, or Export to a CSV file. Shortcut Keys are contained in tables (similar to a look-up table). There is a table for Text editing, Anchor editing, and a Main table. It is possible to have the same shortcut key sequence for a text attribute as you do for a tool or table attribute.

## Drag-and-Drop Customization

You can drag one of the commands from this list to the desktop, and it will create the beginning of a toolbar on the desktop, or you can add it to an existing toolbar.

5. Select the Shortcut Keys tab to the right and in the New Shortcut Key field, enter the letter "W." (I use the letter "W" as it is easy to remember for Wireframe. It will display as an uppercase letter "W.") Click the Assign button.

6. Next, under Commands > View, locate Enhanced. For Enhanced, I do not select the letter "E" as you might think. (It is reserved for Even Alignment.) Instead, I select the letter "Q" and an easy way to remember this is that it is used to quit Wireframe. It is also very convenient because the two keys are beside each other, and it is easy to toggle back and forth quickly. Click the Assign button.

7. The final option from the View menu that we're going to assign a shortcut key to is Page Sorter View. For Page Sorter View, select the letter "S" and then click the Assign button.

So as you can see, it is very easy to customize keyboard shortcuts to allow you to be much more productive. There are two more shortcut keys to assign, and then we can look at toolbars and menus. But first, notice that when you customize a keyboard shortcut, the new shortcut actually is displayed in the appropriate menu (see Figure 3.12).

In this next example, we have a situation where there is already a shortcut key assigned. So you have a choice to either remove the existing shortcut key and replace it with a new one or simply add the one you want (in which case, there will be two). The advantage of keeping both is that you can use either shortcut key sequence.

**To create a new shortcut key and keep the original:**

1. Still in the Options Dialog box, under Commands, where you see the word View, click to open the drop-down and select Arrange. Within the Arrange menu, you will typically find Group and Ungroup.

2. Scroll through the entries, locate Group, and select it.

3. On the right-hand side under Current Shortcut Keys, you will see Ctrl+G. To remove this one, select it and click the Delete button.

4. In the New Shortcut Key box, type the letter "G" on the keyboard.

5. Click the Assign button.

6. From below the Arrange menu, locate Ungroup and select it.

7. On the right-hand side under Current Shortcut Keys, you will see Ctrl+U. To remove this one, select it and click the Delete button.

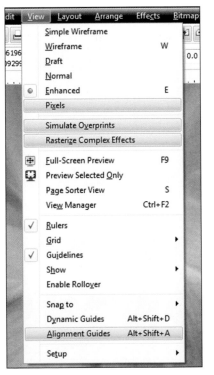

**Figure 3.12**
*In this figure, it is easy to see what shortcut keys are assigned to which features. It's just one more way to design more productively.*

**8.** In the New Shortcut Key box, type the letter "U" on the keyboard.

**9.** Click the Assign button.

## Navigating to Conflicts

If you assign a shortcut key that is currently assigned to another command, the command will be listed under the Currently Assigned to box, as it is with this example. If Navigate to Conflict on Assign is selected, once this shortcut key is assigned, you will then have the ability to assign a shortcut key for the one that was just replaced (see Figure 3.13).

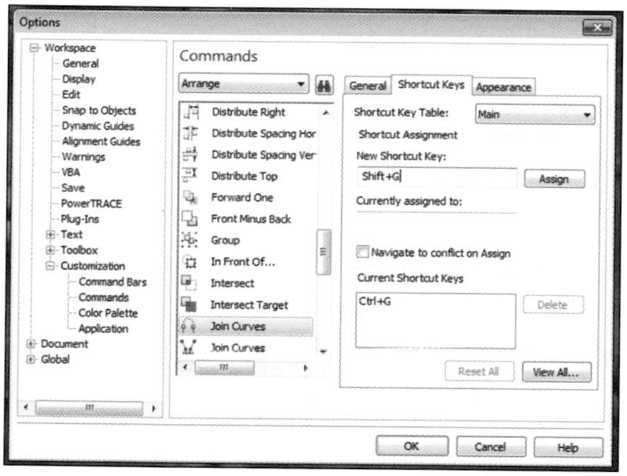

**Figure 3.13**
*Here you can see that a required shortcut key is already in use. In this situation, you have the ability to navigate to the conflicting command so that it can be changed as well.*

## Customizing Icons and Menu Text

Next, we are going to customize the appearance of the various icons, and we will also learn how to change the text within the menus. (I can't think of too many applications that will allow the user to do that.)

If you are not already there, from the Tools menu, select Customization and click Commands; then select the Appearance tab, as shown in Figure 3.14.

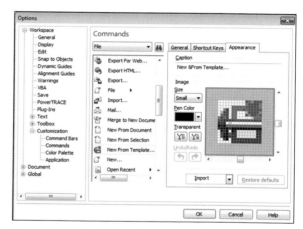

**Figure 3.14**
*The Appearance tab within the customization area is where you can change the command name, mnemonic, and icon.*

Here are the options under the Appearance tab.

▶ **Caption:** Caption is another word for a *label* or *name*, and it refers to how the command, feature, or function is referred to. The ampersand character denotes the mnemonic that is used to activate the command if a mouse is not used. It is the character immediately following it.

▶ **Size:** CorelDRAW has the ability to display small, medium or large icons on the toolbars and within the menus. Changing this drop-down allows you to change the icon for that specific size. Selecting Medium will change it for both Medium and Large.

▶ **Pen Color:** The Pen Color is a palette of 256 colors that can be used to modify the appearance of the icon.

▶ **Transparent:** There are two icons for this option. The icon on the left allows you to select individual pixels to make transparent, while the icon on the right will select individual colors to make transparent.

▶ **Undo/Redo:** This option allows you to correct any changes that have been made to the icon.

▶ **Import:** The Import drop-down allows you to select one of the icons that is installed and currently in use within CorelDRAW. They are there for you to repurpose for other commands. Changing these will not affect how the original that is currently in use will appear. At the bottom of this list is a Files button. Clicking this will help you import a *.bmp, *.ico, *.cur, or *.ani file.

▶ **Restore defaults:** This restores the currently selected item's icon and caption to the default settings.

## Customizing the Caption

Changing the caption is as simple as retyping the command name and replacing the text with what you want.

Let's take a look at some of the menu items in the File menu and change these, just for the fun of it. Probably the only time that someone would want to change the actual name of a command is if he either a) knew the feature by another name and found it easier to remember, or b) wanted to translate the commands into another language.

During the CorelDRAW 10 cycle (if memory serves me correctly), Corel did not release a Dutch version of the application, but an enterprising gentleman from Holland translated all the commands within the application, created a workspace file, and offered it for sale from his website. It was a fantastic way to make use of this feature and earn some revenue.

So let's take a look at how easy this can be. We will customize a few items under the File menu, but the process is identical for anywhere within the application.

**To customize a few items:**

1. From the Tools menu, select Customize.

2. Under the Customize option, select Commands.

**3.** Under Commands, select New from Template and click the Appearance tab.

**4.** Within the Caption field on the Appearance tab, replace the text with Template & Wizard (the & will determine the character that is used as the mnemonic, and in this case, it will be the letter "W").

Now, let's sneak back over to the Shortcut tab while you are working on the Template command, and let's assign a shortcut to it. I have selected Ctrl+T. Remember how to do it?

## Changing the Look of the Icon

It is also possible to change the appearance of an icon with very little effort, and can actually be fun to do (see Figure 3.15).

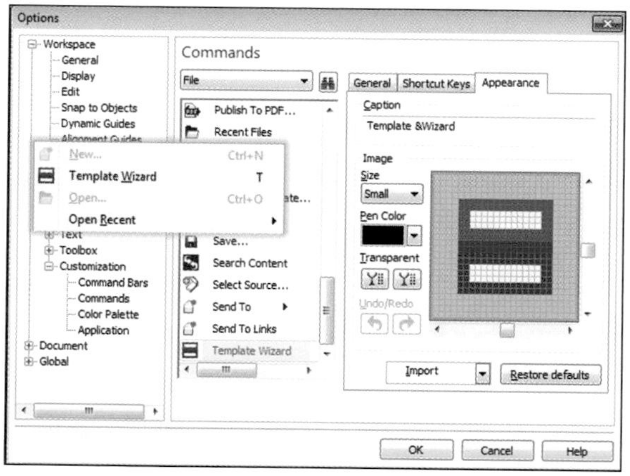

**Figure 3.15**

*You can change the text in the Caption box and assign a mnemonic to it that is reflected in the menu itself.*

**To change the appearance of an icon:**

**1.** From the Pen Color drop-down, select the magenta tile (it is the sixth one down on the right side) and position the cursor over the squares. (These represent pixels within the icon itself and create a frame that is 2 rows horizontal and 2 columns vertical with 3 horizontal rows in the middle.)

**2.** Next, you can create the same size rectangle with a color tile (sixth row down on the left side).

**3.** This created an area between them that I filled with blue, so you can choose your color here.

**4.** Finally, using the Transparent icon on the right, clear out the area within the center of each of the rectangles.

Now that you know how to customize the menu items, go ahead and customize a few more on your own. Don't worry about messing things up because at the end of this section, you'll learn how easy it is to reset the default settings and put things back the way they were in the beginning. While you do this, I'm just going to have some fun (see Figure 3.16).

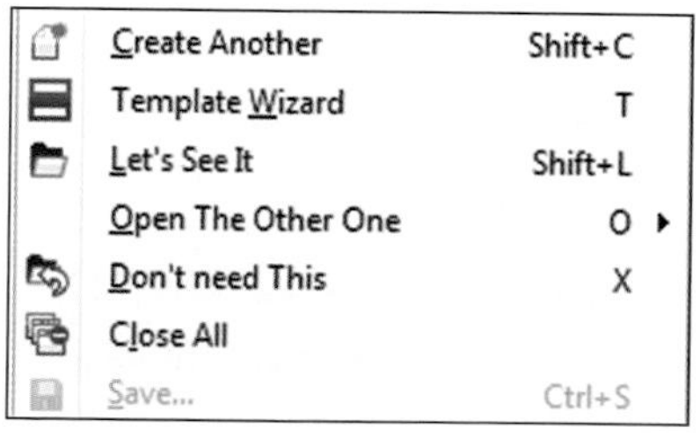

**Figure 3.16**

*It's easy to change the way that a command appears in the menu or change a shortcut key. I have changed a few of the items in the File menu, just for fun.*

# Command Bars

On the left-hand panel of the Options dialog box, select Command Bars. You will notice that in the center there is now a list of the various Command Bars that CorelDRAW includes.

In the center panel you will see a listing of the various Command Bars that are available (see Figure 3.17). These include the following:

- ▶ **Menu Bar:** This is located at the very top of the window, directly below the Application name and the name of the currently opened file.

- ▶ **Context Menu:** The context menu is the menu that appears when you do a secondary (or right) click while you are inside the drawing window.

- ▶ **Status Bar:** The normal position of the status bar is at the bottom of the screen, and it contains information about the cursor position and the object or objects selected.

- ▶ **Standard:** The standard toolbar is located below the Menu bar, and it contains main commands such as New, Open, Save, Print, and so on.

- ▶ **Property Bar:** The property bar is located directly below the standard toolbar, and it is also referred to as the context sensitive or interactive property bar, which contains setting for the specific tool or object that is currently selected.

- ▶ **Toolbox:** Usually located along the left-hand side of the screen, the Toolbox contains the tools that are required to do the design work.

- ▶ **Text:** Contains commands for creating, formatting, and aligning text. This toolbar is not shown in the workspace by default.

- ▶ **Zoom:** Contains the necessary tools to change the view or the objects that can be seen; it is not shown in the workspace by default.

- ▶ **Internet:** Contains Web-related tools for creating rollovers and publishing to the Internet. This toolbar is not shown in the workspace by default.

- ▶ **Print Merge:** Allows you to perform a print merge. Although this toolbar in not on by default, when you select Print Merge from the File menu, this toolbar will be displayed on the screen.

- ▶ **Transform:** Contains commands necessary for skewing, rotating, and mirroring objects. This toolbar is not shown in the workspace by default.

- ▶ **Macros:** Contains commands for editing, testing, and running macros, and it is not shown in the workspace by default.

- ▶ **Layout:** The layout toolbar is new to CorelDRAW X6 and includes formatting tools for Powerclip frames, Text frames, and Columns. This toolbar is not shown in the workspace by default.

## Where Are Those Command Bars?

To quickly access a Command Bar that may not be visible, right-click on any toolbar to open a list of available bars.

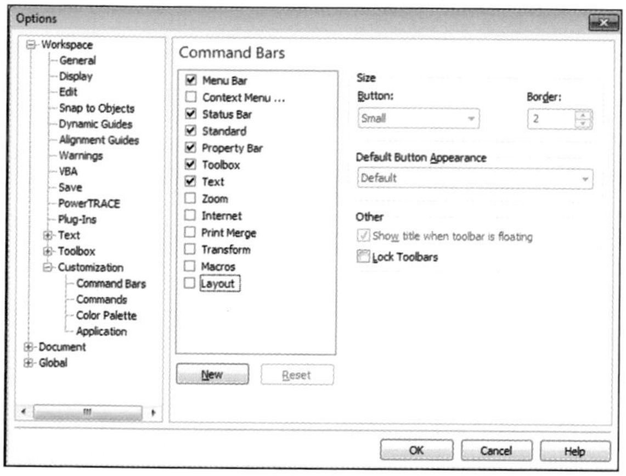

**Figure 3.17**

*The various Command Bars that can be selected, as well as the properties that can be modified.*

## Command Bar Options

To the right of the listing of the Command Bars are the options that can be modified. They are fairly straightforward, so we won't spend too much time on them. They include the following:

▶ **Button:** The options here are Small, Medium, and Large, and they allow you to increase or decrease the size of the icons on the screen for easier visibility or increased workspace (if you make them smaller). This feature only affects the toolbar that is currently selected.

▶ **Border:** Increasing the border will widen the area around the button. This is a great option for those who may have difficulty selecting specific areas. (Range is 0–10.)

▶ **Default Button Appearance:** The appearance will dictate whether or not there is a text description for the button displayed with the button. There are a number of different options here.

▶ **Show Title When Toolbar Is Floating:** This will display the title of the toolbar across the top of it.

▶ **Lock Toolbars:** This option locks the toolbars so they are not inadvertently moved or removed.

▶ **New:** Clicking on New will create a blank toolbar on the desktop that commands can be dragged onto.

▶ **Reset:** This will revert any changes of existing toolbars back to the original state if any of the options were changed. The Reset button becomes a Delete button if you have selected a nondefault toolbar.

## Creating a Custom or New Toolbar

Creating custom toolbars can be easy, and there is more than one way to do this task—just one more reason to use CorelDRAW.

In the Options area, you'll learn how to create a custom toolbar, and then you'll learn an even quicker way to do it (which is the method that I use).

There are two different ways to create a new toolbar within CorelDRAW. As we are currently in the customization area, let's look at this method first, and then we will look at the method that I prefer—because in my opinion, it is much quicker.

In this exercise, we will create a toolbar with the Contour, Boundary, Break Apart, and Hairline Outline tools. If you do not know what these are, don't worry. I can guarantee you that we will cover them in other chapters.

**To create a new toolbar:**

1. Click the New icon. This will create a blank toolbar on the desktop area of CorelDRAW and allow you to provide a name for it. Let's call it Print / Cut. Once you have typed in the name, click outside of the name area to save it.

2. On the left-hand panel, just below Command Bars, select Commands. The first command that you want to add to the toolbar is Boundary. To access it here, select the drop-down under Commands and click All (Show All Items). Commands listed here are in alphabetical order (in CorelDRAW X5 and X6). (Alternatively, you can click on the binoculars to search or select the specific menu if you know where the command is located.)

3. Click on the name Boundary and drag it over to the blank toolbar until you see the I beam insert cursor, as shown in Figure 3.18, and let the mouse button go. This will drop the Command icon onto the new toolbar.

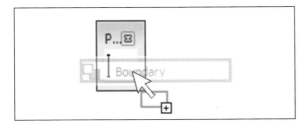

**Figure 3.18**
*Pictured here is the I beam insertion cursor that you will see when you drop a command onto a toolbar.*

4. Next, you will do the same with the other commands. From the Command's drop-down, select the Arrange menu and locate Break Apart and drag this over and place it to the right of the Boundary command.

5. The next command that you will add is the Contour tool. This is located in the Toolbox that is normally on the left-hand side of the screen.

6. From the Commands drop-down, select Toolbox and scroll down to Contour. Drag this one between the Boundary and the Break Apart. (Watch the position of the I beam insert cursor to know where you are dropping it.)

## Optimizing for the Workflow

We are putting these in a very specific order because this is the order that you would typically use them if you were doing a Print / Cut design. We will cover Print / Cut in Chapter 9, "Time to Output."

The last toolbar item that you want to add to this toolbar is the command to change the Width. From the Command's drop-down, select Fill and Outline. Scroll down to Outline Width and drag this item to the far right side of the Print / Cut toolbar. You should now have four commands/tools on this new toolbar, and you should also note that the name of the toolbar can be seen. Click OK to close the Options panel and save this toolbar. Now drag this toolbar to just below the Interactive property bar so that it docks there (see Figure 3.19).

**Figure 3.19**
*Here you can see the toolbar that was just created, before you docked it.*

## Making Custom Toolbars the Easy Way

We will now take a look at an alternative way to create a toolbar and to customize the interface. This method is actually so quick and easy that I use it to add a function when I am working on a specific design and then just delete it when I am done.

Before I show you how to do it, I need to explain a couple of keyboard combinations that you can use to modify commands and what they will do.

▶ **Alt:** Holding the Alt key down while dragging a menu item or icon into the drawing window will delete the command; if you drag it to another location, it will move it.

▶ **Ctrl+Alt:** Holding these keys down while dragging a menu item or icon will duplicate the command.

▶ **Shift+Alt:** Holding these keys down while dragging a menu item or icon will move the command.

Now we are going to create a toolbar that has a combination of menu items and tools from the Toolbox. It will include: Boundary, Smart Fill, Convert to Bitmap, and Fit Text to Path.

**To create a custom toolbar:**

1. To create the toolbar and add your first tool, the Boundary tool, hold down the Ctrl+Alt keys, click the Arrange menu, and move down to Shaping and click Boundary. Drag this onto the drawing window.

2. Next, click the Smart Fill, the sixth tool down in the Toolbox, and hold down the Ctrl+Alt keys. Click it once again and drag it onto the toolbar that you have just created.

The next item to add to this toolbar is Convert to Bitmap. I actually use this one quite a bit because it is a great way to flatten an image or resample a bitmap to optimize the output. (We'll cover optimizing for output in more detail in Chapter 9.)

3. Hold down the Ctrl+Alt keys, click the Bitmap menu, select Convert to Bitmap, and drag it to the toolbar. Now drag the Fit Text to Path.

4. Once in the Text menu, hold down the Ctrl+Alt keys and drag Fit Text to Path onto the toolbar.

5. The only disadvantage of creating toolbars in this way is that there is no option to name them. To do this, you will have to go into Tools > Customize > Command Bars and name it. This is a small price to pay for the convenience of easily creating a toolbar on the fly.

The final step here is to place the toolbar where you want it. We will put it next to the Print / Cut toolbar, as shown in Figure 3.20.

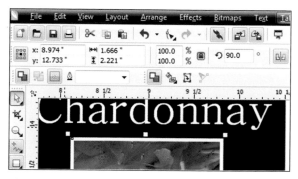

**Figure 3.20**
*The newly created toolbar placed to the right of the Print / Cut toolbar.*

# Rearranging Toolbars

Now that we have created a new toolbar and positioned it, what if we want to move the other ones around. Can we do it? Absolutely. One thing to remember is that with the release of CorelDRAW Graphic X5 and continued in X6, the toolbars are locked by default. This was done to prevent a user from inadvertently removing or accidentally closing a toolbar and not knowing how to get it back.

Figure 3.21 shows a list of the available toolbars.

**Figure 3.21**
*Here are the available toolbars. At the bottom of the list are the two toolbars that we created.*

**To rearrange toolbars:**

1. You will notice in Figure 3.21 that there are some toolbars that have a checkmark to the left of the name; this occurs because they are currently visible on-screen. Lock Toolbars also has a checkmark to the left of it. Before we can move any toolbars around, we'll need to take the checkmark out of Lock Toolbars by left-clicking on it. You can also do this by right-clicking on a toolbar and then clicking on Lock Toolbars.

2. Now that the toolbars are unlocked, you may notice that there are a series of gray dots, known as "grippers" at the beginning of each toolbar. Positioning your cursor over these will change the cursor to a "move" cursor or a cursor with arrows pointing in four directions. Click and drag the toolbar to where you would like to move it.

Play around with the layout. Open more toolbars and place them where you want. Do not worry about accidentally deleting a toolbar because all you need to do to get it back is to right-click on any other toolbar or the menu and place a checkmark back on the toolbar that is missing.

# Rearranging Menu Items

The next thing we'll discuss is how to rearrange menu items. You already know how to move, delete, or copy items to a toolbar. It works the same way for menu items that you want to move around to other menus. For example, in CorelDRAW X5, the Open Recent command is the second to last item in the File menu. It makes sense to move it closer to the top, and this is why it is this way in X6. It is simple to do. Let's take a look.

**To rearrange menu items:**

1. In CorelDRAW X5, press and hold the Alt key; then while still holding it down, click the File menu.

2. Click the Open Recent command and drag it up. As you do this, you will notice a horizontal bar. Place this bar just below the Open command. That's it! Simple, eh!

You now have the Open Recent command directly below the Open command.

The process to move menu items from one menu to another is just as easy. Remember, holding down the Shift+Alt will allow you to delete an item from the menu. This is a great way to remove commands that you will not use. Feel free to play around, as it is easy enough to reset the defaults.

Here, I mentioned CorelDRAW X5, but the process is identical for CorelDRAW X3 and above.

## Customizing a Context Menu

The Context menu is the menu that appears when you do a right-click within CorelDRAW. The contents of the menu will vary, depending on the context of the right-click. Get it? It actually depends on where you right-click within CorelDRAW.

It just takes a few moments to customize the Context menu, and it can save a lot of time while you design. Let's take a look and see just how easy it is.

**To customize the Context menu:**

1. Go to the Tools menu and down to Customization and select Command Bars.

2. Place a checkmark in the Context menu. As soon as you do this, a Context Menu Bar will appear with three options: Workspace, Tools, and Selection. You will not be able to access any of these options until you activate the toolbar. To do this, select Commands in the Options panel. As soon as you do, the toolbar becomes active.

Personally, I find that for the most part, the Context menus have the commands that I need. There is only one that is lacking, and that is the Page Sorter View command.

Page Sorter View allows you to see a thumbnail representation of all the pages within the document and then double-click the desired page to navigate directly to it. As I quite often create multipage documents, having to go to the View menu and then scroll down to Page Sorter View can be a bit of a pain sometimes. To remedy this, I add the Page Sorter View command to the context menu for the Page Tab. Here is how you do it.

**To add the Page Sorter View command to the Context menu:**

1. From Tools > Customization, click on Command Bars and select Context menu. This will bring a small toolbar onto the screen that has three items: Workspace, Tools, and Selection.

2. Click Command in the Options panes to activate the toolbar that you just brought on the screen. You are now ready to customize the Context menu.

3. Under Commands, navigate to the command that you want to add to the Context menu and drag it over to the menu option that you want it to appear in. In Figure 3.22, you can see that I have clicked on the View menu and selected Page Sorter View and dragged it over to the Page Tab context menu. (You will not see the name as it is being dragged, but when the mouse button is released, you will have added this feature.)

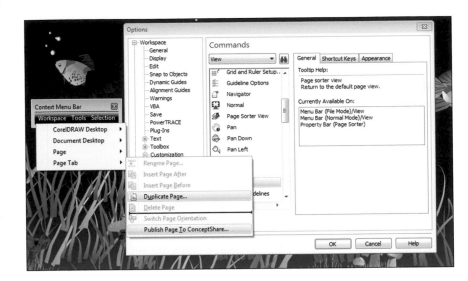

**Figure 3.22**
*Adding an item to the Context menu is just as easy as it is with any of the other menus. Here we add Page Sorter View to the Page Tab context menu.*

## What Are the Options?

There are three main headings on this bar: Workspace, Tools, and Selection. Under these options, there are a number of items that have related context menus. They include the following, as shown in Table 3.1.

### Table 3.1  Context Menu Options

| Workspace | Tools | Selection |
|---|---|---|
| CorelDRAW Desktop | Node Editing of Curves | Graphic Object Selection |
| Document Desktop | Node Editing of Text | Bitmap Selected |
| Page | Effect Selection | Group Object Selected |
| Page Tab | Spelling Errors | Multiple Object Selected |
|  | Grammar/Double Word Errors | Artistic Text Selected |
|  | Ignore – Spelling Errors | Paragraph Text Selected |
|  | Eyedropper | Artistic Text Editing |
|  | Mesh Fills | Paragraph Text Editing |
|  |  | Text Character Editing |
|  |  | Locked Object Selection |
|  |  | OLE Object Selection |
|  |  | Object Manager Selection |
|  |  | Commands to Append |

That brings us to the end of customizing the interface of CorelDRAW. As you can see, the options are endless (pun intended). Now we just have to figure out how to save all of those changes that we made.

## Saving and Exporting Workspaces

So you have spent time customizing your CorelDRAW to function the way that you want to work. It has taken a bit of time and a lot of thought. It would be a shame to lose all this work. Although it rarely happens, it is a good idea to have a copy as a backup in the event that you need to reinstall the application.

**To export the Workspace:**

1. From the Tools menu, select Options (Ctrl+J) and in the tree control in the top left of the dialog, select Workspace. This is where you have the ability to switch between various saved Workspaces and Create a New Workspace, Delete a Workspace, or Import or Export a Workspace (see Figure 3.23). Click the Export button to create a copy of the existing workspace.

2. Now the Export Workspace dialog comes up, and you will need to identify the elements of the Workspace that you want to save. For ease, I usually select all items in the check-boxes. This will include all sub-branches in the tree control that are presented. Select Dockers, Menus, Shortcut Keys, Status Bar, and Toolbars. Now click on Save.

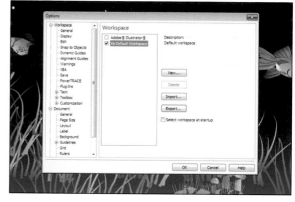

**Figure 3.23**
*Options here provide the ability to switch between Workspaces, as well as Import or Export a Workspace.*

## Sharing Your Workspace

Notice that there are options to Close, Save, and Email. Emailing a Workspace will send the Workspace to a colleague or to another system, possibly a home system if you have another copy of CorelDRAW installed there and want to have the same level experience. For this exercise, we will select Save.

After customizing the workspace, you do not necessarily need to export all of the settings. CorelDRAW allows you to select portions of the workspace (see Figure 3.24).

3. Browse to the location where you would like to save the file, and for now, select the Desktop. You can move it later. As for the name, the best naming convention is just to name the file with the current date, or if the Workspace that you are creating is specific to a certain workflow, then you can name it with that.

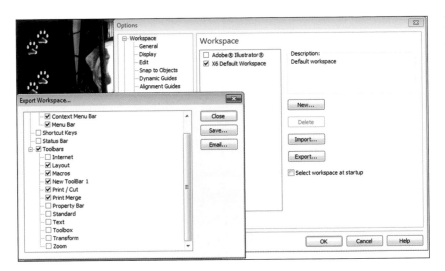

**Figure 3.24**
*It is very easy to select the portions of the Workspace that you need to export.*

**4.** The Workspace that I have created here is more targeted to Print & Cut, so that is the name that I will give it. Once named, simply click Save. After the file has been saved, just click Close to close the Export Workspace dialog box and Cancel to close the Options dialog box.

Now that you know how to Export a Workspace, let's take a look at the process to Import a Workspace.

## Importing Workspaces

The process for importing Workspaces is a bit more involved, but really, it is not very difficult when you take a look at it. Let's do that now.

**To import Workspaces:**

**1.** From the Tools menu select Options (Ctrl+J) and in the Options panel, select Workspace. As mentioned, this is where you have the ability to switch between various saved Workspaces, create a New Workspace, and Import or Export a Workspace (see Figure 3.25).

**2.** Select Import to open the Import dialog box and browse to the Workspace that you have previously exported. For this exercise, you will import the Print & Cut workspace that we created. Click Next.

**3.** In this step, you have the ability to select the elements that you want to import. In this way, if you want to bring in just the Shortcut Keys, then you have the ability to do that. As all items are selected by default, click Next.

**4.** The option for Current Workspace versus New Workspace will determine if you are going to overwrite the existing Workspace or actually add a new workspace. Let's select New Workspace and click Next.

Figure 3.25 shows the Create New Workspace dialog box, which is step 4 in the Import process for a Workspace.

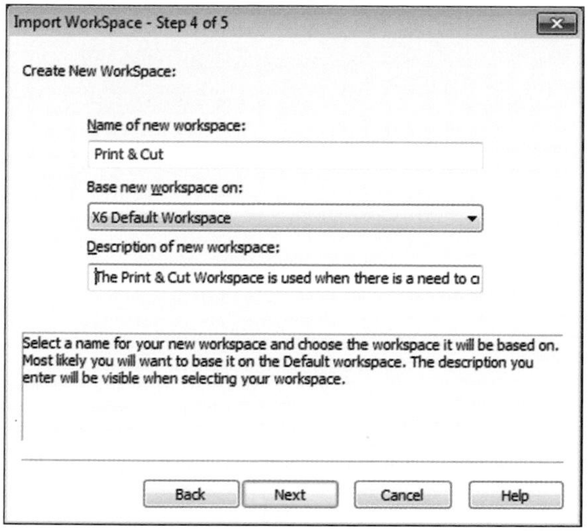

**Figure 3.25**
*The Import WorkSpace dialog box allows you not only to import an existing workspace, but also to dictate what areas of the workspace you want to bring in.*

The Create New Workspace dialog box allows you to name the new Workspace, as well as base it on an existing one. What this means is that while our new Workspace may not have every single tool customized, those that are not customized will be based on a different Workspace. The Description of the New Workspace field is pretty self-explanatory.

Just as we have created a toolbar that is specific to a particular workflow, we can also create an entire Workspace to a workflow as well. This will allow us to have multiple workflows where not only toolbars have been customized, but also shortcut keys and menu items. Let's go ahead and save a custom workspace.

**To save a custom Workspace:**

1. Name the New Workspace "Print & Cut" and base it on the Default Workspace for the version that you are using. Complete the Description of the New Workspace field and click Next. Refer to Figure 3.25.

2. The final step is to confirm the selected options. If everything is as desired, then click the Finish button. Otherwise, use the Back button.

3. You will now see three Workspaces listed; they include the two default Workspaces (plus the new one that we just added, which is currently selected by default).

4. Click OK to close the Options dialog box.

# Default Settings

I SHOULD PROBABLY START by saying that with the release of CorelDRAW Graphics Suite X6, a number of additions have been made when it comes to changing default settings, including the name of the dialog box that is used. It is now called Change Document Defaults dialog, and therefore I am going to provide both a screenshot of CorelDRAW X5 as well as of CorelDRAW X6, to show the differences between them (see Figures 3.26 and 3.27). Also, you should not confuse default settings with Styles, which we will be discussing later in Chapter 8.

## Some Defaults Are Document Specific

A number of the application settings are specific to the current document only. These include page layout options, grid and ruler settings, guideline settings, style options, save options, some tool settings, and Web publishing options.

**Figure 3.26**
*Changing Outline Color defaults dialog for CorelDRAW X5.*

**Figure 3.27**
*The Change Document Defaults dialog box for CorelDRAW X6.*

To set a default for any number of items is very simple and straightforward. The most important thing to remember is that when you set a default, whatever the default is, it has to be with nothing selected.

I would consider using the example of a quill pen and ink—first, someone had to dip the pen in the ink and then draw on the page—that's why you first clear the selection, select the tool in question, make the change to the setting, and then it updates the default.

## Changing Outline Color and Pen Width

I have seen many users struggle with setting the defaults because they forget one simple rule, so I am going to say it again. To set the default of a specific property, *it has to be with nothing selected.*

If I were to draw an analogy, it would be like filling an airbrush with ink or paint. The stroke created will be determined by the color of ink in the brush, as well as the adjustment of the spray pattern control.

Changing default settings in CorelDRAW is very easy to do and relatively straightforward. Probably the hardest thing to remember is that it has to be done with nothing selected in the document.

**To change defaults:**

1. To change the default Outline Pen width, select a blank area on the screen so that nothing is selected, click the Outline Pen tool, and navigate to the Outline Pen dialog box (F12). Depending on whether you are running CorelDRAW X6 or earlier will determine the dialog box that will appear. Please refer to Figures 3.26 and 3.27.

2. Select whichever option or options you would like to modify the outline for and click OK.

3. Select the properties for the outline from the Outline Pen dialog box.

4. Now that you know what the options are, it is time to make some changes to the default outline. I am going to change the color of the outline by clicking the drop-down list beside the label Color, and I will select red.

### The Default Palette Matches the Primary Color Mode

The color palette that is shown here will match the Primary Color mode as selected when the document was created or what is selected under Tools > Color Management > Default Settings. (More on Color Management in Chapter 4, "Elements of Design—File Formats".

5. Next I am going to change the Line style, again by clicking the drop-down. Pick whichever one you want. If you want to use something that is not shown here, simply click the Edit Line Style button, and you will have the ability to change the style as you desire.

6. The final item I want to select here is Scale with Image. As I have already mentioned, if you are creating a design that will be resized at a later time, possibly for another use, it is wise to select this option to save your work down the road.

7. Click OK, and you are done.

## Changing Defaults to Speed Up Designing

Sometimes if I am working on a design where I want a number of my outlines to be the same, say red dashed lines of .05mm in width, I will change the default while I create those objects and then change the default to match the appearance of the next objects I'm going to create. I find that doing this saves a lot of time.

## The Outline Pen Dialog Box

The Outline Pen dialog box gives access to a number of the different settings that are available when using the Outline tool, Freehand Drawing tool, or creating graphic objects that have outlines (see Figure 3.28).

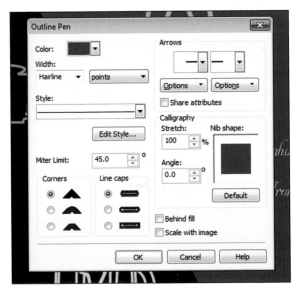

**Figure 3.28**
*Shown here are the various options that are available when setting or changing the Outline Pen dialog box settings.*

Aside from the obvious of being able to change the outline line thickness and color, there is also the ability to change line styles, corners, and the way a line ends, as well as being able to add arrows to the lines that are created.

▶ **Color:** This is self-explanatory; it allows you to change the color of the outline.

▶ **Width:** Again, self-explanatory, but note that by default the unit of measure is points; it might be easier if the units of measure were set to inches or millimeters.

▶ **Style:** Allows you to select the line style or characteristics, whether it is a dotted, dashed, or a dot/dash line. If there is not a style that you want or need, click the Edit Style button just below to create your own.

▶ **Miter Limit:** The Miter Limit controls the angle that a corner gets chamfered or cut off and how it will appear when a line is created and changes the angle. The options are mitered corners, rounded corners, or beveled corners.

▶ **Corners:** Corners defines how the corners should appear (pointy, chamfer, rounded).

▶ **Line Caps:** Similar to the Corner condition controls, it shows how the line endpoint will appear on open paths (see Figure 3.29).

▶ **Arrows:** This option allows you to add specific arrowheads to the ends of lines while you are creating them. This is a great time-saver if you are doing architectural designs or mechanical drawings.

▶ **Options:** The Options button allows you to create new arrow designs and change the attributes of an existing arrowhead.

▶ **Calligraphy:** This section controls the slant or angle used by the software to draw the outline.

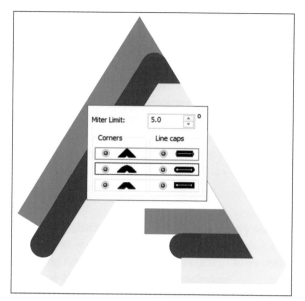

**Figure 3.29**
*Here you can see the various corners and line caps. It should be noted that line caps can only be seen on open paths.*

▶ **Behind Fill:** Outlines are created with a given width and when an outline is created, you have a choice of placing the outline behind the fill or in front. This setting is typically used when you are placing a wider outline on text that uses a font with a light weight (appearance).

▶ **Scale with Image:** This is probably one of the most important in this section (not the most common). As an example, picture a logo that was designed for a sign on the front of a building with some of the outlines .5 inches in width. When this logo is resized to be put onto a business card, if the outlines were not set to scale with the image, the outlines would still be .5 inches. Certainly not desirable. Scale with image is very important!

# Changing Fill Color or Pattern

To set the default of a fill, you must have nothing selected. Click the Fill tool in the Toolbox—it is the second tool from the bottom of the Toolbox on the left side of the screen (unless you have customized it to another location). There are six main settings here, and they include the following:

▶ **Uniform Fill:** Uniform fills are solid colors based on color models and color palettes.

▶ **Fountain Fill:** A fountain fill is a smooth gradient or blend of two or more colors.

▶ **Pattern Fill:** There are three types of Pattern fills. They are two color, full color, or Bitmap fills.

▶ **Texture Fill:** A texture fill is a randomly generated fill that is ideal for creating background textures when designing report covers or Web pages. There are literally thousands of these available within CorelDRAW.

▶ **PostScript Texture Fills:** PostScript fills are "built" with postscript language and can be complex at times. Using certain display modes (under the View menu) will display the fill as the letters "PS." It should also be noted that they are not very popular, but have been a part of CorelDRAW for a number of years.

▶ **Mesh Fill:** The Mesh fill is an innovative fill that allows the creation of subtle shading of colors. Typically, it is used to create photorealistic vector files.

Now that you understand what some of these are, let's put them into action to change the fill. Select the type of fill that you would like to set as default. I am going to click on Uniform Fill.

**To change Uniform Fill:**

1. The next dialog box that appears is one that you have already seen, the Change Document Defaults dialog box. For this exercise, we are going to change the type of fill for graphic objects, so select Graphic and click OK.

2. Next, from the Uniform Fill dialog box, select a color. Here, you will also notice that there are a number of options. We will look at those a bit later, so for now, just click on any color and then click OK.

3. Click the Ellipse tool in the Toolbox and draw an ellipse on the page. Is yours red? Mine is!

# Changing Default Text Properties

If you are not already aware, there are two types of text that can be created in CorelDRAW: Artistic text and Paragraph text. Here is how they differ.

▶ **Paragraph Text:** Paragraph text is text that is typically used for ad copy or sometimes called *body text.* It is used where you need large blocks of text. One characteristic of paragraph text is that it has similar formatting capabilities to that of a word processor.

▶ **Artistic Text:** Artistic text is typically used for banners, title text, or in a situation where you need to create stylized text as in a logo. If you were to look at the text that makes up the Coca Cola logo, it could have been designed in something like CorelDRAW.

By default, Artistic text is set to Ariel 24 point and Paragraph text is set to 12 point. The reason for this is simple: Artistic text is typically used for headlines, text callouts, and creating logo type. It is usually a larger point size as well, where Paragraph text is usually used for body text. From time to time, there is a need to change this size, so let's take a look at how to do it.

To change Artistic or Paragraph text, the steps are the same in CorelDRAW X6 as in previous versions and that is to select the Text Properties docker from X6 or the Character docker from earlier versions, but the types of text that can be changed are slightly different in X6.

In versions prior to CorelDRAW X6, the only text properties that could be changed were Artistic Text and Paragraph text. In CorelDRAW X6, there is now the ability to change Artistic Text, Callout, Dimension, and Paragraph text (see Figures 3.30 and 3.31).

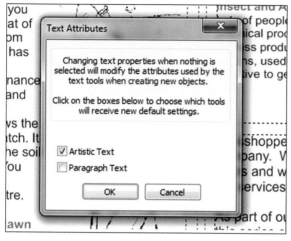

**Figure 3.30**
*The Text Attributes options from CorelDRAW X3 – X5.*

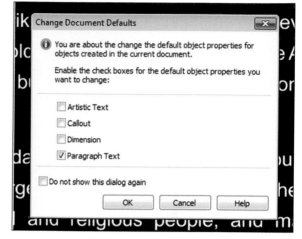

**Figure 3.31**
*The Change Document Defaults dialog box from CorelDRAW X6.*

Now that you have an understanding of what Artistic text is, let's go ahead and change the defaults.

**To change the defaults in Artistic text:**

1. We are going to make some changes to the default Artistic text (like the font and the point size). From the Text menu, select Text Properties (Character Formatting in versions previous to X6) or Ctrl+T. With nothing selected, click the Font drop-down, scroll to Times New Roman, and select it. The Change Document Defaults dialog box will appear on the screen, and we will select Artistic Text and click OK.

2. While we are here, we will change the point size as well. Below the font type, you will see the point size. Set it to 12pt. You will notice that the Change Document Defaults dialog box will appear again. Select OK.

3. Once you have the setting the way that you want, Go to Tools > Save Settings As Default, and your current settings will be used on all new documents.

# Resetting Default Settings

Now that you know how to change the default settings, customize the workspace, and import and export the workspace files, let's take a look at resetting the default settings by resetting the current workspace back to defaults. This is typically used if you want to undo all the changes that you have made to the application and want to get back to "square one" quickly, or if you need to repair the installation. (For more information on repairing the installation, refer to Appendix A, "Troubleshooting 101," or visit www.corel.com/support.)

## Using F8 to Reset the Defaults

I remember a time when it was easy to reset the defaults for CorelDRAW. All you had to do was rename the CDRBARS.cgf, CDRROLLS.cfg, and the CDRMENU.cgf. You then had to locate and delete the CorelDRW.cdt, as well as the CorelDRW.ini. Now you have to hold down the F8 key while launching the application. Times are a changing. OK, seriously, Corel has made it easy to reset to the default workspace.

You can reset to the default workspace by holding down the Function 8 key (F8) while launching the application. When you do this, you will see the message shown in Figure 3.32. Click OK. The workspace and default styles have now been reset to be the same way as the way they were when the software shipped.

Resetting the workspace reverts all shortcut keys back to the original and all toolbars and icons back to where—well, I was going to say back to where they belong, but more accurately where you need them—but it will move them back to their original position before you went in and modified things. It should also be pointed out that this is only for the current workspace, because other workspaces will *not* be affected.

**Figure 3.32**
*Holding down the Function 8 (F8) key while launching the application will reset the current workspace.*

## Restoring All Defaults

Windows has a special folder, referred to as the *Application Data folder* or *appdata*, for short. This folder is where the various applications that you have installed may store their options or settings. From time to time, they may become corrupt, and you might need to reset them. The process is straightforward and thorough.

**To reset your Application Data folder:**

1. With CorelDRAW closed down, on the keyboard, press and hold the Windows key. (This is the key with the Windows logo on it between the Ctrl and Alt keys to the left of the Spacebar.) While holding this down, tap the letter "R". This will open a Run dialog box.

2. In the Run box, type %appdata% and click the OK button. This will open the Application Data folder.

3. With the Application Data folder opened, you will see a number of other folders here. These are created by the various applications that you have installed. Locate the Corel folder and double-click it. This will open the folder, and you will be able to see the folders for any Corel applications that you have installed.

4. Now, you can delete the CorelDRAW Graphics Suite (*version number*) folder, but I *strongly* recommend that you do not do this—just rename it. The reason that I suggest this is that from time to time, you create custom fountain fills, textures, or even palettes. These are stored within this folder structure and in this way, they can be saved.

The next time that you relaunch the application, all settings will be returned to default as though you have just installed the application for the first time.

In this section, we covered quite a bit of information about the Welcome magazine, customizing the workspace, setting various default settings, as well as resetting those defaults.

With a little time and some playing around, you will be amazed at how simple it can be to customize the interface to work the way that you want to work, and in the end, save precious time while you design.

## What's in the AppData Folder?

Some of the customized settings that are contained in the Application Data folder include: Line Styles, Arrowheads, Customized Textures, Fountain Fills, and Quick Correct settings, to name a few.

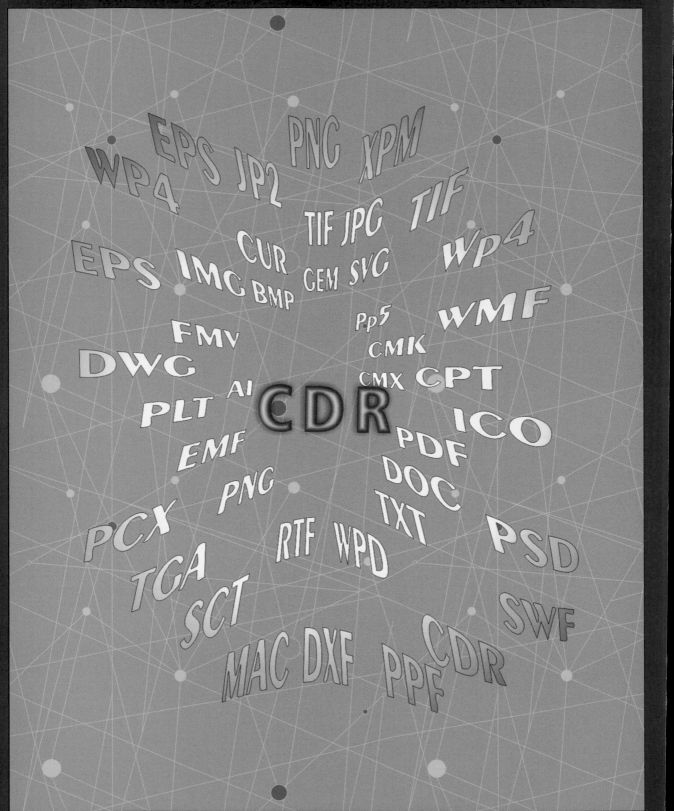

# Elements of Design— File Formats

I N THESE NEXT FEW CHAPTERS, we will take a look at the various elements that are required to create a design and will enable you to take your concept to the next level. Whether it is creating a logo, a business card, or a spec sheet for a real-estate property that you are listing, there are a number of things that you have to keep in mind when creating the artwork for output. We will start with the basics and move on from there. First, we need to cover the various file formats.

# File Formats

A FILE IS A METHOD of storing information on a computer, and there are literally thousands of different electronic formats floating around. For example, you may have a text document on a Windows-based system and then have a graphic file that was created on a Macintosh computer, and then need to combine these on a different Windows-based system. This process can be very complex.

When dealing with different file formats, CorelDRAW has the capability to work with over 100 different file formats, whether you are trying to get something in, or out of, your current document.

Importing versus opening—the difference is simple: If you open a file, such as CorelDRAW (CDR), open that file into a new drawing window. If, on the other hand, you import a file, the file will be placed or imported into the existing, open document. In this way, you have the ability to combine multiple files or pieces of content into a single document, or take an existing work and add it to another document.

Before we look at some of the more common file types that we will be exploring, we need to provide a couple definitions of two of the main type of files that we will be using: vector and raster.

## Vector Files

A vector file format is composed of objects created with line segments or curves (also sometimes referred to as *paths*) that have start and end points, which in CorelDRAW are referred to as *nodes*. These lines and curves are mathematically calculated. A vector image can easily be scaled from 1 inch by 1 inch up to 100 feet by 100 feet (or larger) with no loss of detail or quality. A vector file can make use of a number of color palettes, such as CMYK, RGB, and Pantone. The fact that this file type is basically composed of line segments and color information means that when the file is saved to a disk, it is quite small in size.

## What File Format Is Best for the Printer

There are quite a few supported file formats that cannot be opened and will have to be imported—most notably, the image formats, such as GIF, PNG, JPEG, and TIFF. You can either import these into a new blank document or into an existing document. When creating the final output, you must decide what type of file format to use. Depending on the contents of a document, it is often better to send final artwork to your printer or output print shop in vector format, while other times, a bitmap image will do. If you are unsure, call your print shop and ask them what format they prefer and ask if there are any specific options they would like to have turned on or off when creating the file you are going to send.

Common vector file formats include .PDF, .AI, .CDR, .EPS, and .DXF, just to name a few. You typically will see them as clipart, Computer Aided Design(CAD) drawings, and designs where scalability, easy manipulation, or clean (smooth) lines are required. Programs that create and manipulate vector file formats include applications such as CorelDRAW, Adobe Illustrator, AutoCAD, and QuarkXPress to name a few.

## Raster Files

A raster image or raster file format (also referred to as a *bitmap* or *photo*) is made up of pixels. A pixel is the smallest unit of a picture that can be displayed or modified, and raster images are laid out in a two-dimensional grid. A raster image is typically displayed either in a CMYK color mode or an RGB color mode. Occasionally, it can also be made up of Pantone colors, as in the case of a duotone. An example of a raster image is an image that has been scanned in to the computer, or it can also be an image from a digital camera.

Raster file formats include .JPG, .BMP, .PNG, .PSD, .TIF, or .CPT. The main advantage of a raster image is that it is very compatible with all programs since this is the way that digital cameras and scanners store their files. Also, raster images allow for smooth tonal control (in the case of skin tones in a photograph), and they generally are easy to print, as long as you don't have to resize the picture.

Two main drawbacks of a raster image would be that they take up more hard disk space than a vector file, and you are unable to resize the image (larger or smaller) without image quality loss. Typically, if you are using a raster image, you would not want to resize it any more than about 20 percent larger; otherwise, the image quality will start to suffer (of course, that depends on the original resolution and the resolution required). See Figure 4.1.

**Figure 4.1**
*A vector object on the left and a lower-resolution raster object on the right. Notice the pixilation or "stair-stepping" on the raster object. The various shades of black that can be seen are as a result of anti-aliasing during the rasterization process.*

One other thing to keep in mind is that with technology continually advancing, more and more vector-based graphic design applications are able to manipulate or create and modify raster images as well. There are also application plug-ins and macros that will allow the up-sampling or interpolation of raster images to allow for a higher resolution while maintaining some of the clarity of the image. One example of this would be Photo Zoom Pro by BenVista, an add-on that was included with CorelDRAW Graphics Suite X5.

Now that you know the difference between raster and vector, let's take a look at some of the more commonly used file formats (listed alphabetically) when doing graphic design work.

## The Import Cursor

There are a number of different cursors that can be seen when using the various tools within CorelDRAW. The cursor that appears will depend on the tool being used and the function that you are conducting. As an example, when inserting text, the cursor looks like an "I beam."

During the import of a graphic image into CorelDRAW, you are presented with an import cursor. The import cursor not only provides feedback on the file being imported such as file name and dimensions, but it also provides placement instructions.

Placement instructions include:

Color.tif
w: 12.875 in, h: 15.208 in
Click and drag to resize.
Press Enter to center on page.
Press Spacebar to use original position.

▶ Click and drag to resize.

▶ Press Enter to center on page.

▶ Press Spacebar to use original position.

One other point here is that feedback is provided with respect to alignment with other elements within the existing document. If you are importing text, a separate dialog box is presented that we will discuss later.

# AI (Adobe Illustrator)

THE AI FILE FORMAT is a proprietary file format developed by Adobe, and it is the default format for Adobe Illustrator. It is a single page file format that supports vector and raster graphics.

To export an AI file from CorelDRAW, from the File menu, select Export. In the Export dialog box under the drop-down labeled Save as type, select AI – Adobe Illustrator and then click the Export button (see Figure 4.2).

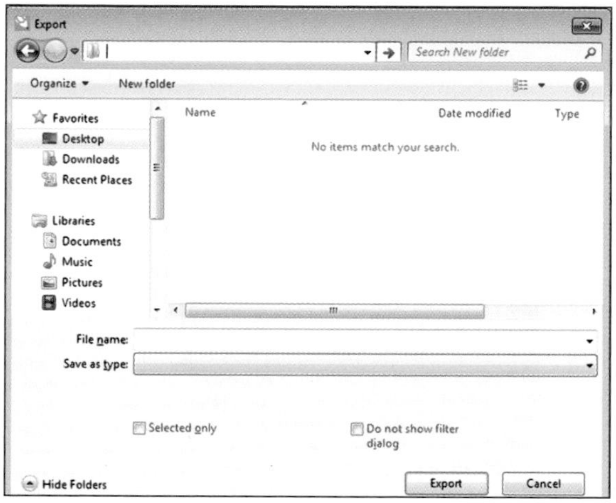

**Figure 4.2**
*The standard Export dialog box.*

Looking at the Export dialog box (see Figure 4.3), the first option is Compatibility. This is where you select the version of the file that is required. Depending on the version of CorelDRAW that you are currently using, this will determine the various versions available here.

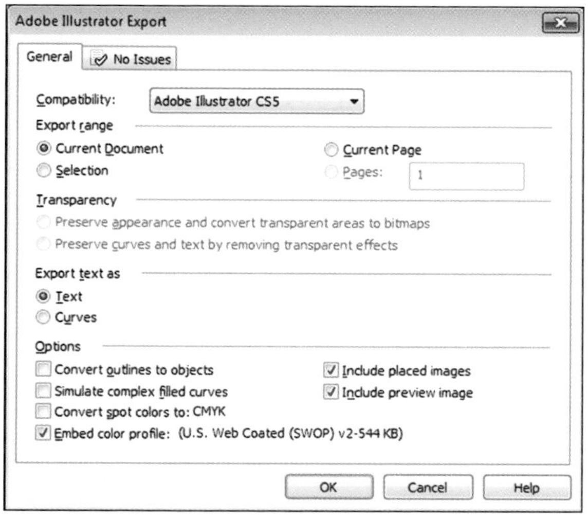

**Figure 4.3**
*Within the Export dialog box, there are a number of options that make it easy to export a design and maintain compatibility with Adobe Illustrator.*

The Export range section controls how much or how little of the document you are able to select for export.

▶ **Current Document:** Exports the current document. In the case of a multipage document, all pages will be exported to single, individual files.

▶ **Selection:** Exports a small portion of a file, for example, a logo from within a larger document. By selecting the logo and then exporting with this option selected, only the logo will be exported.

▶ **Current Page:** Exports the content from the page you are working on.

▶ **Pages:** Selects pages, or page ranges, when exporting to AI from a multipage document. As an example, if you have a 10-page document and want to export odd pages from 1–5, as well as pages 7–10, the format that you would enter into the range box would look like this: 1,3,5, 7–10.

The Transparency section has two options: "Preserve appearance and convert transparent areas to bitmaps" and "Preserve curves and text by removing transparent effects." These options are available when exporting to much older versions of the AI file that do not support transparencies. This would be anything older than version 9.0.

Exporting text as Text or Curves will dictate what happens to text objects. In a situation where you are sending the file to someone who does not have access to the fonts used in the design, it is best to convert the text to curves. A note of caution here: If this option is selected, the person who receives the file will no longer be able to edit the text.

The final section on the dialog box is Options. These are more advanced options, and they include the following:

▶ **Convert outlines to objects:** Converting outlines to objects will remove any outline characteristics and allow the outline to be treated as an object. As an object, there is the ability to apply various textures and effects that otherwise would not be possible.

▶ **Simulate complex filled curves:** As there are some effects in CorelDRAW that are not achievable and may not be supported in another application that may be opening up the AI file, selecting Simulate complex filled curves will do just that—it will "re-render" the content to the fill in a format that can be read by the destination application.

▶ **Convert spot to CMYK:** This option will convert any spot colors in the document to whatever the existing document's color space is. In our example, it would be CMYX. Note, you do not have the ability to embed a color profile when exporting a file to a CS version or older.

▶ **Embed color profile (U.S. Web Coated):** In a situation where a color profile has been applied to the CorelDRAW file, you have the ability to attach that to the AI file when exporting. This is advantageous because that color profile is maintained between applications. In this example, the specific profile is the U.S. Web Coated. Note: By default, CorelDRAW X5 will always apply the profile.

▶ **Include placed image:** This option is selected by default and will create a preview of the file suitable for allowing the file to be seen when imported or "placed" into another program.

▶ **Include preview image:** A preview image is required if you need to be able to review files within a folder structure. The preview is actually a low resolution version of the file. This option is also selected by default.

To complete the export process, click the OK button.

# CDR (CorelDRAW)

THE CDR FORMAT is a proprietary file format developed by Corel Corporation, and it is the default file format when saving from CorelDRAW. The CDR format is a vector format that supports multipage documents, as well as layers and raster images.

The Save dialog box dictates where the file will be saved, as well as giving you a number of other options (see Figure 4.4).

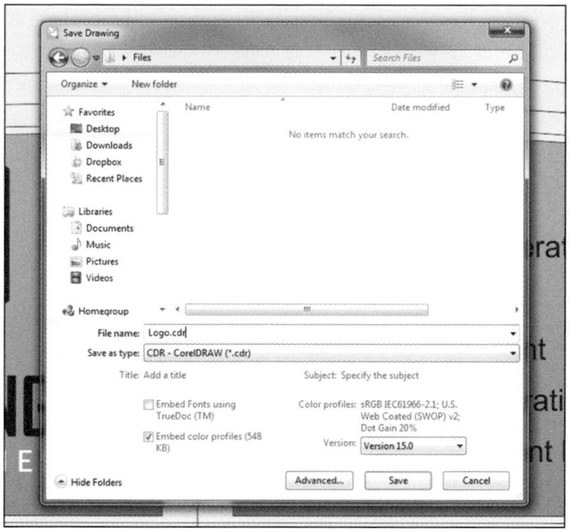

**Figure 4.4**
*The Save or Save As dialog box when generating a CDR file from CorelDRAW X5. It should also be noted that this dialog box is visible when running under Windows 7. The Save dialog box while under Windows XP is slightly different.*

▶ **Title:** Enters a title for the document. This has no correlation to the file name. It is visible when you select properties on the file through Windows Explorer or when viewing the file in a folder where the view is set to Detail view.

▶ **Subject:** Enters a subject for the document.

▶ **Selected only:** If this option is selected, then only the object or objects that are currently selected will be saved into the CDR file. Note: If there is currently nothing selected in the document, this option will not be seen in the Save or Save As dialog box.

▶ **Embed Fonts using TrueDoc:** By embedding fonts using TrueDoc, you enable temporary versions of the fonts to be saved with the file so that if the file is opened or imported on a system that does not have the required fonts, a temporary version of the fonts will be available while the file is open.

▶ **Embed color profiles (548KB):** Embedding the color profile will ensure that the proper color information (or that of the file) is sent along with the file.

▶ **Version:** This drop-down saves the file back to an older version. In a situation where the file is going to a system that has an older version, this should be selected. CorelDRAW enables you to save back as far as version 7 of CorelDRAW and makes file sharing with older versions possible.

### Taking It Back Even Further

In a situation where it is necessary to save as an older version, by using the Export command from the File menu, there is the option to select CMX – Corel Presentation Exchange 5.0. This will enable you to take the file back to a system as far back as version 5 of CorelDRAW. One word of caution here, though: features or effects that are available in newer versions of the application may be lost when saving.

The Save dialog also has three more buttons: Advanced, Save, or Cancel. The Save and Cancel buttons are pretty self-explanatory, but let's take a look at the Advanced button.

When you click the Advanced button, it opens the Save options dialog box (see Figure 4.5). The Save options dialog box has a few options that control objects or elements within the design and how they will be rendered. For the most part, there is no real need to modify or adjust anything in this dialog box, except for possibly the Save presentation exchange (CMX) option. If the presentation exchange data is located within a CDR file, then PHOTO-PAINT can open the file and convert it to a bitmap. If, on the other hand, the CMX information is not included, then PHOTO-PAINT must launch CorelDRAW in the background, convert the file to a bitmap, and then pass the bitmap through to PHOTO-PAINT.

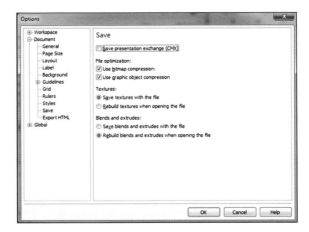

**Figure 4.5**
*These are the advanced options that are available when saving a file in the default CDR format.*

# CMX (Corel Presentation Exchange)

ALTHOUGH THIS PARTICULAR file format is related to bringing files to and from various versions of CorelDRAW, it is worth mentioning here, as there have been a number of changes over the past couple of versions of CorelDRAW. There are currently three versions of the CMX file format. They include Corel Presentation Exchange CMX, Corel Presentation Exchange 5.0, and Corel Presentation Exchange X6. Here is how they break down:

▶ **CMX 5.0:** This is a 16-bit file format and will support CMX files from CorelDRAW 5 and 6.

▶ **CMX:** This is a 32-bit file format and will support CMX files from CorelDRAW version 7 to X5.

▶ **CMX X6:** This supports 64-bit file formats and will only support CMX files created in CorelDRAW X6.

Note that the CMX X6 version is not backward-compatible. It will only open in CorelDRAW X6 and newer versions.

To create a CMX file, start from the File menu and select either Save As or Export—both options will allow you to accomplish the same thing. In the dialog box, under the drop-down labeled Save as type, select the CMX version that you want and then click the Export button (refer to Figure 4.2). There will be no secondary dialog box that will appear, and the file will be created in the location as indicated in the Export dialog box.

# EPS (Encapsulated PostScript)

ENCAPSULATED POSTSCRIPT is a file format that was created by Adobe for the purpose of output to PostScript devices. Files of this type can contain vector and raster information, as well as text. An industry standard, EPS is one of the most commonly used file formats when dealing with graphic design and professional output. When creating an EPS file, the user has the ability to "attach" an image header or preview to the file. As an EPS file is meant specifically for a PostScript printer, sending this information to a non-PostScript printer can pose a problem because the printer won't know what to do with the information it gets. It's like an English person talking to a dolphin—the dolphin might smile and wave, but it has no clue what the person is trying to convey. We have the ability to add what is referred to as an image header or preview, which typically is between 72 and 96 DPI and can be used for placement purposes. It is a representation of the file to show what it looks like. If no preview is selected, typically, there will be a gray box when the file is placed into another program.

When printing to a non-PostScript printer, typically only the preview is printed, but if you print to a PostScript device, you will get the complete, fully detailed image. If I were to draw an analogy, it would be like this: picture a can of soup. The label on the outside gives a picture of the contents and the text tells you what it is; however, you cannot really appreciate it until you open the can. The picture or image header goes to the non-PostScript while the contents of the file go to the PostScript device.

To create an EPS file in CorelDRAW, from the File menu, select Export. In the Export dialog box under the drop-down labeled Save as type, select EPS – Encapsulated PostScript and then click the Export button (refer to Figure 4.2).

The EPS Export dialog box has a number of options, some of which we have already seen in the AI dialog box, but we will go over all of the options here as well (see Figure 4.6).

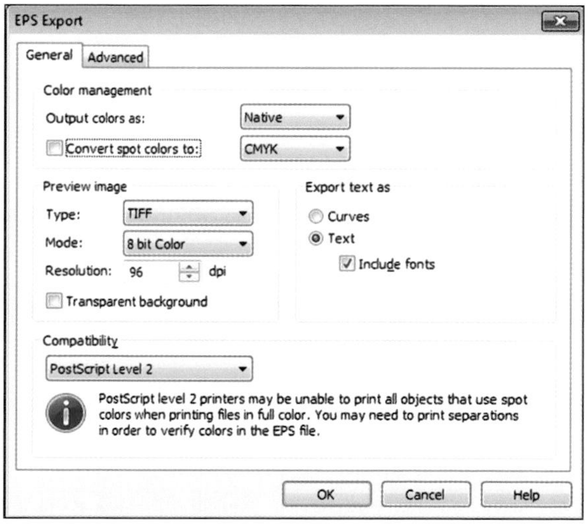

**Figure 4.6**
*The EPS Export dialog box is a tabbed dialog.*

The first tab called the *General tab* has some of the main features or options that can be modified. This tab has four sections: Color management, Preview image, Export text as, and Compatibility.

The Color management section consists of the following:

▶ **Output colors as:** Provides the options to dictate whether you want all colors converted to use only one color model of RGB, CMYK, or Grayscale. There is also the option to keep all colors native, meaning that if there is a mixture of color spaces used in the file, they will be maintained.

▶ **Convert spot colors to:** Allows easy conversion of all spot colors to either RGB (Red, Green, Blue) or CMYK (cyan, magenta, yellow and Black). Spot colors will be covered in Chapter 6, "Designing with Color."

The Preview image includes:

▶ **Type:** Here we can select the format for the image header.

▶ **Mode:** This will dictate the color depth of the image header.

▶ **Resolution:** This will allow you to select the image header resolution, which rarely needs to be any higher than 96dpi.

▶ **Transparent background:** This allows for transparency in the image header.

Export text as includes:

▶ **Curves:** This will convert the text to curves.

▶ **Text:** This will keep the text as text.

▶ **Include fonts:** This will allow you to embed fonts with the file.

The final option on the General tab is Compatibility. Compatibility allows you to set the level of PostScript, either to a level 2 or level 3.

A small footnote here about PostScript levels needs to be made. PostScript Level 1 was the original, basic language developed by Adobe, and it is the language that a PostScript printer "understands." PostScript Level 2 added support for different page sizes and better color printing. Then in 1997, Adobe released PostScript Level 3, and this release included better graphics handling, more supported fonts, and quicker printer times.

The Advanced tab has three main sections (see Figure 4.7). The first section is Bitmap compression, and it allows the user to dictate whether or not the bitmaps in the file are compressed. When selecting the JPEG Quality, the higher the quality, the lower the compression and the larger the file size, so there is a trade-off. Note: It is probably not a good idea to use a high compression if you are going to be sending the file to a printer for output.

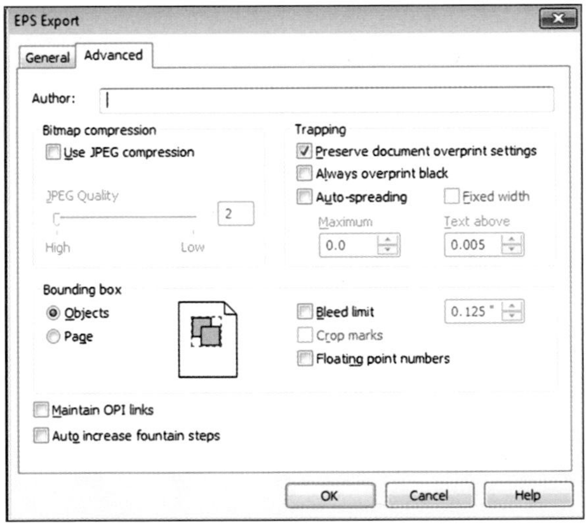

**Figure 4.7**

*The Advanced tab on the EPS Export dialog box provides extended features to the format, which are useful when sending the file to a printer.*

The second section is Trapping. Trapping, also known as *spreading and choking*, is a prepress technique that creates small overlaps between abutting objects and their colors, in order to mask registration problems on the printing press.

Settings within the area of trapping include:

▶ **Preserve document overprint:** An overprint is where one color will print over the top of another color. In CorelDRAW, you have the ability to overprint outlines or fills on individual objects. This option will maintain those settings.

▶ **Always overprint black:** This option allows black (from the CMYK color model) to be overprinted on objects that may be below (or underneath) them. This will ensure a rich solid black.

▶ **Auto-spreading:** This will automatically "spread" the ink when printing. The amount or how it is spread is dependent on the other settings that are associated with it.

The final main section within this tab is the Bounding box. The Bounding box refers to the area that encompasses the object and the page or just the objects.

▶ **Objects:** Only the objects on the page will be exported.

▶ **Page:** This option will export the page and the contents of the page.

▶ **Bleed Limit:** When ink is printed right to the very edge of a page, it is said to have a bleed. Adjusting the bleed will set the distance the object will print off the edge of the page to allow for cropping.

▶ **Crop marks:** Selecting crop marks will place the default crop around the objects when exporting the file.

▶ **Floating-point numbers:** This option is required when exporting for certain software. It will allow for a much higher precision Bounding box definition than is normally required.

These final options under the Advanced tab are more advanced and will probably not be encountered, but I would be remiss if I did not mention them: Maintain OPI links and Auto increase fountain steps.

▶ **Maintain OPI links:** OPI stands for Open Prepress Interface and is a fancy name for a technology that allows the designer to place a low-resolution raster image in the design and manipulate it (for speed and smaller file size). Then on output, if Maintain OPI links is selected, the system will automatically swap out the low-resolution version for the higher-resolution file.

▶ **Auto increase fountain steps:** Auto increase fountain steps is an option that will help to eliminate what is referred to as *banding* on a fountain fill. A fountain fill is a smooth transition from one color or shade to another. Depending on the shades or steps used, it can cause banding (the appearance of bands of color). Selecting this option will help to minimize the effect.

# GIF (CompuServe Bitmap)

COMPUSERVE BITMAP (GIF) or GIF 87a is a file format most used with Web graphics, a later version known as GIF 89a allowed for animation. This file format uses LZW compression, which is a lossless compression, meaning it loses no detail in image quality when saved. The main disadvantage of this file format is that it is limited to 8-bit color, which typically means that it uses only 256 colors, or grayscale (256 shades of gray), and that it is not ideally suited for use with files that contain many colors or high definition within areas that have shades, color, or shadows. Two advantages are 1) that it supports a transparent background and 2) that it is possible to reduce the number of colors in the file and thereby reduce the file size. This is great if you need a design with only a couple of colors and transparency.

To create a GIF image from within CorelDRAW, from the File menu, select Export. Within the Export dialog box, select Save as type (refer to Figure 4.2).

Once the Export button has been clicked, the Export to GIF dialog box will appear (see Figure 4.8).

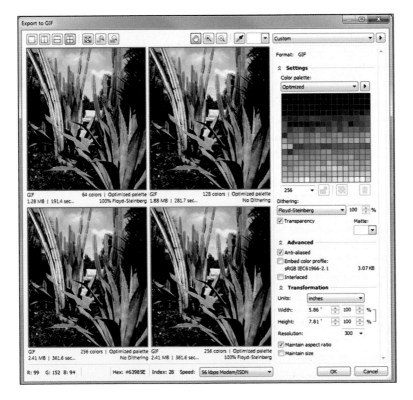

**Figure 4.8**

*The dialog box that appears when exporting a .gif image is the same dialog box that appears when exporting as a .jpg or .png, as well as when using the feature Export for Web.*

# JPEG (Joint Photographic Experts Group)

THE JPEG FORMAT is a common file format when creating images for the Web, but it is not suitable for professional output because it uses what is referred to as "lossy compression."

Lossy compression is a process that removes data from the file to reduce the file size. The drawback is that the quality of the image will be affected, but as mentioned, it will result in a smaller file size (see Figure 4.9).

**Figure 4.9**

*This figure shows an image with the lowest resolution as the main image and the high-resolution version inset. The lowest resolution image is 114KB, while the inset image is 2.2MB. This is a great way to show the trade-off between quality and compression.*

# PDF (Portable Document Format)

## The Portable Document Format

(PDF), like EPS, was created by Adobe and was originally created for the purpose of being able to easily
distribute documents that could be viewed on other
computers and across platforms (for example, PC or
Mac). The PDF format has also become the common
file format for use when preparing files to be sent to
a printer or viewed by other individuals. There are
now a number of settings that include various opti-
mizations. These include document distribution,
Web, prepress, editing, and archiving. There is also
the ability to customize the output to include a
number of settings (see Figure 4.10). We will cover
them in more detail throughout the book, as the
need arises.

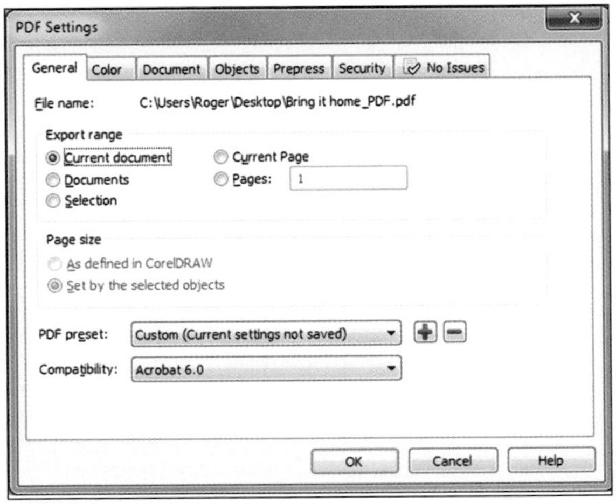

**Figure 4.10**

*The Publish to PDF, referred to as PDF Settings, dia-
log box is a multitabbed dialog. There are a total of
seven tabs, and they include General, Color,
Document, Objects, Prepress, Security, and Issues.*

# TIFF (Tagged Image File Format)

TIFF (OR .TIF) IS PERHAPS the most commonly used bitmap file format when sending information to various applications or to printers, second only to JPEG. The TIFF file format supports a large number of color spaces (including Black & White, 16 colors, 8-bit Grayscale, 8-bit Paletted color, 24-bit RGB, and 32-bit CMYK), as well as a variety of different compressions.

The Export dialog box is fairly straightforward for the TIFF export as well, as can be seen in Figure 4.11. Note the settings include items such as using document color settings, using color proof settings, and embedding color profiles and overprinting black.

That brings us to the end of this discussion on the various file formats that are used when preparing a document for output. The next element and probably the most important element in the entire design process is typography.

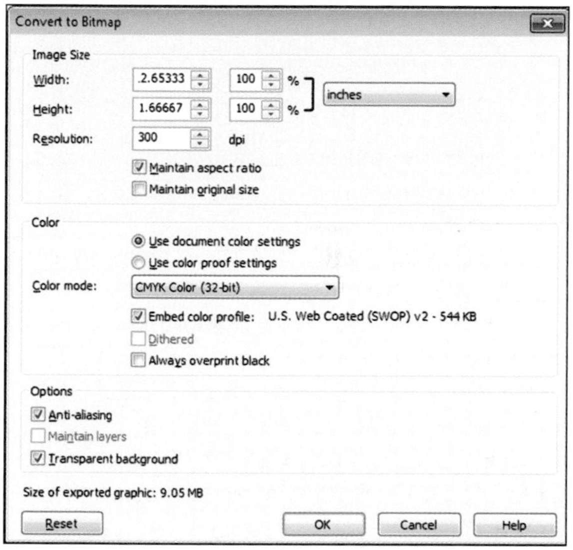

**Figure 4.11**
*These are the settings that are available when exporting as a TIFF file format.*

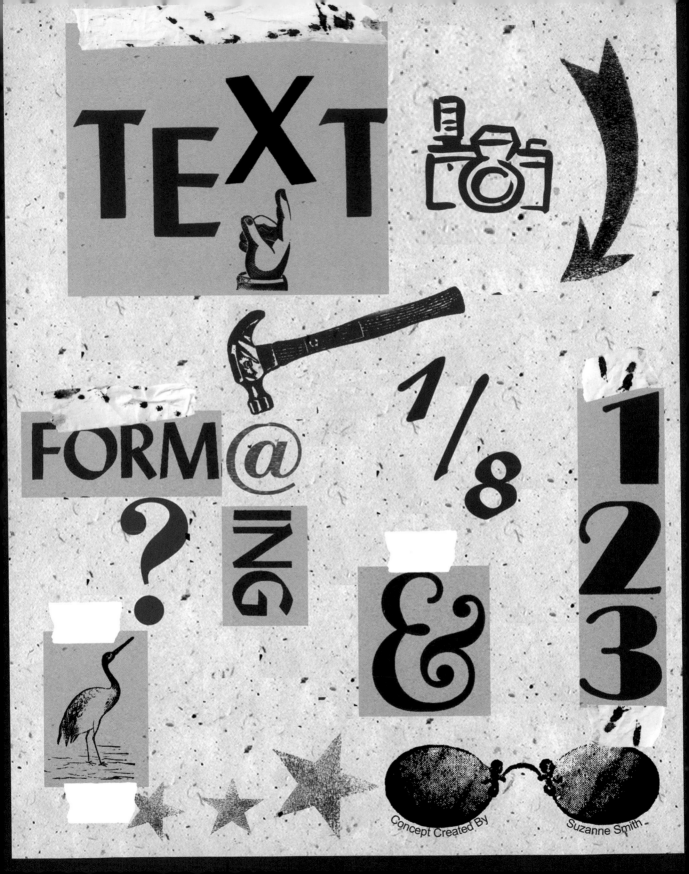

Concept Created By · Suzanne Smith ·

# Elements of Design— Typography

TYPOGRAPHY BY DEFINITION is "the art and technique of arranging type in order to make language visible." Typography involves the selection of typefaces, point sizes, line spacing, line lengths, and spacing between characters. In this section, we will look at some of the rules that are used when dealing with fonts.

# Typography Terms

LET'S START WITH A FEW of the terms you'll need to know when dealing with typography just to make sure that we are all on the same page.

▶ **Font:** A font is a specific typeface in one size, one style, and one weight.

▶ **Font family:** A font family is a collection of all the fonts in a typeface, with different weights (such as bold) and slants (such as italic).

▶ **Kerning:** This is the adjustment that is given to the space between the characters within a word or between words.

▶ **Leading:** Leading originally referred to strips of lead that typesetters placed between lines of type to space them out, and it now refers to the amount of space between lines of text.

▶ **Serif font:** A serif font is one where characters within the font have, well, serifs. A serif is a small line, circles, or swirls that decorates the main stroke of the character, such as the Times New Roman or **Rockwell** fonts.

▶ **Sans-serif:** A sans-serif font does not have serifs at the end of the strokes. Sans-serif fonts are typically used for titles or headlines.

▶ **Style:** Characteristics such as **bold**, *italics*, and the weight of the font are referred to as styles. For example, OpenType has a style called SMALL CAPS. Other font types do not, and as such, there has to be a specific font to display those characteristics.

▶ **Typeface:** Typeface is the designed look of the characters for a specific width and style of a font.

Now that we understand some of the terminology that a designer would typically use when talking about type in a design, let's take a quick look at some other not so commonly used terms. Figure 5.1 shows the Anatomy of Typography with both terms already mentioned and some of those not-so-common terms.

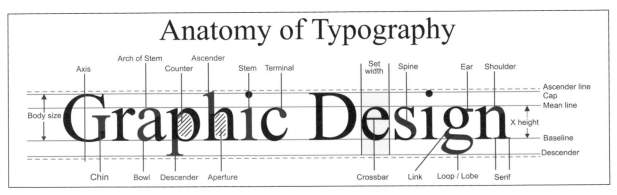

**Figure 5.1**

*The Anatomy of Typography, highlighting the common terms used in typography, as well as some of the uncommon terms.*

# Types of Fonts

NOW THAT WE HAVE THE BASICS down, let's talk type. There are a few different types of technologies currently available (pun intended). They include Type 1, TrueType, OpenType, and Unicode.

▶ **Type 1:** Type 1, also known as *PostScript fonts*, were introduced by Adobe in 1984 as part of the PostScript page description language for use with Adobe Type Manager and PostScript printers. It is a Type 1 font that can support font hinting, which is a method of adjusting ways in which a font is displayed on the screen to produce clearer text. In the earlier days (1984), Type 1 had a reputation for being a higher quality designed font.

▶ **TrueType:** The TrueType font is an outline font standard originally developed by Apple Computer in the late 1980s as a competitor to Adobe's Type 1 fonts. TrueType has become the most common format for fonts on both the Macintosh and the Microsoft Windows operating system.

▶ **OpenType:** OpenType is a relatively new format of scalable fonts, and it was created jointly by Adobe and Microsoft. It was built on its predecessor, TrueType, maintaining TrueType's basic structure and adding many advanced typographic features.

▶ **Unicode Fonts:** What sets the Unicode font apart from the other font types is that Unicode fonts contain a wide range of characters that are mapped to the standard Universal Character Set and include different scripts from around the world, so they are ideal for documents that will be translated into many different languages.

## Did You Know?

### Uppercase Letters

The individual characters that were used with movable printing type presses were stored in large drawers, known as cases. Originally, they were stored in a single case, but since the early 1700s, they have been separated into two cases, by size— uppercase and lowercase.

# Installing Fonts

NOW THAT YOU UNDERSTAND what a font is, the different types of fonts, and some of the characteristics of fonts, the next area to look at, before we look at how to use the fonts, is how to install a font.

Installing fonts into Windows is very straightforward. There are a couple of different ways to do it, and it depends on the version of Windows that you are running.

## Windows 7

Probably the easiest way to install a font into Windows 7 is to double-click on the font file and click the Install button on the upper-left corner of the font. (This is for Windows 7 only.)

**To install a font in Windows 7:**

1. From the START menu, click the Control Panel and then double-click Fonts (or press the letter "R"). This will bring up the Run command. Now just type in the word "fonts" and press Enter/Return on the keyboard.

2. Click File and then click Install New Font. (If you don't see the File menu, press Alt).

3. In the Add Fonts dialog box, under Drives, click the drive where the font that you want to install is located.

4. Under Folders, double-click the folder containing the fonts that you want to add.

5. Under the List of fonts, click the font that you want to add and then click Install.

## Windows Vista or XP

**To install a font in Windows Vista or XP:**

1. For Windows Vista or XP, from the START menu, click Control Panels and then select the Appearance and Themes category.

2. Select Fonts from the See Also panel at the left of this screen.

3. On the File menu, select Install New Font.

4. Click the drive and folder that contain the fonts you want to install.

5. To select multiple fonts, press and hold down the Ctrl key and click on the fonts that you want to install; then click OK.

### Did You Know?

### Temporarily Installing Fonts

If you need to use a few fonts but do not want to install them, and you are using Vista or XP, simply double-click on the font file. As long as you leave the Preview window open, you can make use of the font. When you are done with them, simply close the window. Unfortunately, Microsoft ruined it for Windows 7 users in that this trick will no longer work; however, you could right-click on the font file and select Install.

# Fonts from Other Sources

THERE ARE LITERALLY hundreds of thousands of fonts out there these days. They can come from a variety of sources or locations: installing Office productivity software, other graphic software, various websites, and even from the operating system itself. Even if you have access to all these fonts, there is one thing to remember—fonts that get installed are specific to the computer they are installed on and its operating system, and you may not have access to that font if you take your file to another system.

When you install a new font, the font will only be available on the system where it is installed. Sending a CorelDRAW file to a print shop or service provider that does not have the font will result in problems if they don't have the same font. You could copy the font file from the Font folder and send it along with the file, but this may pose a licensing problem in that you own the rights to use the font where the printer may not. The best resolution is to work with the printer to ensure that they have the fonts or to convert the text to curves.

## TrueDoc

Since the release of CorelDRAW 8, Corel licensed a technology called TrueDoc from Bitstream. By selecting this feature in the Save or Save As dialog box, the fonts within the document are embedded in the document (see Figure 5.2). It should be noted that this feature is no longer available in CorelDRAW X6; however, there is the ability to select Collect For Output from the File menu. We will discuss this a bit later in Chapter 9, "Designing Your Business Graphic."

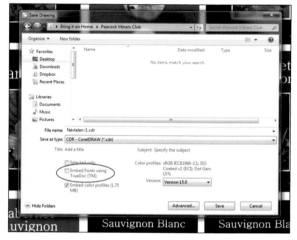

**Figure 5.2**
*The Save Drawing dialog box from CorelDRAW X5. You will notice the selection box to Embed Fonts using TrueDoc. This will cause any fonts that are in the design to be included with that design.*

Fonts, like software, have a license agreement associated with them. As a result, when using TrueDoc, you must agree to the terms of the agreement; otherwise, the fonts will not be embedded with the file.

## Font Collections with Bitstream Font Navigator

As we have discussed, there are different styles of fonts and fonts that convey different moods, and there are also specific fonts for specific purposes (such as single line fonts for engraving). As mentioned, fonts come from a variety of sources and over time, you can amass quite a collection. It is important that you manage the collections properly, and Bitstream Font Navigator is a very capable application to do just that.

Bitstream Font Navigator (Font Nav for short) is a font managing utility that you really cannot do without if you have hundreds or even thousands of fonts. It is a great way to manage the fonts that you would use on any given project. The CorelDRAW Graphic Suite has included it since version 8.

It's a good idea to organize your fonts into collections, possibly by specific types of projects—for example, invitation fonts, poster fonts, or fonts for signs.

## Express Yourself with Fonts

Fonts are a powerful medium of expression. They not only convey the message in words, but also have the ability to convey emotion (see Figure 5.3). The selection of the font family that you decide on when creating your design can make all the difference in the world. It can help your project become more attractive and personalized and help to convey the message that you want.

| Neutral | Classic | Casual |
|---------|---------|--------|
| Arial | Times New Roman | Rage Italic |
| Humerous | Vogue | Elegent |
| Jokerman | Bodoni Bold | Edwardian Script ITC |
| Agreed | Retro | Authoritative |
| Rockwell | Harlow Solid Italic | Swiss 721 Cn BT |
| Friendly | Bold | Technical |
| Tekton Pro Ext | Swiss721 BlkEx BT | Tandelle |

**Figure 5.3**
*This is a small table that shows some font examples and a suggestion as to the type of mood that the fonts may convey.*

# Type Modifications

CHANGING OR MODIFYING the appearance of a string of type or a paragraph text block is fairly simple and straightforward. With the text selected, Ctrl+B will make it **bold**, Ctrl+U will underline the text, and Ctrl+I will *italicize* it, assuming that the font you are using supports it (substitute Cmd for Macs). If you want to do any other formatting, your best bet is to use the Text docker.

Typically, dockers are located under the Windows menu; however, prior to CorelDRAW X6, the two Text dockers were under, well, the Text menu. In Figure 5.4, you can see the Character Formatting docker (Ctrl+T) and the Paragraph Formatting docker. In CorelDRAW X6, these have been put on steroids and combined into one docker called Text Properties (see Figure 5.5). Seriously, the development team has done a tremendous amount of work on CorelDRAW Graphics Suite X6 to make use of the capabilities of OpenType fonts, and the new docker was created to make these features even easier to access.

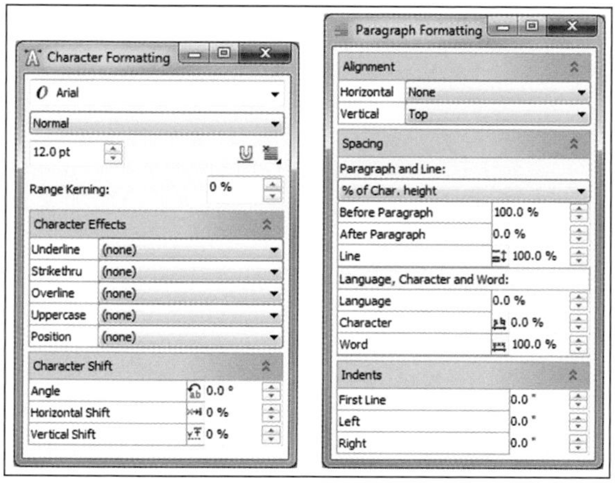

**Figure 5.4**
*Here you can see both the Character and Paragraph Formatting Dockers from CorelDRAW Graphics Suite X5.*

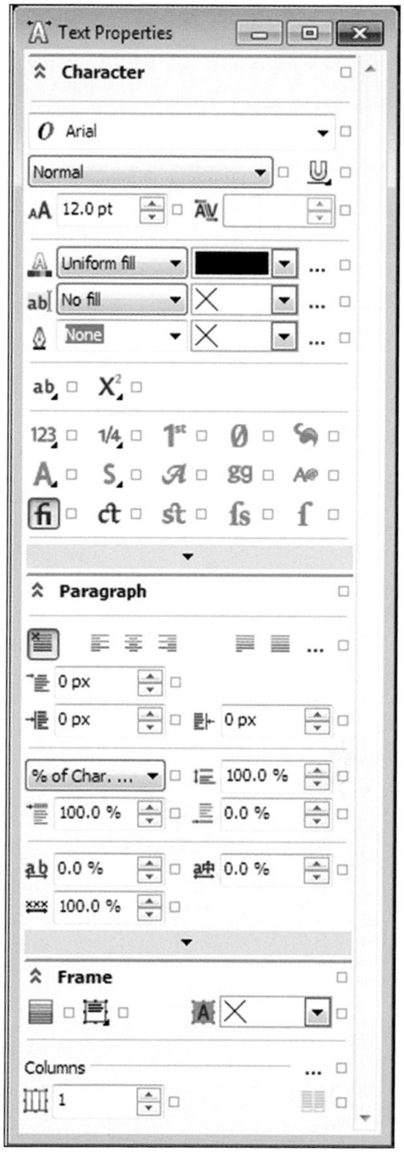

**Figure 5.5**
*The CorelDRAW X6 Text Properties is a single docker that contains all the settings for both Artistic and Paragraph text.*

# Above and Beyond Ordinary Type

LET'S TAKE A LOOK at some of the new features that have been brought to the surface with
OpenType fonts within CorelDRAW Graphics Suite
X6, and then in later chapters, we will make use of
some of these fonts with some practical exercises.

There are many OpenType fonts that have features
built into them that can completely change the
way that the characters appear on-screen or in
print. As an example, you can change the appearance of individual characters or groups of characters, such as numbers, fractions, or ligature sets
(see Figure 5.6). Note that this depends on the font
supporting these features. A ligature set is where
two or more letters are tied together into a single
letter, such as fi and fl.

fling  fling  fling

**Figure 5.6**
*The fl ligature set, as well as something that is referred
to as* swashes, *on the word* fling *can be seen here.*

## How to Access Alternates

Let's take a look at how to add these alternatives to
text and to number sets, and once you start to play
with them for a bit, you will become more com-
fortable at making use of them, and they can greatly improve the appearance of a design piece. Again,
keep in mind that these are new features that have
been added to CorelDRAW X6.

As with almost anything in CorelDRAW, there are a
couple of ways that these can be accessed. They
can either be accessed from the Text Properties
Docker from under the Text menu (Ctrl+T), or with
text selected, you can also go to Windows >
Dockers > Object Properties (Alt+Enter).

**To access alternates:**

1. Using the Artistic Text tool, type the word
   *Melody*. (I'm listening to Melody Gardot at
   the moment.)

2. Set the font to Gabriola and make it 72
   points (see Figure 5.7). Although CorelDRAW
   Graphics Suite X6 ships with a number of
   very nice OpenType fonts, Gabriola is a
   default font that is installed with Windows 7.

3. With the Text tool still selected, select the
   text characters. Note: It only works on single
   lines of text, so double-clicking might get
   you into a situation where the arrow won't
   show. You will notice, unlike in previous versions, the highlighting is a pale powder blue.
   You may also notice that there is a down-
   ward-pointing triangle (or "chicken beak")
   centered below the text. Clicking this handle
   will bring up a new feature called *Interactive
   OpenType*.

4. Click the chicken beak (say that three times
   fast) or Interactive OpenType arrow, and you
   will be able to see a preview of the text using
   features that are available for this font. Note
   that the number of sets will change, depending on the font and characters selected.

**5.** If you scroll the cursor over the previews, the text on the screen will change to reflect the style that the cursor is currently hovering over. Click the one that you want.

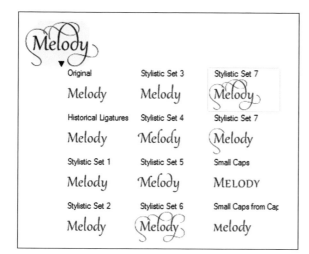

**Figure 5.7**
*This figure shows some of the features that are available with the Gabriola font and the selected text.*

One point here that may be obvious to some, but still needs to be mentioned is that although we have selected the entire piece of text and the desired feature, you certainly do not have to do so. In fact, you can select single character or groups of characters within a word (see Figure 5.8). Once it's applied, you can also use Interactive OpenType to remove features.

**Figure 5.8**
*Selecting individual characters or groups of characters to apply a style can sometimes be more effective within a design, although the suggestions offered depend on the characters selected.*

## Let's Talk Numbers

OpenType fonts can contain ligatures, swashes, and other glyphs for alpha characters. There is also a fair amount of formatting that can be done with numbers. Some of the formatting includes the following information:

- ▶ Numerator format
- ▶ Denominator format
- ▶ Fraction
- ▶ Small Caps
- ▶ Proportional Lining
- ▶ Tabular Lining
- ▶ Proportional Oldstyle
- ▶ Tabular Oldstyle

## A Broken Font

When looking at the various formats that are available with numbers and the Gabriola font, you may notice that with the fraction, the number values are not reflected correctly. This is an issue with the font, and it appears this way within other applications as well.

So, as you can see, there are a number of different characteristics that can be applied to both fonts and alphanumeric characters as well.

# Maintaining Features

IF YOU ARE USING CORELDRAW Graphics Suite X6 and have the need to save your design to a previous version to share with people, with the enhanced text features of this version, there are a couple of options that you should be aware of when saving the file.

When you elect to save to a previous version, the following message will appear (see Figure 5.9). This gives the option to either keep the appearance of the text, in which case the text will be converted to curves, or to keep the text editable, and any new features that you applied to the text will be lost.

If a file has been created in an earlier version than CorelDRAW X6, upon opening, an option bar will appear at the top of the screen that will allow you to update the text (see Figure 5.10). You must update the text if you intend to make use of the OpenType features of CorelDRAW.

OK, that is a brief overview of the OpenType features that have been added to CorelDRAW Graphics Suite X6. Later in Chapter 9, we will delve a bit deeper into the capabilities of the OpenType font features, but for now, because of the importance of typography in design, let's review some of the best practices that should be kept in mind when using fonts and various type characteristics that are available to you.

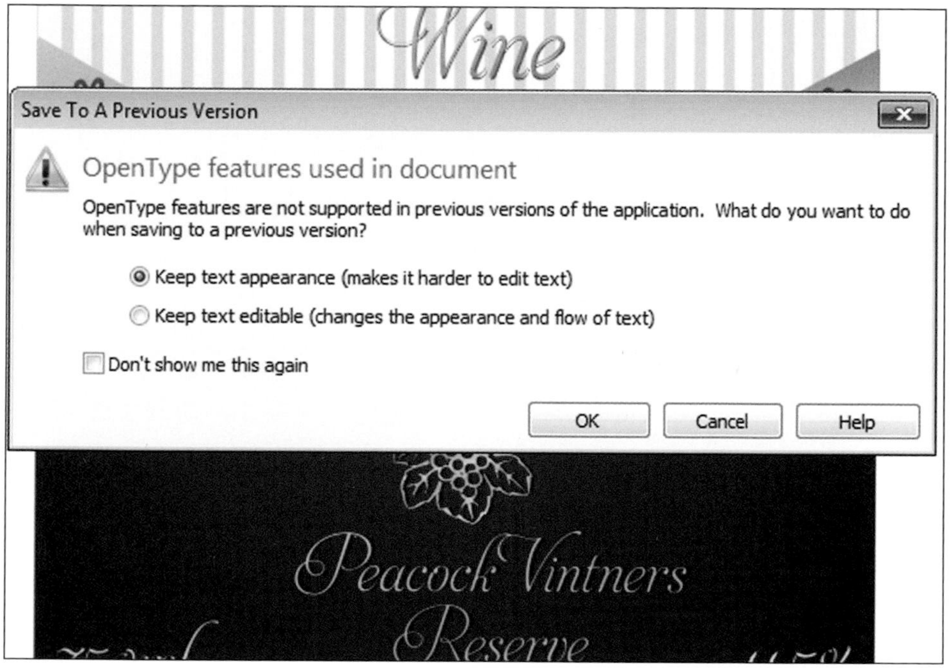

**Figure 5.9**
*If you are saving from CorelDRAW X6, the application will prompt you to make a decision as to what to do with the OpenType features.*

**Figure 5.10**
*If you are bringing in a file from an older version of CorelDRAW to CorelDRAW X6, click Update.*

# Typography Best Practices

WHEN USING FONTS OR TEXT, there are a number of guidelines or general rules that should be kept in mind. Remember that these are only general rules (and rules are made to be broken).

- Don't use too many different fonts; use one font throughout the body and maybe another for the headings. If you use multiple fonts, it can make the reader work too hard to get the message that you are trying to convey.

- Decorative fonts are good for letterhead; use them to frame the message or add emphasis to the text. They should not be used for body or copy text.

- Use serif fonts for body text because the serifs are designed to help the eye track through lines upon lines of text.

- When designing postcards, invitations, or other informal pieces, use unusual fonts, because they will add personality and excitement to the message.

- Handwriting fonts are good for invitations, the backs of postcards, and comments on pictures or photos. Using them for copy text is never a good idea.

- If you need inspiration for icons or logos, look at the dingbat fonts. The shapes and designs found there make them especially useful. These are also very useful for logo design or as icons or symbols in newsletters.

- Cutesy or childish type fonts, such as comic or comic sans, are for kids and kid things. Don't use them for brochures unless it is for a daycare center.

Typically, a serif font is used for body text because it is relaxing for the eye and does not force the reader to have to work too hard to get the message. To add a bit of excitement and flair, a serif font is typically used for titles and headings. It is a science to come up with matching pairs of fonts to make the reading experience more pleasurable (see Figure 5.11).

So in bringing this section on typography to a close, one thing to remember is that the font that you are using in a logo, a newsletter, or a package design is something that will potentially be around for years to come. It is something that will be used to convey the message. Make sure that it is a good one.

## PLEASING FONT COMBINATIONS

Garamond (bold)   **Lorem ipsum dolor sit amet.**
Futura Lt BT   Veniam dolores magna no wisi sit dolor ea. Dolor sed et diam voluptua velit. Vulputate esse magna consetetur. Et dolore sed nonumy. Gubergren dolore dignissim iriure facilisis ipsum duo invidunt.

Bodoni Bk BT   **Lorem ipsum dolor sit amet.**
Futura Lt BT   Veniam dolores magna no wisi sit dolor ea. Dolor sed et diam voluptua velit. Vulputate esse magna consetetur. Et dolore sed nonumy. Gubergren dolore dignissim iriure facilisis ipsum duo invidunt.

Futura Md BT   **Lorem ipsum dolor sit amet.**
Bodoni Bk BT   Veniam dolores magna no wisi sit dolor ea. Dolor sed et diam voluptua velit. Vulputate esse magna consetetur. Et dolore sed nonumy. Gubergren dolore dignissim iriure facilisis ipsum duo invidunt.

Century Schoolbook   Lorem ipsum dolor sit amet.
Franklin Gothic Book   Veniam dolores magna no wisi sit dolor ea. Dolor sed et diam voluptua velit. Vulputate esse magna consetetur. Et dolore sed nonumy. Gubergren dolore dignissim iriure facilisis ipsum duo invidunt.

Gill Sans MT (Bold)   **Lorem ipsum dolor sit amet.**
Calisto MT   Veniam dolores magna no wisi sit dolor ea. Dolor sed et diam voluptua velit. Vulputate esse magna consetetur. Et dolore sed nonumy. Gubergren dolore dignissim iriure facilisis ipsum duo invidunt.

Baskerville Old Face   Lorem ipsum dolor sit amet.
Swiss 721 BT   Veniam dolores magna no wisi sit dolor ea. Dolor sed et diam voluptua velit. Vulputate esse magna consetetur. Et dolore sed nonumy. Gubergren dolore dignissim iriure facilisis ipsum duo invidunt.

**Figure 5.11**

*Here are just a few examples of complementary fonts that can be used when creating documents. Combining a serif and a sans serif gives harmony to the piece and makes it easier to read.*

| | | | | | | | | |
|---|---|---|---|---|---|---|---|---|
| C:0 M:0 Y:0 K:100<br>Black | C:0 M:0 Y:0 K:90<br>90% Black | C:0 M:0 Y:0 K:80<br>80% Black | C:0 M:0 Y:0 K:70<br>70% Black | C:0 M:0 Y:0 K:60<br>60% Black | C:0 M:0 Y:0 K:50<br>50% Black | C:0 M:0 Y:0 K:40<br>40% Black | C:0 M:0 Y:0 K:30<br>30% Black | C:0 M:0 Y:0 K:20<br>20% Black |
| C:0 M:0 Y:0 K:10<br>10% Black | C:0 M:0 Y:0 K:0<br>White | C:100 M:100 Y:0 K:0<br>Blue | C:100 M:0 Y:0 K:0<br>Cyan | C:100 M:0 Y:100 K:0<br>Green | C:0 M:0 Y:100 K:0<br>Yellow | C:0 M:100 Y:100 K:0<br>Red | C:0 M:100 Y:0 K:0<br>Magenta | C:20 M:80 Y:0 K:20<br>Purple |
| C:0 M:60 Y:100 K:0<br>Orange | C:0 M:40 Y:20 K:0<br>Pink | C:0 M:20 Y:20 K:60<br>Dark Brown | C:20 M:20 Y:0 K:0<br>Powder Blue | C:40 M:40 Y:0 K:0<br>Pastel Blue | C:60 M:40 Y:0 K:0<br>Baby Blue | C:60 M:60 Y:0 K:0<br>Electric Blue | C:40 M:40 Y:0 K:20<br>Twilight Blue | C:60 M:40 Y:0 K:40<br>Navy Blue |
| C:40 M:40 Y:0 K:60<br>Deep Navy Blue | C:40 M:20 Y:0 K:40<br>Desert Blue | C:100 M:20 Y:0 K:0<br>Sky Blue | C:40 M:0 Y:0 K:0<br>Ice Blue | C:20 M:0 Y:0 K:20<br>Light BlueGreen | C:20 M:0 Y:0 K:40<br>Ocean Green | C:20 M:0 Y:0 K:60<br>Moss Green | C:20 M:0 Y:0 K:80<br>Dark Green | C:40 M:0 Y:20 K:60<br>Forest Green |
| C:60 M:0 Y:40 K:40<br>Grass Green | C:40 M:0 Y:20 K:40<br>Kentucky Green | C:60 M:0 Y:40 K:20<br>Light Green | C:60 M:0 Y:60 K:20<br>Spring Green | C:60 M:0 Y:20 K:0<br>Turquoise | C:60 M:0 Y:20 K:20<br>Sea Green | C:20 M:0 Y:20 K:20<br>Faded Green | C:20 M:0 Y:20 K:0<br>Ghost Green | C:40 M:0 Y:40 K:0<br>Mint Green |
| C:20 M:0 Y:20 K:40<br>Army Green | C:20 M:0 Y:40 K:40<br>Avocado Green | C:20 M:0 Y:60 K:20<br>Martian Green | C:20 M:0 Y:40 K:20<br>Dull Green | C:40 M:0 Y:100 K:0<br>Chartreuse | C:20 M:0 Y:60 K:0<br>Moon Green | C:0 M:0 Y:20 K:80<br>Murky Green | C:0 M:0 Y:20 K:60<br>Olive Drab | C:0 M:0 Y:20 K:40<br>Khaki |
| C:0 M:0 Y:40 K:40<br>Olive | C:0 M:0 Y:60 K:20<br>Banana Yellow | C:0 M:0 Y:60 K:0<br>Light Yellow | C:0 M:0 Y:40 K:0<br>Chalk | C:0 M:0 Y:20 K:0<br>Pale Yellow | C:0 M:20 Y:40 K:40<br>Brown | C:0 M:40 Y:60 K:20<br>Red Brown | C:0 M:20 Y:60 K:20<br>Gold | C:0 M:60 Y:80 K:0<br>Autumn Orange |
| C:0 M:40 Y:80 K:0<br>Light Orange | C:0 M:40 Y:60 K:0<br>Peach | C:0 M:20 Y:100 K:0<br>Deep Yellow | C:0 M:20 Y:40 K:0<br>Sand | C:0 M:20 Y:40 K:60<br>Walnut | C:0 M:60 Y:60 K:40<br>Ruby Red | C:0 M:60 Y:80 K:20<br>Brick Red | C:0 M:60 Y:60 K:0<br>Tropical Pink | C:0 M:40 Y:40 K:0<br>Soft Pink |
| C:0 M:20 Y:20 K:0<br>Faded Pink | C:0 M:40 Y:20 K:40<br>Crimson | C:0 M:60 Y:40 K:20<br>Regal Red | C:0 M:60 Y:20 K:20<br>Deep Rose | C:0 M:100 Y:60 K:20<br>Neon Red | C:0 M:60 Y:40 K:0<br>Deep Pink | C:0 M:80 Y:40 K:0<br>Hot Pink | C:0 M:40 Y:20 K:20<br>Dusty Rose | C:0 M:40 Y:0 K:60<br>Plum |
| C:0 M:60 Y:0 K:40<br>Deep Violet | C:0 M:40 Y:0 K:0<br>Light Violet | C:0 M:40 Y:0 K:20<br>Violet | C:0 M:20 Y:0 K:40<br>Dusty Plum | C:0 M:20 Y:0 K:20<br>Pale Purple | C:20 M:60 Y:0 K:20<br>Majestic Purple | C:20 M:80 Y:0 K:0<br>Neon Purple | C:20 M:60 Y:0 K:0<br>Light Purple | C:20 M:40 Y:0 K:20<br>Twilight Violet |
| C:20 M:40 Y:0 K:0<br>Easter Purple | C:20 M:40 Y:0 K:60<br>Deep Purple | C:20 M:40 Y:0 K:40<br>Grape | C:40 M:60 Y:0 K:0<br>Blue Violet | C:40 M:100 Y:0 K:0<br>Blue Purple | C:40 M:80 Y:0 K:20<br>Deep River | C:60 M:80 Y:0 K:0<br>Deep Azure | C:40 M:60 Y:0 K:40<br>Storm Blue | C:60 M:80 Y:0 K:20<br>Deep Blue |

# C100 M100 Y100 K100

# Elements of Design— Color

**6**

**W**E ARE ALL IN BUSINESS to make money. Some of us are in sales, others in support, and yet others are in marketing. Regardless of the type of work you do, the one thing we have in common is that we all know what we like to see and make purchasing decisions based on what we like. Keeping this in mind, it is important that the design piece you are creating will capture your viewers' attention, and one of the easiest ways to do that is to use color.

# Color Space vs. Color Model

WE'VE ALL HEARD THE EXPRESSION. "It's right there in black and white," or "he is seeing red," but what does that really mean? What is red, or black, or white?

Let's start with a couple of definitions about exactly what color is and talk briefly about color spaces and color models.

Color is actually a perceived response to various wavelengths of light and the way in which they are transmitted to the brain. Here is how it works: The human eye has two different kinds of receptors—rods and cones. The rods help to distinguish an image in grayscale, and the cones allow the brain to perceive color hues.

There are three types of cones within the human eye that have different sensitivities to different wavelengths of light. The first is sensitive to red light, the second to green, and the third to blue. When a specific type of cone is stimulated, the brain perceives the corresponding color. As an example, if the wavelength of green is perceived, the green cone will be stimulated, and you will see green; the red wavelength, you'll see red; and of course blue, you'll see blue.

A color model is a numerical way to define those colors within the color space. This color model is identified by a series, or sets, of numbers, usually in three or four values that form each color.

In the most generic sense of the definition, color space is the range of colors that one device (eye, printer, camera) can detect. By adding a mapping function to these colors within the color space, you are assigning a "footprint" or boundaries to the model. Any color that falls outside of these boundaries is considered to be out of gamut.

There are a range of color models to choose from when creating graphics. Some are based on the optical components of the colors and others are based on how people "feel" colors are related to each other. For the purposes of this book, we will look at just a few of these.

## RGB

The RGB model is an additive model, which means that you are adding varying amounts of red, green, and blue (see Figure 6.1). You start with black and then you *add* color. This forms the RGB color model.

The main use for the RGB color model can be seen on computer monitors or television screens. Remember those old rear projection television screens with the big red, green, and blue lenses—another example of RGB. The gamut for the RGB model is rather large compared to CMYK, so it is a preferable color model to use when creating images that will be output to a digital device. However, as RGB is device dependent (color can shift or fade on a monitor over time), color management is necessary.

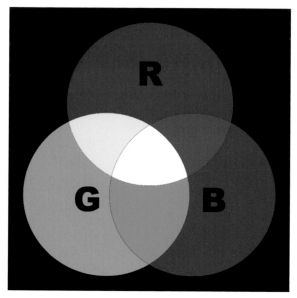

**Figure 6.1**
*A representation of the RGB color model. Note that where the three primary colors overlap, they create the secondary colors of CMYK and white.*

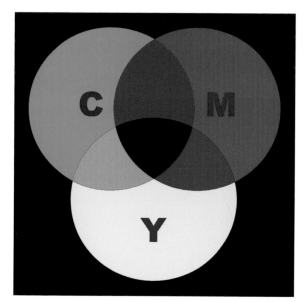

**Figure 6.2**
*A representation of the CMYK color model. Note that where the three primary colors overlap, they create the secondary colors of RGB and black.*

# CMY(K)

The CMY model is a subtractive model that is comprised of cyan, magenta, and yellow. When all three primary subtractive colors are laid down on a piece of paper or a gamut, they block white light from bouncing off the medium. As all the colors have been suppressed, the eyes see black (the absence of any color).

In practice, however, CMY usually cannot be used alone. Because of imperfections in the inks, the material you're printing on, and other limitations of the process, true black or true grays cannot be created by mixing the inks in equal proportions. The actual result is a muddy brown color. In order to get a more pure black and grays, printers accomplish this by adding black ink, indicated as K. Thus, the practical application of the CMY color model when printing is accomplished by using the four-color CMYK process (see Figure 6.2).

## What's with the "K"?

Why isn't it CMYB? The K in CMYK refers to the Key color (not black), and it is the last plate that gets printed. It is this plate that adds the detail to the image—usually black, but not always. The acronym follows the order of print: cyan, magenta, yellow, and finally the Key plate.

As a rule, if the graphic is destined for a print service provider, CMYK would be best.

## Spot Colors

Spot colors are created with custom inks and are typically used when it is not possible to create a specific color using CMYK inks or when color consistency is required. Spot colors can also be used to indicate a specific area of a design that requires a treatment or effect that needs to be applied to the print job, such as applying a gloss lacquer to an object or using a specialty ink to achieve a certain effect, like indicating an emboss on a job. Another use for spot colors would be when applying metallic inks or specific colors, such as the Coca-Cola red or Pepsi blue.

## How Do They Fit Together?

You have just learned a bit about the different color models: RGB, CMYK, and spot, but how do they map to each other and in relation to the visible color spectrum? Why do you see a color shift when printing sometimes? Figure 6.3 shows the different models. Note how many colors fall out of gamut when translating from perceived colors in nature to what the digital camera would capture and to what a printer can print. It is these colors that may be affected when converting from RGB to CMYK, and this is the reason why color management is so important.

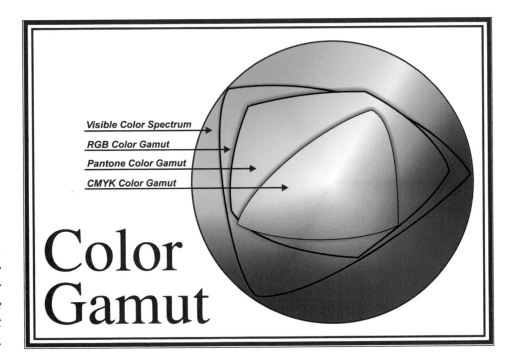

**Figure 6.3**
*Here you can see the visible color spectrum with the various print gamuts.*

# Color Palettes

COLOR PALETTES is a collection of various colors, usually based on a specific color model. There are a large number of palettes that are available within CorelDRAW. These are categorized under various libraries within the Color Palette Manager and include such libraries as Process, which is further broken down to CMYK, Pantone, and RGB. The CMYK library alone has over 45 palettes within it. There is also a Spot library that contains HKS, Pantone, Roland, as well as some individual palettes such as DIC, FOCOLTONE, and TOYO, to name a few. There are also two other palettes that need to be discussed, the Default palette and the Document palette.

## Default Palette

By default, the default palette (can I say that?) is the palette that matches the color model as set by the Primary color mode under Tools > Color Management > Document Settings, or when the document was created. It is this palette that appears on the right side of the screen.

## Document Palette

The Document palette was a new feature that was added to CorelDRAW X5. It gets created with each new file, and the palette actually travels with the document. (I'll explain how this works in Appendix A, "Troubleshooting 101.") This feature is extremely handy because it is much easier to create objects with colors that have already been used in the file, and there is no longer a problem with "missing colors."

By default, in CorelDRAW X5, the Document palette appears undocked near the center of the page, and it is usually closed or docked before you start to create a design. In CorelDRAW X6, the Document palette appears at the bottom of the CorelDRAW window just above the status bar.

## Adding to the Document Palette

As you build a design and add colors, these are added to the Document palette; however, if you import an image, then you must "inform" the palette of these new colors. The Document palette can contain RGB, CMYK, and spot colors. There can also be tints of the spot colors (see Figure 6.4).

Dragging an imported vector image onto the palette will cause the palette to be updated. When you import a raster image into the document and drag it onto the palette, you will need to indicate how many colors from that graphic that you want to have added. By default, 10 colors will be added, but the minimum is actually 0 and the maximum is 256.

It is also possible to add colors using the Eyedropper tool. Selecting the Eyedropper tool within the Document palette will not only allow you to click anywhere within the CorelDRAW screen, but also to click in any application or website. Holding down the Ctrl key will allow you to add more than one color at a time.

## Color Palette Creation

For a great site to create custom color palettes, visit http://kuler.adobe.com. Not only can you create a custom palette, but with the aid of the Eyedropper from the Document palette, you can also save them for projects that you are working on.

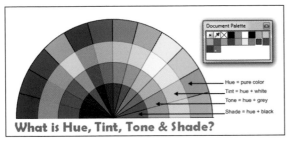

**Figure 6.4**
*Here you can see the current Document palette and the colors that are used in the open document. In the Document palette, you may also notice a small white square in the last color's lower left corner. This is an indication that this is actually a Pantone color. This figure also illustrates the differences between Hue, Tint, Tone, and Shade.*

## Custom Palettes

Custom palettes can be created quite easily in CorelDRAW and can serve a number of different purposes, such as working on current documents and building a palette for a specific customer or for a specific type of document. A custom palette can include colors or color styles from any color model, including spot colors.

There are a couple of different ways to create a custom palette. The three main ways to create a custom palette are the following:

▶ From the Palette Editor, click New Palette.

▶ Choose Windows > Color Palettes > Create Palette from Document.

▶ With objects selected, choose Windows > Color Palettes > Create Palette from Selection.

**To create a palette from a selected image:**

1. First, import a bitmap image into a new document. I am going to use an image that contains a number of yellows and oranges as I want a palette that I can use when I work with images of sunsets.

2. If there are colors that you want to add to the palette that are not contained in the bitmap, either import additional files or create the other objects prior to creating the palette. I have blended two different shades of blue here to give me a number of blues as well.

3. Go to Windows > Color Palettes > Create Palette from Document. By default, the palette will be saved in the My Palettes folder. Give the palette a name and click Save.

4. If the document contains a bitmap, you will be presented with a dialog box asking how many colors from the bitmap you want to include. (There is a limit of 255.) Select how many colors you desire and click OK.

The Color palette (see Figure 6.5) will be created and will be docked to the left of any palette that you may currently have open.

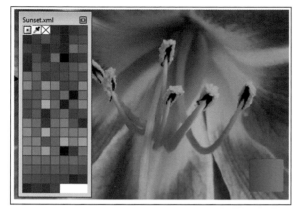

**Figure 6.5**

*You can use any image to create a custom palette. I used an image of a lily to create my Sunset Color palette. You can also see the open and undocked palette. Color palettes from CorelDRAW Graphics Suite X5 and X6 are stored in the .xml format.*

## Specialty Palettes

In CorelDRAW Graphics Suite X5, there were three specialty palettes added to the list of available palettes. These are the Roland Color palettes, and they include the Roland Color System Library, which is a collection of the color available when printing from a Roland device, the Roland Metallic Color System Library, and the Roland VersaWorks palette.

Although these are specialty palettes, and they require specific devices, or more importantly print shops with these devices, they can really add pop to any design that you may create, for example adding metallic ink to a kit folder or report cover.

# Color Styles and Harmonies

I'D LIKE TO SAVE OBJECT STYLES for Chapter 8, "Create Layouts with Ease," as styles really do go a long way toward improving speed and the workflow while designing, but I really cannot leave this chapter without mentioning color styles and harmonies.

The Color Styles docker lets you create, edit, and apply color styles to individual objects or to groups of objects. By creating and applying a color style, it becomes very easy to globally change the color of multiple objects within a document that has that style applied.

Where it really gets exciting is when dealing with color harmonies. Harmonies link a relationship from one color style to another and allow you to edit all colors in a harmony at the same time. For example, if you edit one color within a harmony, another color in that same harmony will be updated as well. Let me show you what I mean with the tutorial in the "Color Harmonies in CorelDRAW X6" section.

# Creating a Color Style

In this tutorial, you will learn how to set up Color Styles and create Color Harmonies. This is something that is way cool, so hang on.

We are going to start by creating a new document. As this is just to demonstrate styles and harmonies, do not be too concerned about the page setup. (We will look at that a bit deeper later on.) Just click OK to select the default page setting. Now, for reference, Figure 6.6 shows the design that we will be creating.

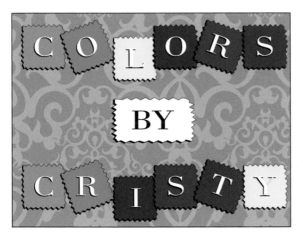

**Figure 6.6**
*This is the design that we will be creating in this tutorial and continuing in the next section to demonstrate the new Color Harmonies that are available in CorelDRAW Graphics Suite X6.*

**To create a color style:**

1. Looking at Figure 6.6 for reference, create a 1" × 1" square. An easy way to do this is to hold down the Ctrl key while dragging with the Rectangle tool to create a square. This will constrain the dimensions. For accuracy, you can also specify exact measurements in the Interactive property bar after it's drawn.

2. Next, let's roughen up the edges by using the Roughen Brush from the toolbox. Click and hold the Shape tool and select the Roughen Brush (the icon looks like a rake); then on the Interactive property bar, set the Nib size to 0.15 (mm). Now run the cursor around the perimeter of the square while holding down the left mouse button.

3. Click the black color swatch on the Color palette. This will fill the object with black.

4. Now press Ctrl+D to duplicate this object (see Figure 6.7).

## Setting Duplicate Distance

If you get a dialog box for Duplicate Offset, set the Horizontal Offset and the Vertical Offset to 0.00. This will cause any duplicate objects in the future to be placed directly over the top of the originals.

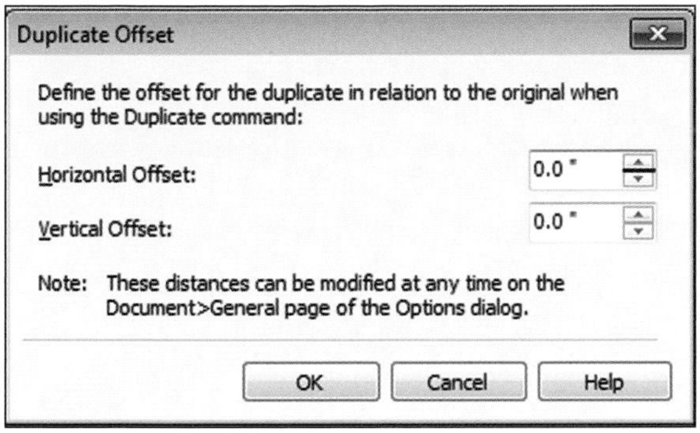

**Duplicate Offset**

Define the offset for the duplicate in relation to the original when using the Duplicate command:

Horizontal Offset:    0.0 "

Vertical Offset:    0.0 "

Note:   These distances can be modified at any time on the Document>General page of the Options dialog.

OK     Cancel     Help

**Figure 6.7**
*In the Duplicate Offset dialog box, set both offsets to 0.00.*

5. Using the arrow keys, nudge this new object up 2 and over 2; then click on the cyan color swatch in the Color palette.

6. Marquis-select these two objects and use Ctrl+D to duplicate them. Now before doing anything else, read the note here.

## A Smart Way to Duplicate

There is something that was added to CorelDRAW 10 and was referred to as *Smart Duplicate*. Smart Duplicate occurs when the application remembers the previous position, as well as the offset (or size change) of the new position, and has the ability to apply that to the new duplicate.

7. Move the duplicated object so that its left edge touches the right edge of the first object (hold the Ctrl key down just after you start the move, which will constrain the movement to one axis). Once you have done that, press Ctrl+D four more times. This will result in six of these elements being created, as shown in Figure 6.8.

**Figure 6.8**
*Your project should look similar to the image shown here*

8. Next, select the Pick tool, click and drag to marquis-select the first two squares (the cyan and the black one below it), and group them (Ctrl+G).

9. Repeat this for the next five sets.

10. Select the second set to the right and rotate it 20 degrees. To do this, make sure that it is selected in the Interactive property bar.

11. Rotate the fifth icon as well, but this time rotate it -20. This will cause a clockwise rotation of 20 degrees.

12. Move the other squares as you see fit.

13. The next step is to apply the various colors to them. Click the second rectangle to the right of the first one, with the Ctrl key held down. This will select the cyan square. Release the Ctrl key and click on a color in the color swatch. Repeat this process for the remaining cyan squares, selecting colors of your choice.

## Selecting Within a Group of Objects

Holding the Ctrl key down while selecting a group of objects will allow you to select an object within the group. You will notice that the sizing handles are black circles rather than the eight small black squares.

## Shading Colors

With an object selected, holding the Ctrl key down and clicking on a color in the Color palette will add 10% of that color to the selected object.

14. Marquis-select these six objects and press Ctrl+D to duplicate them. Move these downward about three inches.

15. Marquis-select the lower row of boxes, as you are going to flip them around. To do this, click on both the Mirror horizontally and Mirror vertically icons on the Interactive property bar.

16. Now let's add the center white rectangle. To do this, simply select one of the rectangles and duplicate it. Move this and center it between the two sets of objects that you have created.

17. To size this, in the Interactive property bar, ensure that the Lock ratio lock is unlocked, change the horizontal object size to two inches, and change the color of the top object to white.

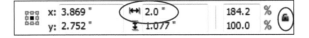

18. Now before we align the objects into the final position, we will add the text. To do this, make sure that you have the Bodoni font installed. (I used the Bodoni Bk BT.) If you do not, go ahead and install it (refer to Chapter 5, "Elements of Design—Typography," if you are not sure how to do so), or if you would prefer, use a different font.

19. Off to the side of the document, type COLORS BY CRISTY on three separate lines. Use the Enter or Return key to create the separate lines rather than creating a new insertion point.

20. Click on the Pick tool, and now from the Interactive property bar, change the font to Bodoni Bk BT (or one that you would prefer to use) and set the point size to 48 pt.

**21.** Now we need to break the text apart in order to place the individual characters. With the text still selected, from the Arrange menu, select Break Artistic Text: Bodoni Bk BT (Normal) (ENU) Apart. Alternatively, simply select Ctrl+K on the keyboard.

**22.** You will notice that the first word is now selected. Now, repeat this step for the word COLORS and CRISTY, but do not do it for the word BY. You should now have individual letters for two of the words.

**23.** It is now time to arrange or align all of the objects. Select the letter C from the word COLOR and while holding down the Shift key, select the first rectangle. Release the Shift key and tap the letter C followed by the letter E. This will quickly align the letter in the center of the first object. Repeat this for each letter in turn.

## Order Is Important

When selecting objects to align, the order of selection is important. The position of the aligned objects when you are done will be based on the last object selected.

**24.** Select the letters O, R, and Y, individually and rotate them to match the angle of rotation for the squares that they are on top of.

**25.** To duplicate these letters, you will need to first select them (sometimes I can really state the obvious).

**26.** Select the letters by creating a marquis selection around *only* the letters, as shown in Figure 6.9.

**Figure 6.9**
*When marquis-selecting, only the objects that are completely surrounded by the marquis will be selected.*

# Selecting an Object in CorelDRAW

As with many things in CorelDRAW, there are a number of different ways to do things, and selecting objects within a document is no different. If you are looking to simply select a single object or a group of objects, it is just a matter of selecting the Pick tool and clicking on the object or group of objects.

Selecting a single object within a group is also fairly straightforward: Hold down the Ctrl key while clicking on the object within a group, and you will select it. Visually, the sizing handles around the bounding box will appear as circles rather than small squares.

Now, when selecting multiple objects that are ungrouped, there are four ways to do this:

- ▶ Hold down the Shift key while selecting the objects that you would like to select.
- ▶ With the Pick tool selected, click and drag around the objects to create a marquis. Release the mouse button, and the objects encompassed by the marquis will be selected.
- ▶ Creating a marquis frame that just touches an object or a number of objects, with the Alt key held down, will select all objects that the marquis touches.
- ▶ In CorelDRAW X6, a new Pick tool has been added. It is called the Freehand Pick tool, and it allows you to create any shape with the selection marquis to select what has been bounded by it.

There is one final tip that I need to mention here when talking about the Pick tool. When you draw a marquis, before releasing the left mouse button, if you also depress the right mouse button, you can freely reposition the marquis. When you have the marquis in the desired, new location, release the right mouse button, and then the left. Cool eh!

Occasionally, you may need to select an object that is behind another object. For example, if you have a large transparent object over the top of a design or an empty paragraph text frame and you need to select an object under it, hold down the Alt key and do a single-click where the object is. This is referred to as the Digger tool. Multiple clicks will dig deeper and deeper, selecting objects that may be layered on top of each other.

Now other than using the Object manager, which we will discuss in Chapter 8, the final way to select an object is by using the Tab key. Holding down the Shift and tapping the Tab key will select individual objects in the order that they were created, and the Tab key by itself will select in the reverse order.

27. Hold down the Ctrl key and press the D on the keyboard to duplicate the text and then tap the up cursor key twice and then the right cursor key on the keyboard.

28. Click on the white color swatch in the color palette.

29. Finally, marquis-select the squares and the text that reads COLOR and group them (Ctrl+G).

30. Repeat the last five steps for the word CRISTY. OK, we are almost ready to take a look at the magic of Color Harmonies.

31. Select the three elements and align them. To do this, tap the letter C. This will center the three elements horizontally. Now, holding down the Shift key, tap the letter C. This will align it vertically and now press Ctrl+G to group the three objects.

32. Marquis-select the three grouped elements and while holding down the Shift key, double-click the Rectangle tool. This is a great way to create a rectangle around the bounding box of whatever you have selected. While still pressing the Shift key, grab the sizing handle on the lower-right corner and pull outward just a bit to increase the size. Not too much now, eh!

33. Now we want to fill this rectangle with a fill. Let's use the full color pattern fill by clicking on the Fill bucket and from the flyout, select Pattern Fill. In the Pattern Fill dialog box, select Full and choose the first pattern. Click OK.

34. Now, from the Arrange menu, select Order and then To Back of Page.

Voila! If your design looks like mine, give yourself a pat on the back, because you've done a good job! Hopefully, you have picked up a few tips and short-cuts along the way.

# Color Harmonies in CorelDRAW X6

We will now take a look at Color Styles and Color Harmonies in CorelDRAW Graphics Suite X6.

If you are using an older version, feel free to read on. Personally, I think that this is really cool and if you are not currently using CorelDRAW X6, this makes the upgrade well worthwhile.

1. From the Windows menu, go to Dockers > Color Styles. Alternatively, press Ctrl+F6. The next step is to create the color styles. It is as simple as dragging and dropping.

2. Drag the image into the box that says Drag here to add color style & generate a harmony. A Create Color Styles dialog box will appear (see Figure 6.10).

3. Slide the slider to 2 and click OK. This will create two harmony sets, which basically allows you to change the text and the squares independently.

4. Click the harmony that has the six colors in it. You will see the Harmony Editor open up (see Figure 6.11). This will control the colors for the rectangles.

Across the top portion of the panel, you can see the color swatches for the currently selected color harmony. Selecting one of these swatches will select the specific color within the harmony. This gives you the ability to change or modify it.

Below the color swatches, there is a representation of the current color model with the various colors graphically identified so that you can see the relationship between each. You can either click on one of the circles at the ends of the arms to select the color or click on a swatch. By clicking anywhere within the color model, it will select all colors.

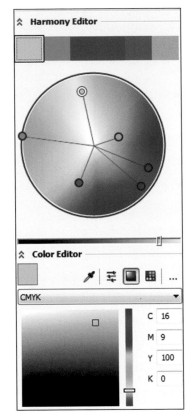

**Figure 6.11**
*The Harmony Editor and Color Editor.*

**Figure 6.10**
*Within the Create Color Styles dialog box, you have the ability to dictate how many harmony sets you want to have, as well as whether or not you want to use outline colors, fill colors, or both.*

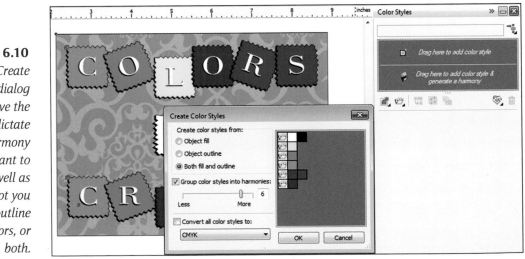

If you select an individual color, use the Color Editor to change that color. Of course, there are a number of options that will allow you to change the color, which include the following:

▶ Color eyedropper

▶ Color sliders

▶ Color viewers, which include CMY, CMYK, RGB, HSB, HLS, Lab, YIQ, and a couple of others

▶ Color palettes—all color palettes are available here, including the spot or Pantone palettes

Time to play! I'm not going to tell you what to do here, just have fun.

Experiment! Try clicking a specific circle and dragging it. Now click on an area where there is no circle. As mentioned, you will notice that it selects all. So now grab one and move it. Watch as it changes all the colors of the design. How cool is that?

I have flashes of staring at a lava lamp!

# Elements of Design— Resolution

D PI, PPI, LPI, HALFTONES? What is resolution? What do all these acronyms mean? In this chapter, I will take a look at these various terms and how they come into play when creating graphic images for print or for the Web.

During my time talking to customers on the support line, at tradeshows, or during training sessions, it has become readily apparent that resolution was and is a confusing subject. Let's see if I can help clear it up.

# Dissecting the Terminology

WHEN YOU LOOK AT a bitmap image or photo, it is made up of pixels (picture elements). A pixel is a single point in an image. Consider monitors and TVs, which are made in a similar fashion. If you get really close to them, you will see many dots of color that run in rows and columns along the surface of the display. Resolution is simply the number of pixels per inch, or PPI. The higher the PPI, the higher the resolution will be. In other words, the more pixels per inch, the more information or detail that you will have in the image. I should point out that what Corel refers to as DPI is in reality PPI, for the most part. For the purpose of this book, I will stay with the term *DPI* as well.

In digital photography, pixels will likely have subtle changes in shade from one to the next. When you zoom out, these subtle changes in shading give the illusion of a continuous tone. For example, picture the shadows on the face of a child playing in the sun. An image with a higher number of pixels per inch will have a smoother transition; conversely, one with a much lower resolution will reveal a jagged appearance between colors.

Many people interpret the above definition as meaning that bitmap resolutions should be as high as possible; however, this is almost never the case.

When determining what the resolution of a bitmap will be, you should consider how the bitmap will be output. If you are outputting to the Web, 72 or 96 DPI is more than adequate, but if it is black-and-white line art, 600 is probably better.

There are some general guidelines when choosing the proper input resolution for the file that will be output:

- ▶ Try to avoid scanning at a resolution that is higher than the scanner will support. This will cause the scanner to create new pixels that don't really exist in the image, and you may see degradation in the quality of the image.

- ▶ Scan at a resolution that is evenly divisible by the optical resolution of your scanner. What I mean by this is that if your scanner has a maximum resolution of, say 600 DPI, do not scan at 437 DPI. Rather, a resolution of 300 DPI or 150 DPI will prevent the scanner from having to recalculate the pixels and potentially reduce image quality.

- ▶ Try to match the size that you scan to the size at which you want to print. For example, if you scan at 4 × 6, try using that size directly in your layout. Otherwise, calculate a factor to resize the image by. Remember not to go larger than the maximum optical resolution of the scanner.

# What Resolution Is Best?

THE ANSWER TO THE QUESTION of which resolution is best really depends on a couple of things: the intended output and the type of image that is being used. For example, a bitmap that will be printed at the same size at which it was captured rarely needs to be more than 300 DPI.

Conversely, if you are using line art (or black and white) and the image has fine lines, you may want to use a much higher resolution when scanning. This will help to avoid jagged edges and the potential for misalignment. Most manuals suggest that you scan at the maximum optical resolution of your scanner.

If you are designing for the Web, or for displaying artwork on a monitor, the optimum resolution would be 72 DPI. That's it!

Why 72? Basically, monitors are 72 DPI, well, more specifically, Macintosh monitors are 72 DPI and Windows-based machines are 96 DPI. So 72 is adequate for both.

## Changing the Image Size

Bitmap resolution cannot be effectively increased beyond its original value without the use of specialized software, unless the bitmap is being reduced in size. If a bitmap is obtained at 72 DPI, changing the resolution to 300 DPI will result in more pixels being added to the bitmap, causing the image quality to degrade as a result. The reason for this is that as the resolution is increased, extra pixels are added using interpolation or resampling routines are used to add these extra pixels that

approximate the detail. Because they don't really add detail back into the image, the larger image actually decreases the quality.

There are some software solutions on the market

### Use Caution When Resizing Bitmap Images

If bitmap dimensions are reduced for the purpose of increasing resolution, the bitmap must remain at its new size in order to maintain this resolution. Increasing the dimensions afterward will only result in a decrease in resolution.

that will effectively allow you to increase the resolution, and in my opinion, they do a pretty good job. BenVista PhotoZoom is one application for this task, and it is included with CorelDRAW Graphics Suite X5, and is accessible through PHOTO-PAINT through the File > Plugins > Export Plugins.

## Be Careful When Resizing Bitmaps

If a bitmap is imported into CorelDRAW and its physical dimensions are too large, many designers will reduce the size of the bitmap by simply using the Pick tool to drag the sizing handles until the bitmap is at the desired size (or typing a value in the Interactive property bar). While this works fine for resizing images, it is important to adjust the bitmap resolution afterward because resizing a bitmap in this way constrains the size and will increase the resolution as the size is decreased. For example, handling it this way could result in a 300 DPI bitmap having a much higher resolution after being resized. To adjust the resolution, select the bitmap, click Bitmaps, and select Convert to Bitmap (see Figure 7.1).

When working with images and preparing or creating designs, it is important to know where these designs are going. Will they be used for screen or print? This is a major deciding factor for how bitmap images will be handled, and it should be determined early in any project.

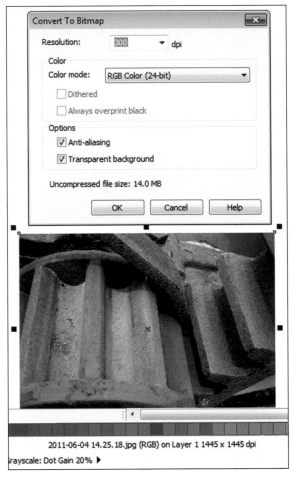

**Figure 7.1**
*The status bar indicates that this resized image is 1445 DPI. This happened because the Pick tool was used to make the bitmap very small on the page. Converting this to 300 DPI, the image size goes from 325MB to 14MB.*

# Halftones

WHEN READY FOR FINAL OUTPUT, your design will need to be separated. This process involves creating halftone screens and separations. We will look at creating halftone patterns more as a design element.

A halftone is an image or object that has been printed using a pattern of dots. In the final printing stage, when these overlapping patterns are viewed together, it gives the illusion of a continuous tone, as shown in Figure 7.2.

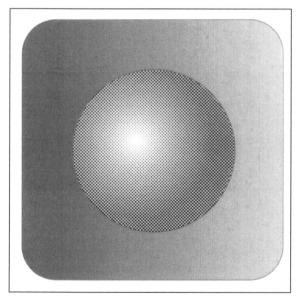

**Figure 7.2**
*The fountain fill here is created with a spot blue color with a frequency of 30 LPI (lines per inch). Note that the spacing of the dots is the same throughout the fill; what differs is the size of the dots. This gives the illusion of a continuous tone when viewed from a distance.*

There are three simple rules for creating a halftone of a vector object:

▶ The output must be going to a PostScript device. You cannot print a halftone pattern to a non-PostScript device.

▶ You must use a Pantone or Spot color.

▶ The spot color must be a percentage or tint of that color.

## View on Output Only

Although you can create a halftone pattern by selecting the proper values, you will not be able to actually view the halftone pattern until you output the file to a PostScript device.

## How Do I Know if It Is PostScript?

To determine whether you are using a PostScript or non-PostScript printer, from within CorelDRAW, with an object on the page, go to the File menu and select Print. Now look at the tabs across the top of the dialog box. If there is no PostScript tab, you currently have a non-PostScript printer selected.

Halftones or halftone patterns are expressed as a screen frequency. This frequency is measured as lines per inch (LPI) or line screen (LS) of a halftone. The typical line screen will vary depending on the quality of the printing required. If the image is grayscale, being printed in the newspaper or onto similar paper, a much lower frequency is used. A higher frequency would place more dots within an inch, and when doing this on a lower quality paper, the printing dots actually leak into each other too much, destroying the print detail on low quality paper. Newspapers typically would be printed at a line screen of 65 to 85. With a higher quality paper stock, such as smooth stock used in magazines or brochures, a higher line screen could be used that would result in much smoother tones. Typically, this line screen would run from 133 to 150.

When preparing images for printed output, it is important to know the screen frequency of the finished halftones so that you can adjust the DPI of your artwork. Once you know the screen frequency of the finished printed piece, you can prepare your images.

As a rule of thumb, scan or size your image to a resolution of approximately 1.5 to 2 times the screen frequency (LPI) of the halftone. As an example, if you had an image that was being printed at a line screen of 133, then it should be scanned or created between 200–266 DPI. If you are going to print the final project at a print shop, call them and ask what the best resolution is to use in your project. If you're going to print on a desktop printer, you will likely be fine with 200 DPI, unless you are using an ultra high-end photo-quality printer.

As I have mentioned, two of the criteria for creating a halftone are that you must be using a spot color and the spot cannot be 100%. Putting down 100% ink on paper will give full coverage, and you will not be able to see the dot pattern. If you reduce the amount of ink, it will allow for "white-space" around the dot, and you will be able to distinguish a pattern.

Go through this tutorial, and it will demonstrate what I am talking about. It can also be used as a reference chart for when you need to create or use halftone patterns for one of your designs in the future.

## Creating a Halftone Reference Chart

Creating a halftone reference chart can be a useful tool if you feel that you will make use of halftone patterns. It doesn't take very much time to make and when needed, it can actually save a lot of time.

**To create a halftone reference chart:**

1. From the File menu, select New. Set the size to Letter and change it to Landscape. Click the OK button.

2. Press the letter D on the keyboard. This is the shortcut key to select the Graph paper tool.

3. On the Interactive property bar, set the columns to 5 and the rows to 4.

4. Draw the grid on the page and then press the spacebar to select the Pick tool.

## Toggle the Pick

Tapping the spacebar will toggle back and forth between the Pick tool and the last tool selected. If the last tool selected happens to be the Text tool, use Ctrl+spacebar.

5. On the Interactive property bar, set the size to 9 inches horizontal by 6.5 inches.

6. Select Arrange > Ungroup, and with the Pick tool, marquis-select the top row of 5 squares. From the Window menu, select Color Palette > Pantone Solid coated. This will open the Pantone palette.

7. Select 100% PANTONE Black C from the color palette. Marquis-select the row below and select 100% PANTONE process Cyan C. For the next row, use 100% PANTONE process Magenta C, and for the final row, select 100% PANTONE Process Yellow C.

8. Select the top row. Then double-click the fill swatch on the right side of the status bar. This will open the Uniform Fill dialog box. Click on the Options drop-down and select Postscript Options (see Figure 7.4). Select Dot for the halftone screen and set the Frequency to 15. Click OK and then click OK again.

## PANTONE Colors

The PANTONE Matching System or PMS is a system that allows designers to accurately match colors within a design when going to output. Also referred to as spot colors, this system is comprised of approximately 1,114 *spot colors* and many cannot be simulated with CMYK (see Figure 7.3).

As a reference, PANTONE has created a number of fan style swatch books that are composed of several sheets that have seven different colors or shades on each sheet with very specific values.

The PANTONE system also has many special palettes, including metallic and fluorescents. While most of the PANTONE colors are outside of the CMYK gamut, in 2001 PANTONE began providing translations of their existing system with screen-based colors (RGB). This is what is referred to as the *Goe system*. The Goe system has been available in CorelDRAW since CorelDRAW X5.

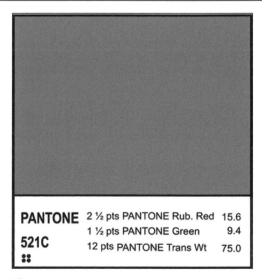

**PANTONE**

**521C**

| 2 ½ pts PANTONE Rub. Red | 15.6 |
| 1 ½ pts PANTONE Green | 9.4 |
| 12 pts PANTONE Trans Wt | 75.0 |

**Figure 7.3**
*The PANTONE matching system.*

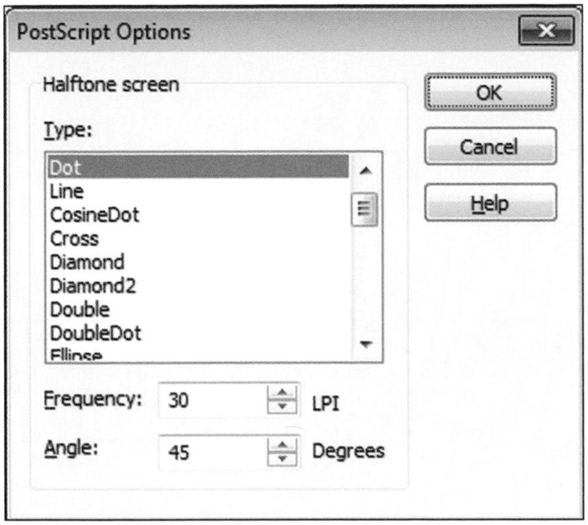

**PostScript Options**

Halftone screen

Type:

Dot
Line
CosineDot
Cross
Diamond
Diamond2
Double
DoubleDot
Ellipse

OK

Cancel

Help

Frequency:   30   LPI

Angle:   45   Degrees

**Figure 7.4**

*Here you can see the various Halftone screen types available, and you will also have the ability to change the Frequency and Angle.*

9. Repeat step 8 for the Cyan row, changing Frequency to 30 and the Magenta row to 45. Because the default is 60, there is no need to change the Yellow row.

10. This next phase is a bit more tedious. Start with the first row and go into the options and change the line screen to 15.

11. Select the first square on the top row, left-hand side so that you can modify the current fill of the black. By double-clicking the Fill icon in the status bar, you can access the Fill dialog quickly. For this first square, on the Tint and Slider, located at the bottom of the Fill dialog, set the value to 10% and then click OK.

12. Repeat this for the remaining squares in the first column, changing then all to 10%.

13. Select the second black square and set the Tint to 25%. Repeat this for the remaining squares in the second column, changing all the tints to 25%.

14. Continue with the third, fourth, and fifth columns changing them to 50%, 75%, and 90%.

15. Now it is time to evenly space out the squares. To do this, marquis-select all the squares in the first column and in the Interactive property bar, delete the value in the x position and type .5 and then press Enter. This will move the entire column to the right by $1/2$ inch.

16. Next, marquis-select the entire first row and then press the Shift key and the E. This will evenly space the squares. Repeat this for the next three rows.

17. Next, we want to space the columns. To do this, marquis-select the first column and hold down the Shift key while pressing the C to evenly space the column. Repeat this for the remainder of the columns.

18. Across the top, using the Text tool, click above the first column, type in 10, and then click the Text tool over the next column and type 25. Over the next columns, type 50, then 70, and finally 90.

19. Arrange the numbers centered over each column by selecting the number and then selecting the first square and pressing C on the keyboard. Repeat this process for the rest of the numbers.

20. Next, we want to put the line screen values down the left side. To do this, type 15 and then click beside the next row and type in 30, beside the next type 45, and then type 90.

21. Select the first frequency and then the rectangle to the right of it and press Ctrl+E to center the text. Repeat this step for the rest of the rows.

22. Marquis-select the numbers that were just entered and press the letter C to center align everything. Now use the right or left cursor key to position the text close to the rectangles.

23. Once you have finished the positioning of all the objects and the text to your satisfaction, it is just a matter of setting the labels.

24. Type the text Percentage (%) and along the vertical of the chart, type Line Screen (LS). You are done and should see something similar to Figure 7.5.

Now it is important to offer a reminder. You will not be able to view the halftone pattern on the screen, and you will not be able to output this to a non-PostScript printer.

After you print out the halftone reference chart, you will better understand the correlation between frequency and LPI. Keep this chart handy so that you can refer to it when you need to be able to create a halftone pattern and want to get some idea as to what settings to use.

## Black-and-White Halftone Images

We have taken a brief look at creating halftone patterns with vector objects, so now let's take a quick look at creating a halftone with a raster or bitmap image.

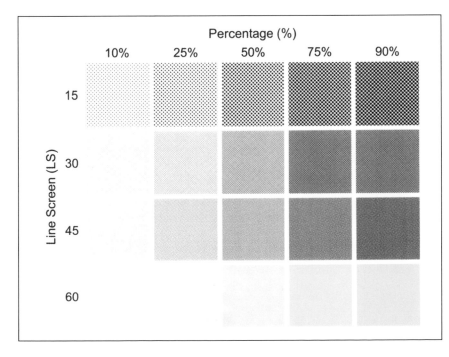

**Figure 7.5**
*Your completed project, a Halftone Reference chart. Print this out and keep it handy in your work area. It can be referred to when you need to create a halftone pattern for a vector object. (Please note: This figure is printed with a four-color process.)*

Creating a halftone of a bitmap is best done in PHOTO-PAINT, but I will show you a technique that will provide a similar result. In CorelDRAW, we will convert the image to black and white and select a halftone pattern. For this exercise, we will create a custom page size, and once we are finished, we will save the file and make use of it for a project later in Chapter 9, "Designing Your Own Business Graphics."

**To create a black-and-white halftone image in CorelDRAW:**

1. Start a new document by selecting File > New.

2. Set the width and height to 5 × 7.

3. Under Number of Pages, set this to 2. Set the Primary color mode to CMYK and the Rendering resolution to 300. Click OK.

4. I'm going to use an image of a mannequin's face. The size of this image is 3 inches × 3.5 inches and the resolution is 300 DPI. Please use an image of your choice. (If you select an image of a female face, it will work better when we use it a bit later on.)

5. With the bitmap selected, from the Bitmap menu, select Mode > Black & White.

6. In the Conversion Method drop-down, select Halftone.

7. Leave the degrees at 45, but set the lines per inch to 20 and click OK.

8. With the black-and-white image still selected, left-click on the yellow swatch in the color palette and right-click on the magenta (just below the white). See Figure 7.6.

9. Finally, click on File Save and save the file to a location on the hard drive that you will remember. You could create a folder on your desktop and call it "*Bring it Home Projects.*" As I have mentioned, we will use this file in Chapter 9.

## It's Not Always Black and White

As a black-and-white bitmap is a one-bit image, it is possible to change the foreground and background or fill and outline colors of a 1-bit image by clicking on the swatches in the Color palette. A left mouse click on a color will change the white within the image and a right-click will change the black.

OK, we have spent a bit of time looking at some of the important elements that should be taken into consideration when designing, such as color, typography, and resolution. Later, we will take a closer look at CorelDRAW, but for now let's look at some of the different ways that we can minimize the amount of time that is spent in CorelDRAW by using some of the many templates, scripting, and other tools that are available, so that more time can be dedicated to the actual process of designing.

**Figure 7.6**
*The completed image that we will be using in a later project.*

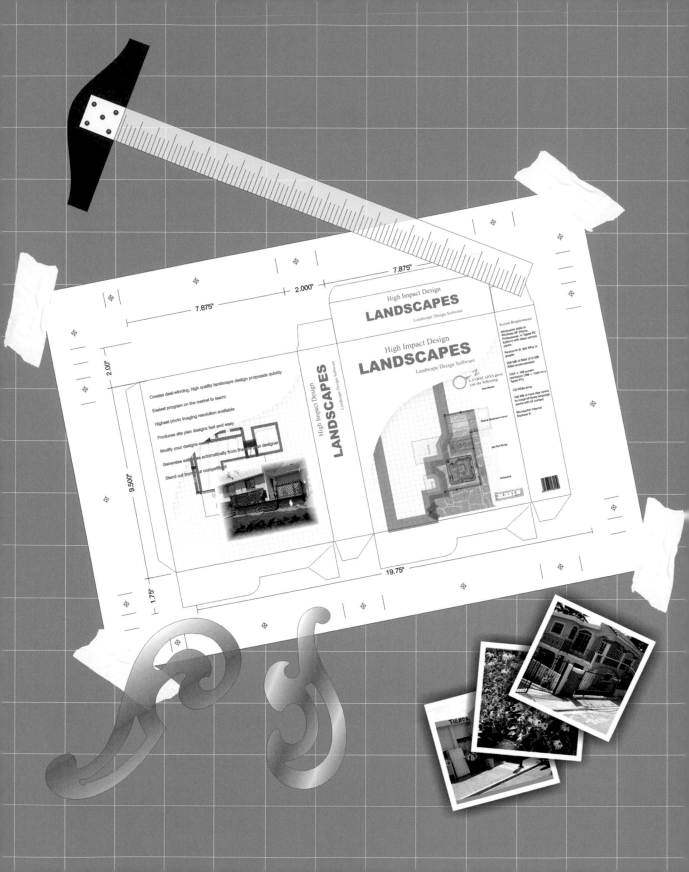

# Create Layouts with Ease

I N THIS CHAPTER, we are going to take a look at some of the tools and features that will allow you to create the layout that you want (and need) with the minimum amount of effort. After all, a graphic design program should be all about designing and not hinder the creative flow, and that is exactly what CorelDRAW does. It allows you to design freely without having to stumble through many steps to get there.

At the stage where drawing begins, most users will already know what size and type of page they will be working with. The controls provided in the New Document dialog of CorelDRAW make it easy to configure page settings exactly as you want. We have already seen the page layout options in Chapter 3, "Set Up and Start Smoothly," so we will move on to creating documents from a template. But I cannot stress this enough: Take a look at the many default settings that are available within the New Document dialog.

# Working with Templates

EVERY CORELDRAW DOCUMENT created
is based on a template, which is a pattern or mold
for the text, graphics, and formatting contained in
a particular document. The default template that is
used in CorelDRAW is a file named CorelDRAW.cdt
(this is the last time I will mention that).

Templates are based on sets of styles that govern the
appearance of specific types of objects including
shapes, lines, and text. When a style is applied to an
object, the object takes on that particular style.

By creating a design around a template, the attributes of the document can be controlled by the user.

Designs can be started using a preset template for
a specific type of design or using a custom template. If used properly, templates can form the
foundation for most of your documents.

In Chapter 3, we took a look at the New from
Template dialog box. Let's now take a look at the
Save as Template options and later in this chapter we
will create a template that we can save for later use.

## Saving a Template

Once you have the design created, remember that
the template does not need to be completely pol-
ished; it just needs to include the elements that
you want and where you want them. Keep in mind
that a template is a starting point. When you have
the layout ready, from the File menu, select Save.
In the Save as type, select CDT – CorelDRAW
Template and click Save.

## Template Properties

The Template Properties box lets you enter the
information that identifies the type of document
that is being created (see Figure 8.1).

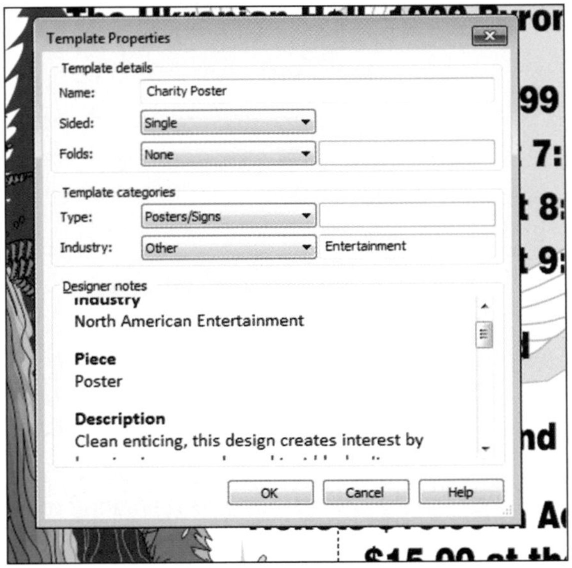

**Figure 8.1**

*In the Template Properties box, you can enter infor-
mation that will identify the type of document that is
being created, as well as details about the project.*

► **Name:** The name is not necessarily the file
name, but is the name that will be displayed in the New from Template dialog.

► **Sided:** This refers to whether the document
is a single-sided document or double-sided
document.

▶ **Type:** Here you can indicate a type of project such as a Brochure, a Business Card, Stationary, a Flyer, and that sort of thing. If you select Other, there is the option to indicate what it is.

▶ **Industry:** This area gives you the ability to classify the templates by industry, such as Education, Recreation, and Retail to name a few. You can also select Other and create an industry that may not be listed.

▶ **Designer Notes:** The final area is very important and useful. Here you can provide all the details on the template that will make it easier to identify and determine if it may be the ideal template to use when creating a project.

After the template has been created, if you select File > New from Template and then select My Templates, you should see them listed here. If not, ensure that you have the filtering set properly, as we discussed in Chapter 3.

---

### A Template for the Template

Create a text document in Notepad that has the main headings that you want to use for the Designer notes, including headings such as Description, Style, Color Choice, Fonts, or Special Instructions. When it comes time to create a new template, copy this text into the Designer Notes field and fill in the blanks. Of course, if you are only creating one template, just create a text block off the drawing page that holds this information.

---

# Layout Toolbar

THE LAYOUT TOOLBAR is a new feature to CorelDRAW X6 and was designed to help speed up the design process; it can be invaluable when creating templates and any design that uses PowerClips and Text boxes.

So what is a PowerClip? Essentially, a PowerClip is an object that can hold other objects. Think of it as a matte in a picture frame. Anything that is in the middle of the mate will be visible and if something slides under the matte, it will be hidden to the user. The objects can be vector, raster, or a mixture. The container can be a single vector shape or a group of vector objects.

## PowerClip in X5 and Earlier

PowerClip is an effect that has been around for a number of versions (see Figure 8.2). I'll explain to you how to create a PowerClip in X5 and earlier versions.

**To create a PowerClip:**

1. With a new document open, import a picture. This can be any image that you want, as it is just going to be used to demonstrate this effect.

2. From the Interactive property bar, make sure that the Lock Ratio button is depressed and change the size of the picture to be 6" horizontally.

3. Select the Text tool and click anywhere on the page away from the image and type the word POWER in capital letters.

4. Set the font to Arial Black and set the point size to 100 points.

5. Select the bitmap with the Pick tool.

6. Move the text over on top of the picture.

7. With the bitmap selected, from the Effects menu, select PowerClip > Place Inside Container.

8. You will be presented with a large black arrow pointing to the right. Use this arrow to click on the edge of the text.

### The Disappearing Content

With PowerClipping, there is an option to center the contents when the image is clipped. In CorelDRAW X5, this feature is turned off by default. As a result, it may appear that your image has disappeared.

**Figure 8.2**
*The PowerClip cursor allows you to indicate which object or group of objects will become the container when creating a PowerClip.*

9. You may need to edit the contents of the container. From the Effects menu, select PowerClip and then select Edit Contents.

10. Prior to CorelDRAW X6, objects on the page will seem to disappear, and you will see a blue outline of the container and the contents that you have clipped. Now you can resize and position the picture. (In CorelDRAW X6, the objects on the page will appear ghosted.)

11. When you are satisfied with the size and position of the contents, from the Effects menu, select PowerClip and then Finish Editing This Level, or click the "Finish Editing" button in the lower left of your screen, next to the page tabs (see Figure 8.3).

**Figure 8.3**
*The finished PowerClip.*

## Make It Quicker

There are a couple of shortcut keys that will speed up the process:

▶ To make it faster to place the picture inside a PowerClip container, right-click the image that you want to place in the container and at the same time, drag it over on top of the container and release the mouse button. A pop-up context menu will appear; select the option to PowerClip Inside.

▶ To edit the PowerClip that already has something inside it, hold the Crtl key down and left-click on the PowerClip. This will automatically take you into the Edit mode.

▶ To finish editing the PowerClip, hold the Ctrl key down and click outside of the container boundary; CorelDRAW will return to the full-page view. How easy is that?

## Back to X6 and the PowerClip

In CorelDRAW X6, you can use the same process to create a PowerClip as you used in earlier versions, or you can use the new Layout toolbar. Right-click on any of the toolbars and select Layout. This will open the Layout toolbar, and this is where the magic in X6 is, because you can have an "empty container" as a PowerClip placeholder (see Figure 8.4). In previous versions, there had to be content inside a PowerClip container.

Once the Layout toolbar is on the screen, you will notice the following controls (from left to right):

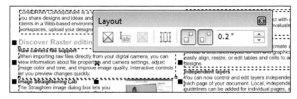

**Figure 8.4**
*The Layout toolbar makes it easier to create Power-Clip and Text frames, as well as having additional features.*

▶ **PowerClip frame:** This will convert the selected object into an empty PowerClip frame.

▶ **Text frame:** This will convert the selected object into a text frame.

▶ **No frame:** Use this in a situation where you want to revert to a PowerClip frame or a text frame.

▶ **Columns:** This option allows you to adjust the number of columns, width, and gutter.

▶ **Alignment guides:** Alignment guides appear if this is toggled on. When positioning, these guides "pop" onto the screen to provide interactive feedback while moving and drawing objects. It's a great timesaver and aid to accurate alignment.

▶ **Alignment guide margins:** By default, Alignment guides will make objects align right next to each other, and this control allows you to add a margin to control the distance from the edge of another object.

# Rulers, Grids, and Guidelines

LOOKING AT THE DEFAULT workspace within CorelDRAW, you cannot help but notice the ruler across the top of the desktop area, as well as the one located down the left side. By default, the 0:0 position of these rulers is at the bottom left corner of a new document that is created (regardless of document size), as shown in Figure 8.5.

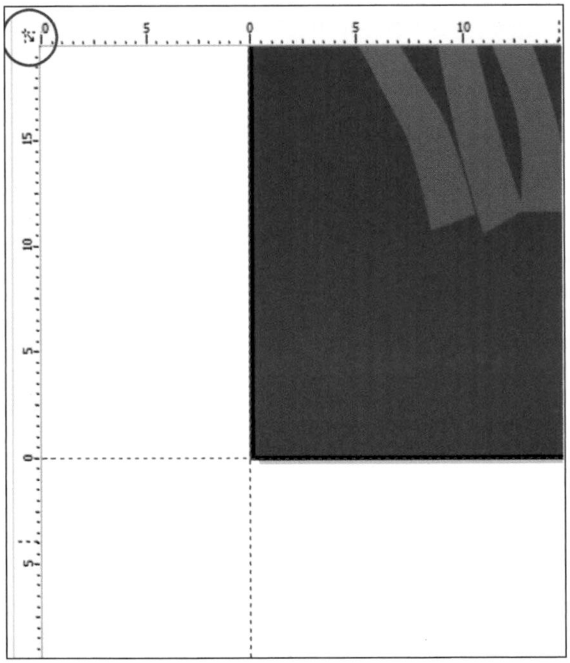

**Figure 8.5**
*Here, you can see a portion of the rulers. Notice that the 0:0 position is the bottom left corner of the document.*

## Adjusting the Rulers

To adjust the rulers, from the Tools menu, select Options. When the Options panel opens, expand Document and highlight Rulers. You will see options that will allow you to adjust the rulers and a number of other settings, as shown in Figure 8.6.

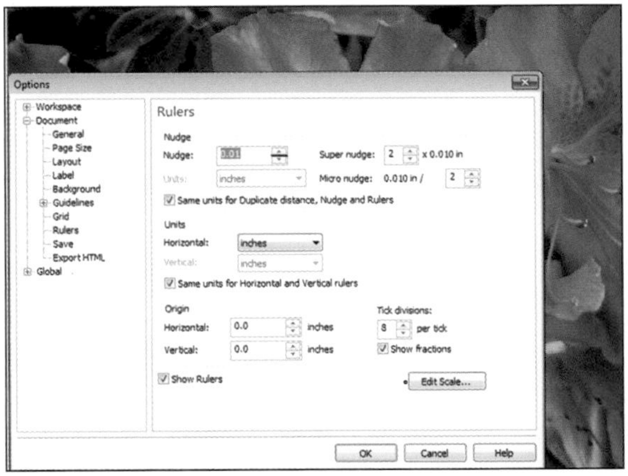

**Figure 8.6**
*Options that allow control over how the rulers are calibrated, as well as units of measure within CorelDRAW.*

## Using the Nudge

Nudging allows you to move an element on the page by a specific amount, using the cursor keys or arrow keys on the keyboard. Pressing the Shift key at the same time acts as a Super Nudge and pressing the Ctrl key with the cursor key or arrow keys acts like a micro nudge.

Let's cover the various options in the Ruler settings panel:

▶ **Nudge:** Each tap of the arrow key will move the element in the corresponding direction the distance that is set here.

▶ **Super Nudge:** Holding down the Shift key while tapping the arrow key will perform a Super nudge. A multiplying factor is used to calculate the distance. In Figure 8.6, the distance would be $2 \times 0.010$ in.

▶ **Micro Nudge:** Holding down the Ctrl key while tapping the arrow key will perform a Micro nudge. A dividing factor is used to calculate the distance. In Figure 8.6, the distance would be 0.010 in / 2.

▶ **Units:** This will set the units of measure within the application.

▶ **Origin:** The Origin will dictate what inch mark is the lower left corner of the document.

▶ **Tick Divisions:** This will indicate the number of marks on the ruler between inches (or unit of measure).

▶ **Edit Scale:** Opens a dialog box that allows the user to set a scale factor. This is useful when creating a large drawing such as an architectural design or where a scaling factor is required.

---

## Quick Access

For quick access to the Ruler setup options, rather than going from the Tools menu, select Options. When the Options panel opens, expand Document and highlight Rulers; then simply double-click on one of the Rulers.

---

From time to time, it is necessary to move the rulers or readjust them. In CorelDRAW, it is very easy to do. To move the 0:0 position, simply click where the rulers intersect (refer to Figure 8.5) and drag the crosshairs out onto the position within the page and release the left mouse button.

If you would like to move the actual rulers onto the page, you can do so by clicking on the same location with the Shift key held down. To return the rulers, simply repeat the process and drag them back, or simply Shift+double-click where they intersect, and they will dock in the original location.

## Grid

The grid is useful if you have a requirement to lay out a number of objects in a matrix. To view the grid (as they are not on by default) from the View menu, select Grid.

If you are in CorelDRAW X6, there are three different grids that are available.

▶ **Document grid:** The Document grid is the main grid that can also be seen in earlier versions of CorelDRAW.

▶ **Pixel grid:** The Pixel grid is used when creating designs at the pixel level, usually for Web design. This option becomes available when two conditions are met: 1) Under the View menu, Pixels is selected and 2) The Zoom level is greater than 800%.

▶ **Baseline grid:** The Baseline grid will place horizontal gridlines within the page only and is used to line up text effectively.

## Setting the Grid Spacing

To set up the grid, from the Tools menu, select Options (see Figure 8.7). When the Options panel opens, expand Document. Then just double-click on a Ruler from the Drawing window and in the Options panel, select Grid, just above Ruler. Much quicker!

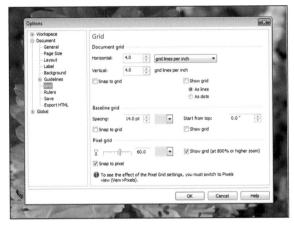

**Figure 8.7**
*Options that allow you to control how the grid is set up. New to CorelDRAW X6, as shown here, is the Baseline Grid as well.*

There are three sections here: Document grid, Baseline grid, and Pixel grid.

▶ **Document grid:** Here you have the ability to select the Horizontal and Vertical values for either the gridlines per inch or the spacing between grid lines. You can also turn on Snap to grid and Show grid. I should point out that these last two settings can also be accessed from the View menu so if you need to turn them on or off, you do not need to access them here. You can also show the grid as a series of lines or a dot pattern.

▶ **Baseline grid:** As mentioned, the Baseline grid allows you to set up horizontal lines for aligning text, so here you'll find the first setting, which is spacing and is measured in points (pt). You also can indicate color and how far from the top the grid is, as well as Snap to and Show grid. Note that individual text frames need to have "Align to baseline grid" enabled for the text to use the Baseline grid.

▶ **Pixel grid:** Transparency is the first option shown here, and you also have the ability to set the color of the grid. The ability to turn the grid on if the zoom lever reaches 800% can be selected here as well, or it can be done under the View menu. Snapping to pixels can be selected and when snapping to the grid, you can align the pixel to the center, as well as the pixel edge.

# Guidelines

Guidelines are extremely useful for aligning objects quickly and accurately. Guidelines can be placed anywhere in the drawing window, either horizontally, vertically, or angled. You can literally set up a guideline wherever you need one, on individual pages, master pages, or with preset guidelines.

## Creating Guidelines

With the Pick tool, click on the horizontal ruler anywhere and drag down about an inch and release the mouse button. That's it.

OK, seriously, guidelines typically are used to align objects, so when you take a guideline onto the drawing page, you can make use of the rulers to position them where you want them. You can also color guidelines by simply dragging a color from the Color palette onto the guideline, and you can adjust their placement by editing their position on the property bar (see Figure 8.8).

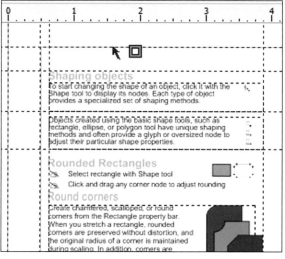

**Figure 8.8**
*Guidelines can be used for positioning frames of paragraph text. You can also see how I dragged the color green from the swatch to color one of the guidelines.*

## Presets

The quickest and easiest way to set up multiple guidelines is to use the presets. You can either create your own presets or use the Corel default presets. Preset guidelines have certain advantages, since they will keep the same margins and position from the edge of the page should you resize the page. The Corel presets include the following:

- ▶ One-Inch Margins
- ▶ Bleed Area
- ▶ Page Borders
- ▶ Printable Area
- ▶ Three-Column Newsletter
- ▶ Basic Grid
- ▶ Upper-Left Grid

You can use more than one preset at a time or manually add guidelines to a Corel or user-defined preset.

## User Defined Guidelines

Setting up User Defined Presets is just as easy, but a lot more flexible. You can set the following options, as shown in Figure 8.9.

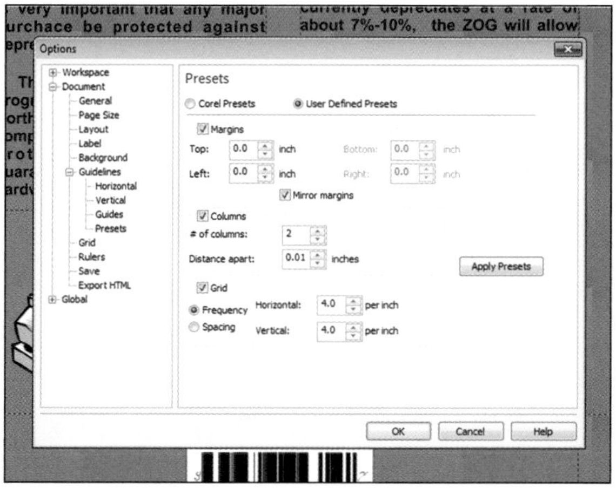

**Figure 8.9**
*There are a number of options for setting up the User Defined Presets.*

- ▶ **Margins:** Top, Bottom, Left, and Right (including the option to Mirror margins)
- ▶ **Columns:** Number of columns, Distance apart
- ▶ **Grid:** Frequency (Horizontal and Vertical) or Spacing

# Object Manager

THE OBJECT MANAGER is a very powerful but greatly misunderstood docker that you can see parked on the right side of the screen when you launch the application for the first time. I have heard many users say they never use it, because they don't understand it. Here I will try to explain what it is, and you can see just how powerful it can be.

In a nutshell, the Object Manager allows you to create layers within the document either before you start to design or during the design process. A layer is like a piece of tracing paper where you can have a separate design on each layer and control each layer independently. Objects are drawn on layers, and you can move objects from one layer to another layer. You can also set layers to be invisible or set them not to print.

## Let's Examine It

If the Object Manager is not docked and open on the right-hand side of the screen, from the Windows menu, go to Dockers and then to Object Manager.

Starting at the top of the Object Manager, there are three icons on the left. They are the following, as shown in Figure 8.10.

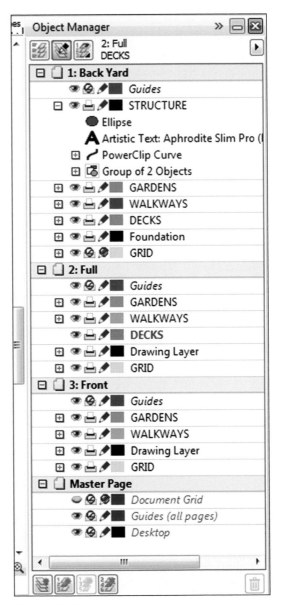

**Figure 8.10**
*In the following section, you can use this figure for reference.*

▶ **Show Object Properties:** A toggle that turns on and off the Object Properties. In Figure 8.10, it shows that they are turned on, and this is why you see a rectangle *and* a color value.

▶ **Edit Across Layers:** In a situation where there are multiple layers on a page, with many objects on each layer that may overlap, turn this off to make it easier to work on a specific area of a document. By default, it is enabled.

▶ **Layer Manager View:** Hides all the content from view in the Object Manager and only shows the names of the various layers. In this way, it makes it much easier to reorder layers if required.

To the right of the three icons is the name of the current page and the name of the layer that is currently active. This layer is also indicated in the Object Manager as being in red text. To the far right of this is a small right-facing triangle, which allows access to the Object Manager options. Within the Object Manager Options, you'll find the following, as shown in Figure 8.11.

▶ **New Layer:** This allows for the creation of a new layer on the currently selected page. Seriously, it does!

▶ **New Master Layer (all pages):** This allows for the creation of a Master page. Any content on this page will appear on all pages. Prior to CorelDRAW X6, this item was simply referred to as New Master Layer. In CorelDRAW X6, the next two items were added.

▶ **New Master Layer (odd pages):** This will create a Master layer that is used for all odd-numbered pages.

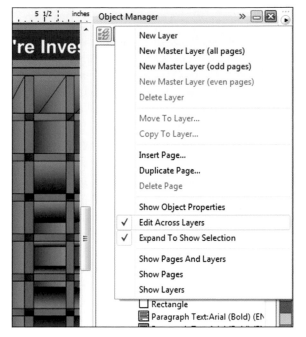

**Figure 8.11**
*There are a number of options available within the Object Manager Options menu that make it easier to control layers and pages.*

▶ **New Master Layer (even pages):** This will create a Master layer that is used for all even-numbered pages.

▶ **Delete Layer:** This will delete a layer and all the contents on that layer.

▶ **Move to Layer:** With an object or group of objects selected, they can easily be moved from one layer to another by selecting this option. The objects can be selected within the document or directly in the Object Manager.

▶ **Copy to Layer:** Selecting Copy to Layer will allow the objects that are selected in one layer to be copied to a another layer.

▶ **Insert Page:** Selecting this option will allow you to insert a single page or multiple pages into the document and dictate page size and orientation.

▶ **Delete Page:** This will allow you to delete a single page or a range of pages.

▶ **Show Object Properties and Edit Across Layers:** These are the same options that are available by selecting the first two icons that appear across the top of the Object Manager.

▶ **Show Pages and Layers:** This option will expand collapsed pages to show the layers on them.

▶ **Show Pages:** This option will collapse the Object Manager to show only pages, which is useful for navigating within a multipage document.

Now, referring back to Figure 8.10, within the Object Manager, below the three icons, you can see the first page name and below this are layers. Each page within a document has two layers associated with it by default (Layer 1 and Guides); additional layers can be added. Following all pages within the Object Manager, there is the Master Page. On the Master Page, there is a Guides layer, a Desktop, and a Grid (called *Document Grid* in CorelDRAW X6).

Each layer has six options that allow the user to identify and control how the elements on the layer appear or are treated, and they include the following:

▶ **Expand or Collapse Layer:** Expands a layer to see the objects within a layer (if collapsed). It makes it easier to select or locate

objects that may be hidden by others or to locate groups of objects.

▶ **Show or Hide:** Selecting the "eyeball" makes a layer visible or hidden. Any objects on the layer will still be printable and may be exported. You will be unable to edit anything on an invisible layer.

▶ **Printing or Exporting:** Disables printing and exporting. It is useful for objects that you do not want to print in the final output. For example, sometimes you might have an object that is used for reference or placement, such as a background bitmap.

▶ **Lock or Unlock:** Locks a layer so that the objects on it will not move. This is useful if you are placing a bitmap that you may want to trace over, or possibly a layer of a floor plan that you do not want to accidentally move while you are creating other objects.

▶ **Layer Color:** The layer color is very useful if you are using View > Wireframe. Changing this color will cause the objects to display in the color selected. It is layer specific and a great way to see which objects are on what layers while in Wireframe view. This feature can also be used to help organize layers when dealing with a document that may have many layers by using it for color coding, for example, floor plans.

▶ **Layer Name:** By providing a layer name, you can locate a specific layer that you may want to modify. By default, the layer names are Layer 1, Layer 2, and so on. Right-click and Rename will allow you to change the layer name, and you can change the page name in the same way.

In Figure 8.10, by examining the Object Manager, you can see that this document has three pages. Page one, called Back Yard, has seven layers including Guides and Grid. You will note that the layers are expanded to show some of the objects on them. Items that have a plus [+] to the left indicate that they are either grouped or linked objects (for example, Powerclip, Blend, Contour, and Extrude). The layer on page 2: Full is called DECKS, and it is in red, which is an indication that this is the layer that is currently selected.

The final options on this Docker are icons that match the first five items within the Object Manager Options drop-down. They include the following:

► **New Layer:** Creates a new layer.

► **New Master Layer (all pages):** Creates a Master page. As mentioned, prior to CorelDRAW X6, this item was simply referred to as *New Master Layer*. In CorelDRAW X6, the next two items were added.

► **New Master Layer (odd pages):** Creates a Master layer that is used for all odd-numbered pages.

► **New Master Layer (even pages):** Creates a Master layer that is used for all even-numbered pages.

► **Delete Layer:** Deletes a layer.

With a bit of practice using the Object Manager, you can save a lot of time when you need to move objects from one layer to another, change the order of layers, or simply create and manipulate files.

# Setting Up a Page

I HAVE SAID THIS BEFORE: There is more than one way to create multiple page documents in CorelDRAW, and here are a few of them:

► From the Object Manager Options drop-down, you can use Insert Page.

► From the Layout menu, select Insert Page.

► From the Document Navigator in the bottom-left corner, click on the [+].

By importing a multipage document, you will also increase the page count.

## Quickly Inserting a Page

If you're on the last page of the document and press Page Down, you will be asked if you want to insert pages. If you're on the first page of the document and press Page Up, you will be prompted to see if you want to insert pages in the beginning of the document.

Let's take a look at some of the options on the Interactive property bar that relate to the setup of a page or pages within a document (see Figure 8.12). To get to this property bar, you need to have no objects selected. The easiest way to do this is to select the Pick tool and click on the whitespace beside the page.

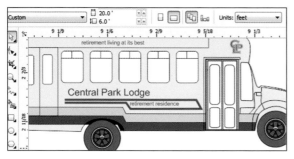

**Figure 8.12**
*It is very easy to set page size and orientation and indicate whether there are mixed page sizes within the document.*

Here are some of the options in the Interactive property bar:

▶ **Page Size:** There are in excess of 65 preset page sizes that you can choose from. They include everything from the standard letter, legal, and tabloid to envelope sizes, Web page sizes, and Web banners, as well as architectural sizes. If there is not a preset that you need, select Custom and enter the size that you would like.

▶ **Page Dimension:** By simply entering the page dimension, it automatically sets the page size that you dictate.

▶ **Portrait:** Sets the page so that the page is taller than wide.

▶ **Landscape:** Sets the page so that the page is wider than tall.

▶ **All Pages:** When All Pages is selected, any page that is added to the existing document will be the same size as all of the others.

▶ **Current Page:** Only applies changes to the existing page. This option is used when you would like to create a document with varying page sizes and orientations.

## How Small Can You Go?

You can actually create a page that is .001" × .001", although I am not sure what you would use it for. As mentioned earlier, the maximum page size is 150' × 150'.

# Working with Multipage Documents

WORKING WITH MULTIPLE PAGE documents is very easy when in CorelDRAW. While inserting and deleting pages can be done through the Object Manager, anything beyond that should be done through the Document Navigator.

## Document Navigation

The Document Navigator is located in the lower-left corner of the CorelDRAW window, as shown in Figure 8.13.

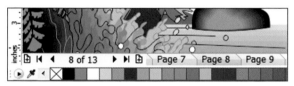

**Figure 8.13**
*The Document Navigator allows you to insert pages into various locations within a document, move between the pages, and do a number of other things.*

The Document Navigation area will enable you to add pages and move between pages. Let's take a closer look:

- ▶ **Add Page Before Current:** Adds a page before the current page.
- ▶ **Beginning of Document:** Regardless of where you are in a multipage document, moves you to the first page.
- ▶ **Back One:** From the current page, moves you to the previous page.
- ▶ **Current Page:** Gives an indication as to the page that you are currently on.

- ▶ **Forward One:** From the current page, moves you to the next page.
- ▶ **End of Document:** Regardless of where you are in a multipage document, moves you to the last page.
- ▶ **Add Page After Current:** Adds a page after the current page.
- ▶ **Page Tabs:** Indicates the page that you are currently on within a multipage document.

## Page Sorter View

There are a number of different options accessible from the Page Sorter View menu, but basically, the Page Sorter View allows you to review thumbnails of all the pages within a multipage document (see Figure 8.14).

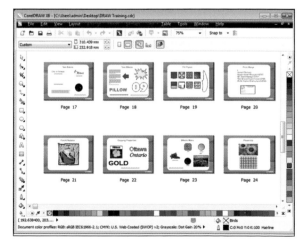

**Figure 8.14**
*Here you can see thumbnails of a multipage document using the Page Sorter View.*

From within the Pager Sorter View, you have the flexibility to reorder the pages simply by dragging the page image to another location. When you do this, you will see a red vertical insertion beam appear between the two pages. This is where the page that you are dragging will end up when you release the mouse button.

Right-clicking on one of the pages will reveal a context menu with a number of options that are available to you.

- ▶ **Rename Page:** Renames the page (there I go again).
- ▶ **Insert Page After:** Inserts a single page after the currently selected page.
- ▶ **Insert Page Before:** Inserts a single page before the currently selected page.
- ▶ **Duplicate Page:** Opens up a secondary dialog box that allows you to have the duplicate page positioned either before or after the current page. There is also the option to duplicate the layer with or without the existing content.
- ▶ **Delete Page:** Sorry, I have to say it—deletes the page.
- ▶ **Switch Page Orientation:** If the current page is landscape, it will switch it to portrait. One note here is that if the Current Page icon on the Interactive property bar is selected, only the selected page will be affected; otherwise, all pages will be rotated.
- ▶ **Publish Page to ConceptShare:** Publishes what you design to ConceptShare, which allows you to share your design with invited participants for review and markup.

# Page Numbers

Page numbers are often required when creating multipage documents. In versions of CorelDRAW prior to X6, there was a macro that enabled the creation of page numbers (more on that a bit later in this chapter).

In CorelDRAW X6, creating page numbers could not be easier. Simply click on the Layout menu and select either Insert Page Number or Page Number Settings. You'll find one dialog box and one menu item that are related to page numbers, as shown in Figures 8.15 and 8.16. You can add a page number to odd pages, even pages, or all pages, and you do not necessarily have to start page numbering on the first page. This option allows you to have a cover page or a table of contents in the front of your project, and those pages don't have to be included in the page number count.

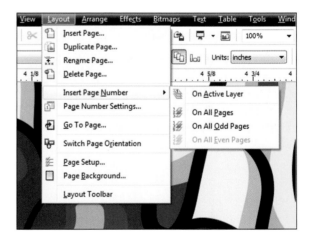

**Figure 8.15**
*From the Layout menu, select Insert Page Number to dictate where you would like the page numbering to start and whether you want it on all pages, even pages, or odd pages.*

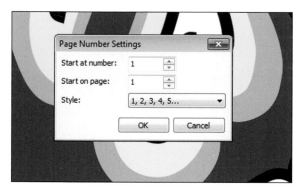

**Figure 8.16**
*The dialog box is used in conjunction with the Insert Page Number menu options.*

## Adding Page Numbers

As I mentioned, adding page numbers is very easy. From the Layout menu, select Page Number Settings. Here you will want to indicate which page to start the numbering on, what number you would like to start with, and the style of numbering. This is useful if you are creating a larger publication, and you do not want to start the numbering on the first page.

Next, from the Layout menu, select Insert Page number and indicate whether you want numbering on the Active Layer (meaning current page only), On All Pages, On All Odd Pages, or On All Even Pages. I should point out that if you are currently on an even page, Odd Pages will be grayed out.

When selecting any option other than On Active Layer, the page number is put onto a Master layer. The advantage here is that you can go to the Master layer in the Object Manager, modify the

appearance of the page number, and it will be reflected on all pages. As pages are added, removed, or reordered, page numbers are automatically updated.

## Page Numbering Prior to X6

Page numbering in CorelDRAW prior to X6 was done using a VBA macro that shipped with the application. The script was somewhat limited in what you could do. Running the script was a bit trickier than it is in X6. Here is an example of how to do it:

### X6 Page Numbers in X5

If you were to save a file that had page numbers on it to an earlier version of CorelDRAW, the page numbers would be maintained; however, if you then added a page, you would need to update the numbers manually.

1. From the Tools menu, select Macro and then Run Macro.

2. Under Macros in, select GlobalMacros (GlobalMacros.gms).

3. Under Macro Name, select CorelMacros > PageNumbering.

4. Click Run. This will run the macro, which will present you with the settings that will be applied to the page numbering.

5. On the General tab, indicate the page number where you want to start (ensure that you are currently on that page before launching the script).

6. Left/Right and Top/Bottom margins are used to position the page number within the document.

7. The Fonts tab enables you to set the font, Font Alignment, Size, and Font color.

8. The final tab is the Effects tab. Here, you have the ability to rotate the text on any angle.

# Working with Styles

CORELDRAW PROVIDES STYLE capabilities that allow you to globally make changes to any of the properties of the objects within your drawing. Every object within CorelDRAW has a set of properties related to it, and these properties can vary based on the type of object (for example, an ellipse or rectangle can have an outline color, outline thickness, fill type, and fill properties, among other things). Text can have these same properties, as well as size, font, kerning, and spacing (leading).

In CorelDRAW X6, it is possible to create both a Style and a Style Set. A Style captures the value of one specific property, whereas a Style Set allows for multiple object properties to be captured as a style. To open the Object Styles Docker from the Windows menu, select Dockers > Object Styles (Ctrl+F5).

In versions prior to CorelDRAW X6, dealing with Styles was a bit more restrictive. You did have the capability to create a Graphic, Artistic text, or Paragraph Text style. To open the Styles Docker from the Windows menu, select Dockers > Graphic and Text Styles (Ctrl+F5).

By applying a style to an object, or multiple objects, it is very easy to make the change to the style, which will change all objects that are using that style. Let's take a closer look, and we will see how we can set that up.

## Object Properties Docker

The Object Manager Docker shows all of the objects that are within the document (see Figure 8.17). Although you can select the Show Object Properties icon to see the properties, to see more detail and be able to easily change a number of the properties for a given object, you need to go to Window > Dockers and open the Object Properties Docker (Alt+Enter).

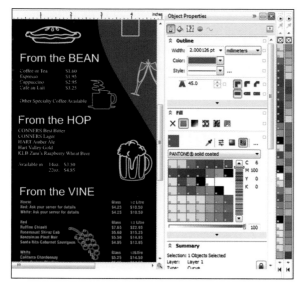

**Figure 8.17**
*The Object Properties Docker gives a central location where the various properties for an object can be modified.*

With the Object Properties Docker, you can change all the properties that are associated with an object in one central location. These would include the following:

- ▶ Outline
  - ❏ Width
  - ❏ Color
  - ❏ Style
  - ❏ Miter Limit
  - ❏ Corners (X6 only)
  - ❏ Line caps (X6 only)
  - ❏ Nib shape (X6 only)
  - ❏ Nib Tilt (X6 only)
  - ❏ Behind Fill
  - ❏ Scale with Object
  - ❏ Overprint outline (X6 only)

- ▶ Fill
  - ❏ Fill Type (No fill, Uniform, Fountain, Pattern, Texture, Postscript)
  - ❏ Color model selectors
  - ❏ Fountain fill options
  - ❏ Pattern fill options
  - ❏ Texture fill options
  - ❏ Postscript fill options
  - ❏ Fill Winding (X6 only)
  - ❏ Overprint fill (X6 only)

- ▶ Summary
  - ❏ A summary of the current object
  - ❏ Type of object
  - ❏ Type of text wrapping
  - ❏ Connector line wrapping
  - ❏ Selection dimensions

- ▶ Internet
  - ❏ Behavior (Link or Bookmark)
  - ❏ URL
  - ❏ Target
  - ❏ Defining hotspot
  - ❏ Cross-hatch
  - ❏ Background

- ▶ Curve
  - ❏ Specifications of the curve

## Object Styles Docker

The Object Styles Docker allows you to create, modify, and delete styles. You can also export a Style or Style Set as a Style Sheet so that it can be imported into a new document. This is a great way to ensure that you maintain consistency across many documents.

## Creating a Style in CorelDRAW

Let's say that you have a document that you need to format that has multiple pages and contains many headings, graphic objects, and text blocks. If you were to format each element manually in each paragraph, defining attributes such as text font, color, alignment, line spacing, and indentation, it would be a very time-consuming process and allow much room for errors. Using a style to accomplish this would make the whole process much quicker. Not only that, but if you decided to change any of the attributes at a later time, all that would be required would be to simply change the style and then the text throughout the document with an update. The Object Style will dictate exactly how the object will appear. If there are many attributes that you want to maintain within styles, such as character and paragraph settings, then you will use Style Sets.

The process to create a style is fairly simple. Once you have an element created, with the text or graphic and the properties set the way that you want, simply drag it into the Graphic and Text Styles (earlier version) or Object Styles in X6 Docker (Ctrl+F5). Alternatively, right-click on the object and select Object Style > New Style (or Style Set) from Document. To apply a style to an object, it is just a matter of double-clicking on the style when the object or objects that you want to affect are selected (see Figure 8.18).

In CorelDRAW X6, Styles contains one setting, for example, Fill. If you need to store an Outline and Fill, it would be in a Style Set. If you wanted to have a complete appearance saved for paragraph text, including font, point, justification color, and so on, you would need to save the character and paragraph styles inside a Style Set.

Prior to CorelDRAW X6, the only styles that could be created were for graphics and text (bullets were text styles). With the release of CorelDRAW X6, you also have the ability to create styles for Callouts, Dimension lines, and Artistic media. The process to create a style in X6 is the same.

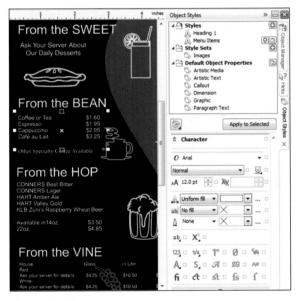

**Figure 8.18**
*The Object Styles Docker allows you to create, edit, use, or delete Styles and Style Sets.*

An appropriate workflow for creating styles would be to decide what characteristic you would like the titles or headings in the document to have. After you have those established, you can then create a style for each one of them. Next, create a style for paragraph text (remember you might need a Style Set that holds character and paragraph settings) and for the graphic elements (which might need a Style Set for Fill and Outline) as well. As you build the document, apply the style to the text and objects. If you need to change any of the settings, updating the style will update the objects on the drawing page. With a bit of preplanning, using styles can go a long way toward saving countless hours of design time.

# Creating and Using Scripts

VISUAL BASIC FOR APPLICATIONS, or VBA, can be used to create macros that can automate more complex tasks and save countless hours of design time when used properly.

A macro is a series of commands that are compiled into a single action that will allow you to save a lot of time—sort of like setting up a speed dial number on a telephone. Entering a one- or two-digit code will quickly dial a ten-digit number. Here we will look at two macros that can save a lot of time. One of them, I use quite a bit.

Before we step into this exercise, I would just like to point out that there are a few macros that are available in CorelDRAW; however, it is relatively easy to create your own or to add macros from third-party websites, such as www.macromonster.com. This is something that we will not be covering here, but the Help file is fairly extensive in this area, and there are a couple of websites where you can access additional scripts (see Appendix D, "Additional Resources and Web Links" online).

## Creating a Calendar in CorelDRAW

The hardest part about creating a calendar in CorelDRAW is deciding on the document size. Once you set the page size, the script will take care of the rest, whether it is for the back of a business card or a 4' panel highlighting monthly specials.

The script that is included with CorelDRAW is capable of creating a calendar almost any size that you may require; it is just a matter of setting the page size and then configuring the proper settings.

Here, we are going to create a tabloid size wall calendar that displays the entire year.

**To create a tabloid size wall calendar:**

1. Start by creating a new document. In the New Document dialog, select Tabloid from the Page Size drop-down (Portrait or Landscape). As this is intended to be a small

print run (only 200 copies) on a color printer at the local print shop, select RGB from the Primary color mode and click OK.

2. From the Tools menu, select Macro > Run Macro.

3. When the Run Macro dialog box opens, from the Macros in drop-down (at the bottom of the dialog), select CalendarWizard (CalendarWizard.gms) and click Run. This opens the Oberon Calendar Wizard as shown in Figure 8.19.

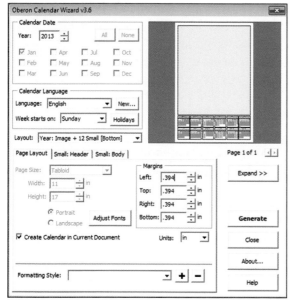

**Figure 8.19**

*The Oberon Calendar Wizard is a fairly extensive macro that allows you to create a single monthly calendar, 12 individual months, or an entire year and in 15 languages!*

4. Looking at the interface, the top left corner enables you to select the year and the specific months. Click the All button in the upper right if you want to create an entire year. Below this is the Language drop-down menu.

5. Under Layout, you will see a number of different layouts. Experiment for a moment and then select Year: Image + 12 Small [Bottom].

6. On the Page Layout tab, click the button that reads Adjust Fonts. This will automatically adjust the fonts to fit within the various regions. Alternatively, you can select the Small: Header and Small: Body tabs and manually adjust them. You also have the ability to select the color of the text.

7. After you are happy with the settings, click the Generate button. It will probably take no more than about 15 seconds until you see the message Finished Generating Calendar; then click OK and select Close.

8. Now it is time to dress it up. Resize the larger gray rectangle to 10" × 8" using the Pick tool and place it toward the top of the page. This will leave space to add your logo, address, and the year.

9. If you are using CorelDRAW X6, right-click on the rectangle and select Frame Type > Create Empty PowerClip Frame.

10. Go to File > Import and select an image that you want to use on the Calendar and place it beside the rectangle.

11. If you are using CorelDRAW X6, drag the image on top of the PowerClip Frame and release the mouse button. Go to step 16. If you have an earlier version, you will need to follow the next few steps to manually create the PowerClip. (I'll walk you through them.)

12. Select the bitmap and select Effects > PowerClip > Place Inside Container. Use the large black arrow to click on the gray rectangle.

13. If your image seems to disappear and you see an empty frame, do not worry. A Powerclip is like a porthole where you can hide items behind it. If the image does not sit in the middle of the porthole, you won't be able to see it.

14. With the frame selected, from the Effects menu, select PowerClip > Edit Contents. Now you will be able to see the image and the PowerClip frame. Drag to position and size the image where you would like it and then from the Effects menu, select PowerClip > Finish Editing This Level. Prior to CorelDRAW X6, you may also notice that there is also a little Finish Editing button above the Document Navigator.

15. Once your image is inside the PowerClip and centered where you want it, the final step is to add a background.

16. By double-clicking on the Rectangle tool, you will create a page frame the size of the page that will be placed behind other objects in the document. Select the Eyedropper tool from the toolbox and pick a color from within the image and then click the rectangle that you just created.

17. Now, it's just a matter of printing out a proof, and if everything is OK, send it off to the printer or copy center. This calendar works well printed on card stock, and it is quite reasonably priced even in small runs (see Figure 8.20).

## PowerClip Tip

If you click on an image with the right mouse button and drag a bitmap onto an object (or group of objects), when you release the mouse button, you will have an option in the context menu to PowerClip Inside. Once PowerClipped, Ctrl+clicking on the PowerClip will take you into the Edit mode. Ctrl+clicking outside of the container will finish editing the PowerClip.

**Figure 8.20**

*Using macros can speed up the design process and allow you to finish a project quickly, as you can see.*

It is easy to see how using a script can save a lot of time when designing a layout or performing tasks. Let's take a look at one more script before we move on.

## Sample Color Swatches

There may be times when you need to know how a certain color will print out to a specific type of material, whether it is on vinyl, paper, or fabric. Creating a sheet of color swatches can save you time and potentially money. It can be an expensive mistake to print the wrong color on a dozen tradeshow shirts, brochures, or shirts for the sales people.

**To create a color swatch:**

1. Start by creating a new document. Set the page size to letter.

2. From the Tools menu, select Macro > Run Macro.

3. When the Run Macro dialog box opens, from the Macros in drop-down, select GlobalMacros (GlobalMacros.gms).

4. In the open window, select CorelMacros.CreateColorSwatch and click Run.

5. Under the Palette drop-down, select the palette that you want to create the swatch for (see Figure 8.21). All open palettes will be available. If you want to print out a swatch sheet for a palette that is not open, click on the Open button to browse to the palette that you want.

**Figure 8.21**
*Color Swatch dialog box.*

6. Header information will allow you to add a date and the printer information.

7. Thumbnail spacing and Outline is pretty self-explanatory.

8. Select the settings that you want and click OK. That's it. The number of colors within the palette will determine how long the process will take and how many pages the document is when complete. As an example, with a spacing of 2, using the Pantone solid palette, the script created a 16-page document. Figure 8.22 shows the Default Palette Color Swatch.

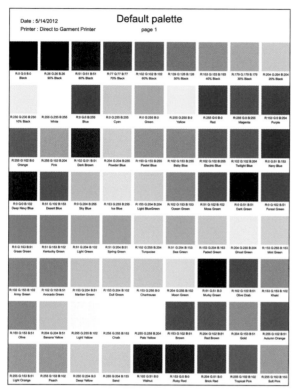

**Figure 8.22**
*The completed output from the Color Swatch script when printed on a t-shirt or other substrate would make a great reference tool to see how specific colors will look.*

## Quick-Launch a Script

If you need to use the Calendar script on a regular basis (or any other script), it might be a good idea to create an icon to launch it. Remember how we customized the Workspace? Let's do it one more time.

From the Tools menu, select Options (Ctrl+J) and then select Commands. Under the Commands drop-down, select Macro. Here you will find the Wizard.CreateCalendar. Drag this icon to a toolbar and close the options panel. That is all there is to it.

In CorelDRAW, the use of scripting can be a very powerful tool if learned to use properly, as shown in Figure 8.23.

**Figure 8.23**
*Yet another example of what can be done with scripting. Here a script from www.oberonplace.com is used to transform this Aztec calendar design into a functional wooden jigsaw puzzle in CorelDRAW and then output it to a laser engraver.*

# Corel Connect

COREL CONNECT is a full-screen browser or finder that synchronizes with both CorelDRAW and Corel PHOTO-PAINT. Corel CONNECT provides an easy way of finding content on your computer, local network, Flickr, Fotolia, iStockphoto, and the Corel content DVD. In CorelDRAW X6, you can also gather content from online sites.

Corel CONNECT gives you the ability to browse or search for clipart, photos, fonts, symbols, photo objects and file formats that are supported. Once you find the content that you need, you can import it into your current document, open it, or collect it in a tray for future reference.

## Searching for Content

With Corel CONNECT, searching is very easy and quick (see Figure 8.24). You have the ability to search in one of three locations:

▶ **Libraries:** In the Libraries location, you can search for content located on Flickr, Fotolia, iStockphoto, and the content that's included with CorelDRAW Graphics Suite. (Corel CONNECT with CorelDRAW Graphics Suite X6 allows you to search content as far back as CorelDRAW Graphics Suite 11.)

▶ **Favorites:** Searches for content in your favorite locations. Favorites are created by dragging and dropping from the Folders section.

▶ **Folders:** Searches for content in the folder structure available on your computer.

Once you select the source, just below the Search field is the Filter toolbar. You can search folders, vector files, bitmap images, fonts, and other files. To search for content, enter a word in the Search box and press Enter. Files that match the search term

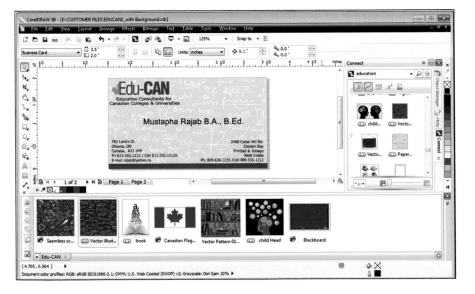

**Figure 8.24**
*Corel CONNECT is an application that can be launched as a stand-alone or as a docker within CorelDRAW or PHOTO-PAINT.*

appear in the Viewing pane. With CorelDRAW Graphics Suite X6, you also have the ability to search for a specific URL (website address) and view the images on that page, for example, www.corel.com will show all the images on Corel's website.

## Adding Content to the Tray

The Content Tray is useful for gathering content from various folders or libraries. While the files are referenced in the tray, the images actually remain in their original location. You can remove content from the tray by simply right-clicking on the content and selecting Remove from tray.

In CorelDRAW Graphics Suite X6, you can have multiple trays. This is huge because you can create a separate tray for each of the projects that you may be working on.

By positioning your pointer over a selected thumbnail, either in the Viewing pane or in a Content tray, you can display file information, such as filename, file size, dpi, and color mode. At the bottom of the docker is a slider that will allow you to zoom in on the thumbnail to make recognizing a particular file easier and faster. Once you decide which image you want to make use of, it is simply a matter of dragging it into your design.

Although Corel CONNECT is a stand-alone application, once you launch either CorelDRAW or Photo-PAINT, accessing the Tray from the Windows > Docker menu will open it with all of the content that you have added.

With CorelDRAW X6, it is also possible to have multiple trays within Corel CONNECT. The advantage here is that you can have a separate tray for each project that you may be working on.

### Easy Access Trays

By changing the default location where Corel CONNECT saves the trays to a Dropbox, they can be accessed by any computer that is also pointing to this same location. To change the location, from within Corel CONNECT, click the gear in the upper-right corner and select Options. Then it is just a matter of pointing this location to your Dropbox.

With a little practice, it is easy to see how Corel CONNECT can save countless hours of design time by making it easier to browse or search for clipart, photo images, fonts, symbols, objects, and websites. Corel CONNECT allows you to import these into your document, open them in their associated application, or collect them in a tray for future reference.

We have covered a lot in this chapter, including working with templates and setting up the page to make the design process run smoother. We covered page setup, looking at the grids, rulers, and guidelines, and also dealing with multipaged document. We'll finish off this chapter with an exercise on creating a template that we will be able to make use of in the next chapter.

# Creating a Custom Template

NOW THAT YOU UNDERSTAND some of the tools and features that can be used to create a template for a brochure, you can save literally hours of design time down the road.

## Three-Fold Brochure

There are many types of brochures that can be created using CorelDRAW. They can be two-fold, tri-fold or four-fold. The size depends on the amount of information and the target audience. For this exercise, we are going to create a three-fold or tri-fold brochure that will serve as an educational pamphlet.

**To create a three-fold brochure:**

1. If CorelDRAW is already launched, from the File menu, select New and give the file a name. Call it 3-Fold. Set the size to Letter and the orientation to Landscape. Set the Primary color mode to CMYK. (You would usually do this when creating a brochure or pamphlet because you would probably be printing larger quantities, and, as such, a larger printing press might be required.) If you know that you will be using a digital workflow (like in print shops or copy centers), then change it to RGB. This can be changed just by going to Tools > Color Management > Document Settings and changing the Primary color mode to RGB. Click OK.

2. The next step is to divide the page into three panels. There are a couple of ways that you can do this, but the quickest and most accurate is to make use of the Guideline presets. Either go to Tools > Options > Guidelines > Presets and select the Three Column Newsletter or double-click on either one of the rulers or the shadow of the page.

3. Once in the Options panes, click the + to the left of Guidelines to expand the Guidelines option and select Presets. Under Presets, I'll select Three Column Newsletter, click the Apply Presets button, and click OK. This will create guidelines that I can use to position the text and the other graphics for my pamphlet.

4. Click on the horizontal ruler and drag another guideline down about 1/2" below the top guideline (use the vertical ruler for reference).

5. Because this is going to be a double-sided document, click the + to the left of the Page 1 tab so that it adds it after the current page.

## Creating a Multipanel Document

When creating a document with multiple pages or panels, it helps to visualize it by taking a sheet of paper and folding it similarly to how the final output will look; then number the panels or pages. Use this as a guide when laying out your panels.

6. To make it easier to plan the layout of the individual pages, I am going to temporarily number the panels right on the document. Remember, when the brochure is folded, panel 1 is on the same side of the page as panels 5 and 6. I'm going to access Corel CONNECT from the Windows > Docker menu. And then I am going to start with panel 1 and import my business card. If you are following along, import your own business card if you have one; otherwise, search for content to use. I can repurpose some of the content for this. After ungrouping the elements of the business card, I will position the objects on panel 1 with my company name at the top, make sure that I have centered it, insert my logo, and then I will add the title of the publication, and finally my tagline at the bottom. Because I want the text to be easily read, I will use a sans-serif font in a larger point size. The text that reads "Customer Information Leaflet #3" is Arial 40-point. Below that I have the title "Lawn Care Basics," and I am using a 55-point Arial Black.

7. To color the text, I want to ensure that it is using the same color as my logo. So select the Eyedropper tool from the toolbox, click on the logo, and then click the text that I created for the titles. You'll see the result in Figure 8.25.

**Figure 8.25**
*The completed first panel of my pamphlet.*

8. Next, we'll create some text and graphic frames to use. As this is just going to be a template and not a final design, I will create empty frames that can be populated later. Remember in CorelDRAW X6, you have the ability to insert placeholder text.

9. From the view menu, select Snap to > Snap to Guidelines.

10. Select the Text tool and on Page 2, panel 2, create a text frame that snaps to the preset guidelines that were added earlier. Repeat this for the remaining four panels. For the text frame on panel 5, make sure that the bottom of the frame is level with the "Lawn Care" text on the first panel. This will ensure that there is enough space for our company contact information.

Paragraph text gives you the ability to format it as you would in a word processor. As such, it is possible not only to have multiple panels (as we have here), but also to link these panels so that the text will flow from one panel to the next as you edit or format it.

**To create paragraph text:**

1. Starting on Page 2, with the Pick tool selected, select the first frame and at the bottom, center, you will see a small rectangle. (If this text frame had too much text in it for the size of the frame, you would see a small downward pointing triangle.)

### Text Overflow

When dealing with paragraph text, it is possible to have too much text in the frame for the size of the frame. In this situation, it is possible to have the text flow into another frame. If you already have the text frame created, simply click on the frame with the overflow cursor. It will look like a big fat black arrow pointing to the right. If you do not have a frame created, clicking into the overflow rectangle will provide you with a cursor that will allow you to draw a text frame and have the text automatically flow.

2. Click on this rectangle, and your cursor will change to an overflow cursor.

3. Click on the paragraph text frame on panel 3.

4. Select the rectangle at the bottom of panel 3 and click on panel 4.

5. We now want to link panel 4 on page 2 to panel 5 on page 1. To do this, click the rectangle at the bottom of panel 4 and then tap the Page Up key on the keyboard and click on panel 5. One thing that you will notice is that there is a visual indication to show that the text for panel 5 is flowing from page 1. If we move to page 2, it will show that the text from panel 4 flows to page 1.

6. Link the last panel, panel 5 to panel 6.

7. Next, create a rectangle about 1.5" × 1.5" on panel 1 and right-click on it. Select Wrap Paragraph Text and then duplicate the rectangle and place one on each of the panels (except panel 1, as there is already a graphic there).

8. If you are using a version of CorelDRAW prior to X6, ignore these next three steps. Right-click on one of the toolbars and select Layout to open the Layout toolbar.

9. One at a time, select each rectangle and convert them to a PowerClip frame by clicking the PowerClip frame icon on the Layout toolbar.

10. Next, fill the text frames with Placeholder Text. Right-click on the frame on panel 2 and select Insert Placeholder text.

11. After adding Title 1 and Title 2 text and formatting them, right-click on each of them

individually and create a style for each. Also, create a style set for the body text.

12. The final step before saving is to remove the panel numbers that we put on at the beginning as a guide.

13. You can now save the file as a template. From the File menu, select Save As and in the Save as type drop-down, select CDT – CorelDRAW Template and save the template to your MyDocuments folder so that the New from Template will be able to locate the file. Click Save.

14. The final step is to complete the Template Properties dialog box with the information for your template.

You can see side one of the completed template in Figure 8.26.

Well, another chapter is finished, and hopefully you have picked up some more tips and techniques along the way that will enable you to create layouts with ease.

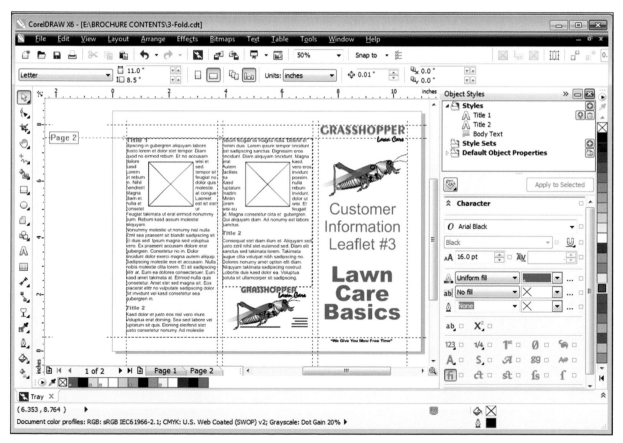

**Figure 8.26**

*Side one of the completed template. When it comes time to add the text and images, all of the layout work is already done. Note the indication that text is flowing from Page 2, as well as the styles that have been created.*

Edu-CAN
Education Consultants for
Canadian Colleges & Universities

Sub-Conscious
A HEALTHY WAY TO FEED THE BODY
123 MAIN STREET, OTTAWA, ON K2J 3P8 (613) 555-5515

GRASSHOPPER
Lawn Care

Customer
Information
Leaflet #3

Sub-Conscious
A HEALTHY WAY TO FEED THE BODY
Robin Stewart
Sub Tzar
THATCHER STREET, NEPEAN ONTARIO, CANADA K2B 1R4

awn
are
sics

"...e You Mow Free Time"

Sacha's
Lemon Pepper
Oil

Ingredients
Sun dried hot chillie peppers, roasted
garlic, blended 5 grain peppercorns,
lemons and lemon...

750...

Cabernet
Merlot

12.5%

...ck Vintners Reserve

Themes...
Creating Memori...

Load Current
Onyx Record
No    Yes

Customer
Search/Pin Review

Yes

Review Profile
content

...te Profile

Edit
Record

Pre-Sales

E-mail

First Name

Last Name

Privacy Settings

...ucation    Government

...com login    No    Organization Name

GRASSHOPPER
Lawn Care

Josh Panoch
Greely, ON
613-821-5885
613-850-5674

"...u Mow Free Time"

Edu-CAN
Education Consultants for
Canadian Colleges & Universities

Mustapha Rajab B.A., B.Ed.

24 Cedar Hill Rd.
Claxton Bay
Trinidad & Tobago
West Indies
Ph. 868.555.4726 /Cell 868.555.0893

162 Larkin Dr.
Ottawa, ON
Canada, K2J 1H9
Ph 613.555.54140 / Cell 613.555.7480
E-mail:rajabsr@email.com

• 162 Larkin Dr. - Ottawa, Ontario - Canada - K2J 1H9 - Ph 613.555.41... - E-mail:rajabsr@email.com

• 24 Cedar Hill Rd. - Claxton Bay - Trinidad & Tobago West Indies - Ph. 868.555.4726 / Cell 868.555.0893

# Designing Your Business Graphic 9

W ELL, HERE WE ARE—we've come a long way from covering the basic concepts of design such as color, typography, and page layout. We have also examined some of the common file formats that are used when creating or distributing files to the various vendors for the actual output, assuming that you are not doing the output yourself.

Now, it's time to apply some of the information that you have learned in order to create some of the documents and designs that are required to promote what you do and the business that will help you sell yourself, your product, and your company.

This section contains a number of tutorials, exercises, and projects that, when completed, will help you learn the features within CorelDRAW that will allow you to produce a design piece that will be informative and functional.

# The Corporate Identity Package

FOR A NEW BUSINESS, it is important to create a corporate identity package, which consists of a variety of forms, letterhead, or stationary that is all tied together with a common appearance and color scheme. Also part of the package is a style guide that dictates how and when to use specific collateral—for example, how colors, fonts, and logos are used when creating printed material or when using the company brand for advertising or promotion. We discussed the style guide in Chapter 1, "The Design Process."

You don't have to be a big company to need a corporate identity package; you just need to care about your image and the effort that it takes to develop one. Creating a clean, professional-looking corporate image can go a long way toward helping to promote your business as a successful professional organization. Let's look at some of the content that makes up the corporate identity package.

## What Makes a Corporate Identity Package?

There are a number of elements that go into a corporate identity package to make it a tool for success. The obvious elements would be a logo and a business card, but there are a number of other elements as well. Here are just a few:

- ► Tagline
- ► Letterhead
- ► Envelopes
- ► Purchase order and invoice
- ► Estimate sheets (if necessary)
- ► Fax cover sheet
- ► Mailing labels
- ► Presentation slide formats
- ► Websites
- ► News release (if necessary)
- ► Press kit folder (if necessary)

For the next few tutorials, we will be creating a few of these deliverables. Remember that we're not going to concentrate too heavily on the design aspect, but rather on the techniques for getting the most out of CorelDRAW.

## Logo Creation

In this tutorial, we will look at creating a logo for an electrical contracting firm and then use that same logo to design a business card and a purchase order. Once we are done with these items, you will have enough knowledge to create the rest of the collateral yourself.

The owner of the company is Gordon Lighthouse. (I know, I know, it's a Canadian thing.) Our goal is to create a logo that is clean and easily recognizable.

**To create a logo:**

1. We will start with a new document and because we are creating a logo, at this point, page size is not really important so just set it to letter and set the Primary color mode to

RGB. We can change it to CMYK later for some of the other pieces that we need to create. Remember, RGB has more colors in the visible spectrum or a much larger color gamut.

2. We want to create a lighthouse image with rays emanating from behind. To do this, we will start with an ellipse that is 3" in diameter. Select the Ellipse tool and while holding down the Ctrl key (remember this will constrain and create a perfect circle), create a circle that is 3" in diameter. To verify the size, look in the property bar. If it is not 3", simply type the value in the horizontal and vertical Object size boxes.

3. Next, with the Freehand tool, click the left mouse button once to the left of the "9 o'clock" position of the ellipse while holding down the Ctrl key and draw a horizontal line completely through the ellipse.

4. With the line still selected, hold down the Shift key and select the Pick tool. Click on the ellipse so that both objects are selected and press the C key to center and the E key to align it evenly.

5. Now before duplicating this element, you will need to make sure that the nudge value is X:0, Y:0. On the Interactive property bar, with nothing selected, set the duplicate distance to 0.0 (by default it is .25 × .25).

6. Hold the Ctrl key down and press the D key to duplicate this line. Without deselecting it, set the angle of rotation to 12 degrees and press the Enter key.

7. Smart duplicate is something that was added in CorelDRAW 10. Basically, the way that it works is that once an object is duplicated,

the next transformations made to the object are "remembered" and applied to any subsequent duplicate. With this in mind, if you press Ctrl+D again, it will duplicate this second line and rotate it 12 degrees as well. Repeat this 13 more times until it goes full circle (pun intended).

8. The next tool that we'll use is the Smart Fill tool. The Smart Fill tool lets you create objects from an enclosed area and apply a fill. Select the Smart Fill tool (the sixth tool in the toolbox).

9. On the Interactive property bar with the Smart Fill tool selected, under the drop-down to change the fill color, select the darkest yellow (R:255 G:204 B:0).

10. Under the Outline Options, change it to no Outline.

11. Click within the triangular area at the "9 o'clock" position and then click every second one going clockwise until the "3 o'clock" position is reached (see Figure 9.1).

12. Next, we want to delete the lines and ellipse. There are a couple of ways to do this. We could select each individual object, but that would take time. In versions prior to CorelDRAW X6, marquis-select the objects below the horizontal line that runs from the "9:00-3:00 o'clock" position with the Alt key held down and then press the Delete key. Then all you need to do is select the horizontal line and delete it. In CorelDRAW X6, click and hold on the Pick tool to reveal the new Freehand Pick tool (see Figure 9.2). With the Alt key held down, marquis-select the objects and press the Delete key.

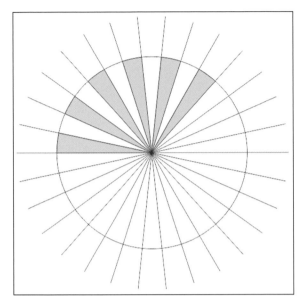

**Figure 9.1**
*Creating the "rays" becomes very easy when using the Smart Fill tool. It is just a matter of clicking within every second "triangle" to create them.*

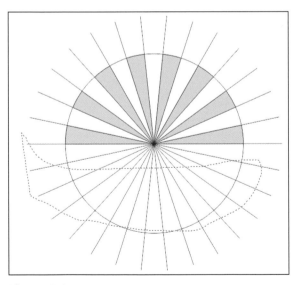

**Figure 9.2**
*The Freehand Pick tool in CorelDRAW X6 makes it easy to select objects.*

## Precision in CorelDRAW

After creating an object, you can change the width and height in the Object size on the Interactive property bar to edit the object with precise measurements. If you do not want the measurements to remain proportional, deselect the Lock ratio. Now group these elements together.

13. The next step is to draw a rectangle that will form the lighthouse base. Using the Rectangle tool, create an object that is .5" × 1.3" and center it along the base of the "rays." An easy way to ensure that it is properly positioned is to select the rectangle first; then with the Shift key held down, select the grouped rays. Next, simply press the C key (center) and the B key to align with the bottom.

14. Create another rectangle that is .5" × 0.125" and a third that is .25" × .25". Stack the second rectangle on top of the first and the third on top of the second.

15. Select the triangles with the Shift key held down, select the rectangles in reverse order, and select the yellow objects last. Press the C key to center them based on the last object selected.

16. Select the larger rectangle, go to the Arrange menu, and select Convert to Curves (Ctrl+Q).

17. With this rectangle still selected, click on the white in the Color palette and then using the Shape tool (F10), pull the two noted at the top of this rectangle in toward the center, about 1/8". (Zoom in and use the rulers as a guide, or you can view the distance moved in the status bar.)

18. For the very top rectangle, select the Shape tool, and on the Interactive property bar, click on the "Edit corners together" button (it looks like a little lock) and then set both the upper-left and upper-right values to 50. Give this object a yellow fill and then deepen the yellow color a bit. Hold down the Ctrl key and click on the orange color swatch in the Color palette. Doing this will add 10% of that color each time you click it.

### Did You Know?

## Using Mathematical Formulas in CorelDRAW

Did you know that you could actually use mathematical formulas in the X:Y position boxes and the Object size boxes? If you have an object that is .5" vertical and you enter to the right of this *1.5 and press Enter, the object will increase by 50%.

19. Duplicate this object and give it a black fill. Now increase the height by 50%.

20. Move this last object to the bottom of the design by selecting it, holding down the Shift key, selecting the largest of the rectangles, and pressing the B key (bottom align).

21. Select the smaller rectangle and give it a white fill.

22. Select the three objects that make up the lighthouse and right-click on the "no fill" swatch (which looks like an X) in the Color palette to remove the outlines. We are going to use the rays to provide the illusion of an outline, as shown in Figure 9.3. The only thing left now is to add the text below it.

23. So let's add the company name. As the company name is simply "Lighthouse Electric," type this in using Artistic Text. I have used the Moolboran font and set the point size to 40 points. Now select the text, and from the Arrange menu, select Convert to Curves (Ctrl+Q). This will avoid any problems if you should bring this file on to a system that does not have the font installed.

24. Save the file out to a folder that you have created to store your artwork.

**Figure 9.3**
*If you are following along, your design should look something like this.*

With an idea in mind and a few simple tools, it can be fairly easy to create a logo that will be remembered for years to come. Now we will take the logo that we just created and see how we can use it within a business card design.

## The Business Card

When creating a business card, you want it to stand out. To coin a phrase, "You never get a second chance to make a good first impression,"—that is exactly what you want to do—make a good first impression.

When looking at the design, the keys to a good design are to look clean, uncluttered, and easy to read.

For this design, we will use the logo that we just created, but first, let's consider a few design options.

▶ Will the card be single- or double-sided? If double-sided, what information is to go on which side?

▶ Flat or folded? Folded cards give more space for content and will stand out, but they are also more expensive to print.

▶ If you really want your card to stand out, consider getting specialized printing. Embossed, die-cut, magnetic, plastic transparent cards, or laser engraved on metal are some of the more noticeable business cards in use today.

## What Goes Where?

The front of the card should be reserved for the standard information—the logo, your name, address, and contact info (including office phone, cell phone, and fax). Also you should include your email address and website.

On the reverse side, try to keep it free of any printing and not have a lacquer finish, so that people can write on the back of the card if they'd like.

So let's lay out the card. We have decided to make it a single-sided card with a full bleed. A full bleed is where the ink goes beyond the edge of the card. This is done so that you're guaranteed edge-to-edge color on the card after trimming. Without a full bleed, the cutting process can leave white lines along the side of the card after trimming. Typically, the bleed would extend about 1/8" beyond where the stock is being cut.

When we set up the file, we will need to decide whether it should be CMYK or RGB. Here are the considerations. Typically, business cards are run in batches of 250, 500, or 1,000. For runs of this size,

## Scan It!

In this day and age of iPhones and smart phones, you have to make sure that it is easy for prospective customers to capture your contact information. The easiest way to do this is to put a QR code on the card (see Figure 9.4). A QR code can contain all kinds of information—from phone numbers to a linkable Web address, a list of services, a hidden message, an email address, a Twitter address, or links to other social medial sites. You could also include a QR code on a real-estate feature sheet to link to a virtual tour, a website, or to get a phone number.

**Figure 9.4**

*A QR code or Quick Response code was first used in the automotive industry, but since then it has been adopted by many other industries for use in publications to present a lot of information in a small space. What does this one say? Grab your phone, scan it, and see.*

economically it makes more sense to go with digital printing.

Another option is to print 5,000–10,000 or more with the main artwork and then just print the employee name and contact info on it afterward. This way could work out to be cheaper in the long run, but the blanks will need to be stored at the printers. This method is best if there are a number of employees who will require business cards. In this situation, it would be best to go with CMYK and use offset printing.

**To make the business card:**

1. You can either start with a template or a new document. From the File menu, select New.

2. From the Size drop-down, select Business Card.

3. For this project, set the Primary color mode to RGB and click OK. Next drag out two horizontal guidelines and two vertical guidelines and place them 1/8" in from the outer edge of the page.

4. From the File menu, select Import (Ctrl+I) and browse to the folder where you saved your logo. Then import it in.

5. From the Interactive property bar, set the Object size (horizontal) to 0.8", but make sure that the Lock Ratio button is locked first. Position the logo in the upper-left corner of the card.

6. Below the logo, with the Text tool selected, type the address of 123 Midi Street, Oakland, CA 12354 on three separate lines and set the font to Arial Black 7 point and the justification to Center Justify on the property bar.

7. Below this, we are going to place a QR code. Now, if you have a smartphone, there are a number of applications that will allow you to create one. There are also a number of websites that have free generators. One such site is www.qurify.com.

8. In the QR Code, add the complete address and all contact information, as well as your email address and website. This makes it easier for prospective customers to add your contact information to their database. Generate the code and import that into the card. (I am not going to go through the steps as they will vary, depending on the tool that you use to generate the code.)

9. Place the code on the left side of the card under the logo.

10. Next create a rectangle that is 3.6" in length and .32" high. Position this so that it is centered horizontally on the card and about 1/8" is off the edge of the card. This will be used as the bleed. To fill this rectangle, you want to ensure that you are using the same color of yellow in the logo. To do this, use the Eyedropper tool. Select the fourth tool from the bottom in the Toolbox and click on one of the rays within the logo. If you are using CorelDRAW X5 or X6, simply click on the rectangle to apply the color. If you are using X4, hold down the Shift key to switch to the paint bucket before you click on the rectangle.

11. Type the slogan "Bring Light to your Electrical Needs" and set the font to Arial 10-point Bold and make it white by clicking on the white in the Color palette with the left mouse button.

12. It is now time to type the rest of the text, and you can see how it looks before laying it out for printing.

**13.** Type the name Gordon Lighthouse and set the font to Arial Black 15 point. Below this, type Electrical Contractor and set the font to Arial 12 point. Below this, type both the phone number and the cell number. I have used 613-555-1212 and 613-555-1234. When adding phone numbers, always use two or three letter prefixes to designate what the number is and be sure to use hyphens. It makes it easier to read and some card scanners have problems with numbers that do not have the hyphens in them.

**14.** Finally, type Commercial, Industrial, and Residential as three separate pieces of text.

**15.** For positioning these elements, we are going to use a couple of keyboard sequences.

**16.** Center the name horizontally between the right edge of the logo and the right of the card. With the name still selected, hold the Shift key down and select the logo. Press B. This will align the name with the bottom of the logo.

**17.** Select Electrical Contractor and Shift-select the name above. Press C to center under that name. Deselect both objects and select the Electrical Contractor text again and the address below the logo. Press T to align with the top of the logo. (I hope that you are seeing a pattern here. The alignment is based on the last object selected.)

**18.** Finally, select the word *Commercial* and then the name. Press L to left align. Now do the same for Residential, but press R. Now, select the three words at the bottom (in any order) and then holding down the Shift key, press E, which will evenly space them. With these words still selected, select the QR code and press B to align the words with the bottom of the QR code.

**19.** The final step is to add the two bullets between the three words at the bottom. Select the Text tool and click on the card. Holding down the Alt key, type 0115 on the numeric keypad. Select this character (the bullet) and change the font to Wingdings. Size this character and duplicate it by pressing Ctrl+D on the keyboard (see Figure 9.5).

**Figure 9.5**
*Here is the completed business card—a clean appearance with all the necessary information to present to a prospective customer. I have created lines to indicate where it will be cropped to provide a full bleed (illustrative purposes only). The advantage with the full bleed is that if your card is in a stack of cards, this will help it stand out.*

## Now That It's Created

Now that you have created the business card, there are a few options for output that you should consider.

How many copies do you want or need? If this is going to be a very small run, say under 100, and you have access to a color laser printer, it is possible that you can do it yourself. You can purchase card stock from a print shop or a "quick copy" center such as a UPS store or Kinko's or specialty paper stores in your city. Then, once they are printed, you only need to cut them. There is also the option to purchase card blanks from stationary shops or office supply stores that are pre-perforated. The problem with this is that the stock is usually a lighter weight and you may end up not having a clean-cut edge.

Do you have the equipment to do the printing yourself? Assuming that you have a quality color laser printer and want to print your own, it is simply a matter of printing them on the appropriate stock. To do this, you will have to use 100-pound stock paper that is either gloss or matt coated. Next, you will need to lay it out in CorelDRAW using the Imposition layout tool.

## Impositioning in CorelDRAW

Imposition is one of the basic steps in the prepress printing process. It consists of arranging the printed pages on the printer's sheet, in order to obtain faster printing, simplified binding, and less waste of paper.

Imposition is affected by a few variables:

► Finished page size

► Number of pages

► How the CorelDRAW pages are placed on the printed page

► Finishing and or binding (how the publication is assembled)

To better visualize how the pages are put together, it may be necessary to create a dummy. We already looked at this in Chapter 8, "Create Layouts with Ease," when we created the three-fold or tri-fold brochure template.

**To output the files you just created:**

1. From the File menu, select Print (Ctrl+P). I am going to make a couple of assumptions here: First, you have a color printer to print to and in the Printer drop-down, it has been selected. And second, the printed page size has been set to match what is in the printer currently.

2. In CorelDRAW X4, you will see a message that asks if you want to match the current page layout with the default. Answer "No" to this. What this means is that the application knows that your document is a landscape format (wider than longer) and the printer is printing in a portrait fashion. In CorelDRAW X5 and X6, below the Printer drop-down, you will see a Page drop-down. Select Use Printer default (Portrait) and then click OK.

3. Click the Print Preview button in the lower-left corner of the Print Dialog box (see Figure 9.6).

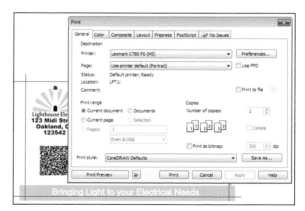

**Figure 9.6**
*The Print Dialog box allows you to gain access to all of the controls required to output any design that you may have created. Here is where you will access the Print Preview button.*

## Did You Know?

### A Signature Layout

A signature layout is a layout that printers will create to put multiple pages on a single piece of stock with specific placements so that when the stock is cut and folded, it will contain all the pages in the proper order and with minimal paper waste. The term *signature layout* comes from the fact that the pressman would have to put his signature or "sign off" on the layout before it was actually put into production.

4. In the Print Preview window, click on the Imposition layout tool, which is the second tool down in the toolbox (see Figure 9.7).

5. On the property bar at the top, set the Pages for 2 across and 5 down. This will lay out 10 cards on a letter-sized piece of paper.

6. Click on the Template/Document Preview icon and set the rotation of specific cards to be able to create the bleeds properly.

7. If you visualize the cards having numbers 1–5 for the column on the left and 6–10 for the right-hand column, then click the arrow above the numbers for cards 2, 4, 7, and 9. Rotating the cards like this, the bleed will be shared, and there will be no need to create gutters for cropping.

8. We can now add crop marks and then print. To do this, click on the Marks Placement tool from the Toolbox and then select Crop Marks from the property bar.

9. You can now print.

Once the cards are printed, it is just a matter of cutting them out using the crop marks as a guide.

Now that you understand what it takes to create a good layout for a business card and what elements should be included, go ahead and create your own. Also, as you can see, the Imposition tool makes it very easy to create special layouts and is a great way to save not only media but time as well.

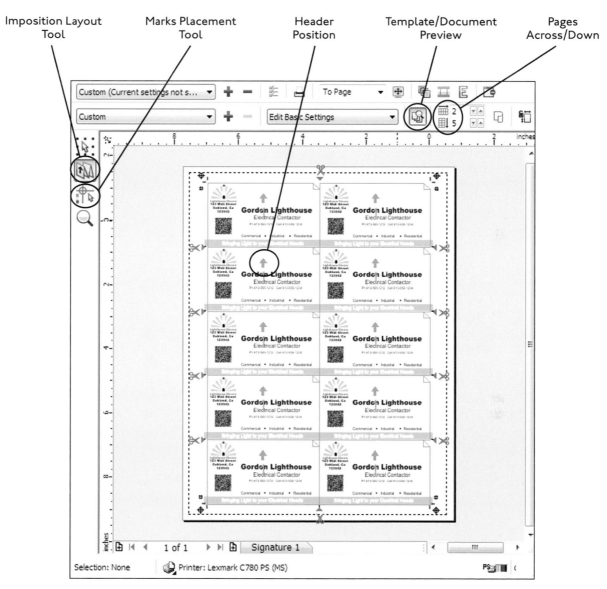

**Figure 9.7**

*The Imposition tool within CorelDRAW enables you to create signatures and styles of binding. It makes it extremely easy to layout a signature the way that you want.*

## Let's Impose Again

During the release cycle of CorelDRAW Graphics Suite X6, I had the opportunity to create what I referred to as a Quick Reference card. The

CorelDRAW marketing manager referred to it as a Quick Reference brochure, and I guess when you think about it, that is probably closer to the truth (see Figure 9.8).

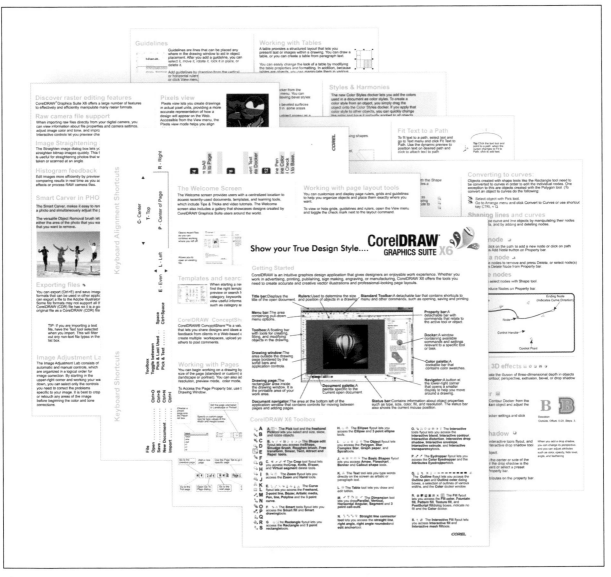

**Figure 9.8**

*This is the Quick Reference brochure. It is an invaluable tool for those learning CorelDRAW or for those who want to pick up some additional tips and tricks.*

The Quick Reference card was something that I had originally helped to create for CorelDRAW X3 and then took over to keep it up to date and current with the versions as they were released.

You can download your copy of the Quick Reference card from www.courseptr.com/downloads.

Once you have the file downloaded, follow these steps to output your own reference card to use while working in CorelDRAW.

### Know Where the Numbers Go

When creating a signature layout, it is easier and a lot less confusing if you create a dummy. A dummy is where you take a piece of paper and fold it as to how you envision the output should look. Next, number the pages in order. When the paper is then unfolded, you will know exactly where the pages and page orientation go prior to printing.

**To output your reference card:**

1. Once the file has been downloaded, copy it to the desktop where you can access it easily.

2. Create a new document in CorelDRAW and set the page size to Letter and the Primary Color mode to RGB.

3. From the File menu, select Import (Ctrl+I) and browse to the file on your desktop. Import it. You will notice as you import the eight-page document, it will automatically add pages to the existing document.

4. For the purpose of this exercise, we are going to assume that you have access to a printer that is capable of handling tabloid stock or 11 × 17. So from the File menu, select Print and click on the Print Preview icon.

5. In the Print Preview window, click on the Imposition layout tool.

6. On the property bar at the top, set the Pages to 2 across and 1 down.

7. Set the icon to the right of this (Single/ Double-sided) to Double-sided.

8. You will notice that there are two tabs at the bottom, Layout Template (Front) and Layout Template (Back). On the front, ensure that the page on the left is 1 and the page on the right is 2.

9. Select the tab that says Layout Template (Back). Ensure that this reads page 3 on the left and 4 on the right.

10. From the File menu, select Print this sheet now (Ctrl+T).

11. Set the next sheet up with page 7 on the left and the page on the right as page 8.

12. Select the tab that says Layout Template (Back). Ensure that this reads page 5 on the left and 6 on the right.

13. From the File menu, select Print this sheet now (Ctrl+T).

14. Position these two sheets with page 8 facing up and page 1 to the left of it. Tape them together and then fold each of the tabloid pages in half (see Figure 9.9).

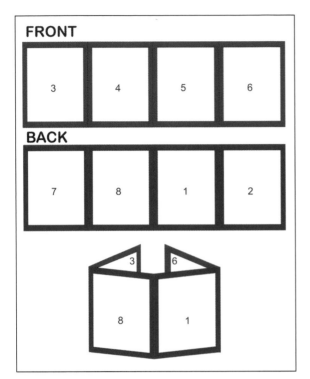

**Figure 9.9**
*Once you have your impositioned pages laid out, assemble them as shown to create a valuable tool to assist you when using CorelDRAW.*

The Quick Reference card is now completed. Keep it handy at your workspace, and you will always have some of the more common tools, tips, and tricks ready at your fingertips.

Now that you have a better understanding of what imposition is all about, it should be relatively easy for you to lay out another project down the road. Just remember to take your time, create a model or mock-up, and above all have fun doing it. When it is done correctly, it can look very professional and be rewarding.

# Letterhead

Creating a layout for letterhead is fairly straightforward, and there are no real hard and fast rules. You would probably not design letterhead for a bridal shop, daycare, or automotive garage using the same layout, but they will probably have the same type of information included.

I do not think that there is a need to get into a tutorial to show you how to import an image or position it on a page, so I will just provide you with a few guidelines that should be kept in mind when laying out your letterhead.

You need to be able to create a design that is pleasing to look at and functional at the same time. The choice of fonts is important. For example, you do not really want your address or phone number in a font that is almost impossible to read when it is displayed in a small point size. The style of your letterhead should also match your business card and website if you have one set up.

There are certain elements that should be included on the letterhead, including the company name and logo. But there are some other more common, and some not so common, elements that should be included as well.

- ▶ Company name
- ▶ Logo
- ▶ Tagline
- ▶ Mailing address
- ▶ Shipping address
- ▶ Office phone number
- ▶ Mobile number
- ▶ Fax number

▶ Email address

▶ Web address

▶ Facebook address

▶ Twitter handle

Another consideration should be placement. When we look at a document, instinctively our eye goes to the upper-right corner, which is a scientific fact. Is this the best spot for the logo? Should the address go here? Use colors and lines to separate elements and provide a clean professional look.

Another important area to remember is when you create your letterhead's design in CorelDRAW, make sure that you set the Primary Color mode to CMYK. When the design is printed, it is more economical to go with a four-color print rather than digital, since you will typically be printing in excess of 1,000 copies.

We are going to switch gears now and take a look at creating a mail-out piece for a business that is just starting out.

# Creating a Postcard Invite

IN THIS TUTORIAL, we are going to create a postcard mailer to be sent out to a select client database to announce the fall fashion lineup for a small fashion house. We will look at the power and flexibility of Print Merge to be able to merge an address database and add sequential numbers to a multiprint job.

## Make Your Postcard Stand Out

When people pick up the mail, they typically sort it into three piles: the good, the bad and the ugly. The good are checks and letters from friends (people still send those, right?). The bad are bills and past due notices, and the ugly is junk mail (oh, and maybe some of those past due notices). The ugly usually ends up in the recycle bin. Your goal is to make your marketing piece noticeable or memorable enough so that the message does not get lost. Here's how you do that.

▶ **Highlight the benefits:** When conveying your offer to the client, highlight the benefits in bullet point form. People don't always have time to read what they see. Make it stand out.

▶ **The offer:** Make them an offer they can't refuse, and make it easy to obtain. A one in fifty thousand chance won't cut it, but one in fifty might.

▶ **Make it big:** Size matters! A small postcard can get lost in a pile of junk. Make it big. Make it bold!

▶ **Use color to grab attention:** Certain color combinations can grab attention. Orange and blue, black and orange, yellow and black, purple and yellow, or red and green are all combinations that will get attention.

▶ **Double-sided:** Double the exposure by using the other side. You never know which side will be up when your customers pull the mail out of the mailbox.

▶ **Unique imagery:** Use unique imagery to make your piece stand out. I still have a tourism postcard from the city of Denver, CO that I got over two years ago, only because they used lenticular printing (the type of printing where the image changes depending on the angle of view).

As mentioned, Charlotte's Fashion House is launching its fall season with a special fashion show. During the show, there will be a drawing for a $1,000 gift certificate to spend at the boutique. We want to send out a mailer to a select list of key customers.

**To create a postcard:**

1. Before starting this tutorial, ensure that you have downloaded the Chapter 9 tutorial files from www.courseptr.com/downloads.

2. Start a new document in CorelDRAW and set the page size to 5" × 8" and set the Primary Color mode to RGB.

3. Double-click the Rectangle tool to create a page frame around the page and give it a solid black fill. Right-click on this object and select Lock Object. This will keep it from moving around while we create our design.

4. I am going to import the image that I saved from Chapter 7, "Elements of Design–Resolution," into the document and resize it to 2" horizontally (make sure that Lock ratio is selected on the Interactive property bar).

5. I'm going to import the original image of the model and continue to make use of it. First, I will resize it to the same size as the image I just brought in (2" horizontal). This will eventually be placed behind the mono-chrome bitmap image.

6. Duplicate the image six more times by holding the Ctrl key down and pressing D.

7. Convert three copies of the image to black and white using the following settings. From the Bitmap menu, select Mode and then Black and White. Make sure the Conversion Method is Halftone, the Screen type is Round, the degrees are 45, and lines per inch are 20.

8. Position the four copies of the image that have not been converted on the center of the 5 × 8 card in a pattern of 2 across and 2 down (see Figure 9.10).

9. Select the first image that was converted to black and white and then with the Shift key held down, select the color bitmap top left and press the letter C and then E (this will align Center and then Even). Now select the second black-and-white bitmap, Shift-select the color image, and press the letters C and E again. Repeat this for the last two images.

10. Before we start to color these, right-click the top of the Color palette just below the little black triangle. A menu will appear. Scroll down to Rows and select 3 Rows. This will make it possible to see all colors within this palette.

11. With the black-and-white image in the top right selected, left-click on the yellow one and right-click on magenta.

12. With the bottom left image selected, right-click on the blue purple.

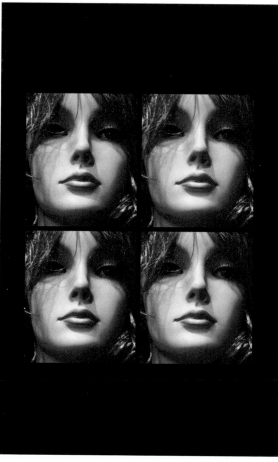

**Figure 9.10**

*Now that you have the base images down, you can put the halftone bitmaps on top and select the proper colors.*

**13.** With the last image selected, left-click on cyan. You should now have four very colorful images.

**14.** Select the four images and then from the toolbox, select the Transparency tool. (It is in the Interactive tool flyout along with the Blend tool. Once the tool is selected, on the property bar, set the Transparency type to Linear and the starting Transparency to about 20. This will make them just transparent enough to allow some of the detail from the image below to show through.

**15.** Using the Artistic Text tool, type the text "A Private Gathering for a Very Private Collection." Set the font to Calibri 24 point and center justify it. Left-click on the white in the Color palette. Now you need to adjust the leading. This adjustment can be done through the Text Properties docker, but instead, select the Shape tool. Reduce the leading slightly and center the text in this area (see Figure 9.11).

## Did You Know?

### Put the Lead In

The term *leading* comes from the earlier days of traditional typesetting when a typesetter would add bars or strips of lead to a layout, in between the rows of type slugs, to increase the spacing, hence adjusting the leading.

## Finding Colors

Holding down the Shift key while clicking on a color will not only tell you the name of the color you selected, but if you type the name of a color that you want, CorelDRAW will also navigate to it.

**Figure 9.11**

*It is easy to adjust the kerning or leading manually by selecting the text with the Shape tool selected and pulling on either the arrowhead pointing to the right for kerning and the arrowhead pointing downward for leading.*

16. With the Text tool selected, type in the text "Fashion Extravaganza." If you are not using CorelDRAW X6, select an ornamental font or a script font. I have used a font called Burgues Script, set the point size to 33, and clicked on the white in the Color palette both with the left mouse button and the right. This will give the text an outline and the appearance of bolding. With the text selected and the Text tool, triple-click on the text. This will select the entire string of text (well, both words). And if you have used the same font or another OpenType font, you will see a downward pointing arrow that you can click on to see other Stylistic Sets. Select one that you like.

17. The final step with this side of the card, before we start the back, is to resize the background to act as a bleed. Right-click on the background with the Pick tool and select Unlock Object.

18. In the Interactive property bar, in the horizontal measurement just after the 5.0", type +.25 and press Enter. Do the same for the vertical measurement. This will cause the rectangle to increase in size by .125" on all sides.

19. Save the file as Fashion Extravaganza front.CDR. You can see the completed fashion piece in Figure 9.12.

**Figure 9.12**

*The completed image.*

## Double That Exposure

As I mentioned, you can double the exposure by using the back of a postcard as well. In our project, we created a design that would hopefully catch the attention of the target audience and be something that the recipient might want to hold onto for the artistic value. Now, it is time to get the message out.

Because this card is going through the mail system and will have postage attached to it, there are certain guidelines that should be taken into consideration. In the United States, for example, it is required that a 3.75" wide area be left blank for the postage and address. This is typically on the right-hand side of the card. It is also important to have a minimum of 5/8" for a postal barcode along the bottom. With that in mind, let's begin side two.

**To create side two of the postcard:**

1. From the File menu, select New and set the page size to 5" × 8" and set the Primary Color mode to RGB.

2. As we are putting mainly text here, it will be easier if we are working with the same orientation in which the text will be read. Double-click the Rectangle tool to add a page frame. Now move this frame off the page and rotate it 90 degrees by typing 90 in the Angle of Rotation box on the property bar.

3. Draw a .75" × 1" rectangle and place it in the upper-right corner about .5" in from the right edge and .5" down from the top. This will be the area for the postage. Nothing fancy.

4. Now because we need 3.75" "clear space," draw a vertical line with the Freehand tool (F5). Then holding down the Ctrl key, click

once and then move to the new position and click again to ensure that your line is perfectly straight. Make sure that it is at least 4" long.

5. With this line still selected, press the spacebar to return to the Pick tool. Hold the Shift key down and press the letter R on the keyboard. This will move the line to the right edge of the rectangle.

6. As you can use mathematical formulas and operators in the size box on the property bar, you can also use them in the Object position box. With just the line selected, in the X position box to the right of the value that is there, type -3.75 and press Enter. This will move the line to the left by 3.75 inches. Your working area is to the left of this line.

7. We will start with the text and then add the logo later. Select the Text tool and click a blank area on the page. Then type Fashion Extravaganza, press Enter on the keyboard, and type Event of the Year. Change the text to Calibri bold and center justify it. The point size should be 18pt.

8. Type the remaining text in as follows:

   As a valued customer, please be our guest for the unveiling of a very special collection. Where: Charlotte's Fashion House When: September 15, 2012 Time: 7:30 p.m. (cocktails served at 6:00 p.m.) R.S.V.P.

   The invitee has a chance to win a $1,000 gift certificate.

9. Position this text block about .5" from the bottom and about .5" in from the left side.

**10.** Format this text as follows: use Times New Roman 12pt and ensure that the text is left justified.

**11.** Charlotte's logo consists of a piece of clipart that has been modified along with the company name in a specific font. To create this, we will modify a piece of clipart that comes with CorelDRAW. From the Standard menu bar, just below the Text menu, click on the Application launcher and select Corel CONNECT. Now there are a couple of ways that the CONNECT interface can be accessed—either through the Windows Docker menu in DRAW or Photo-PAINT or from the icon on the standard toolbar. And, of course, you can access it from the Application launcher (see Figure 9.13).

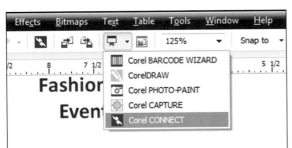

**Figure 9.13**
*One of the many ways to launch Corel CONNECT is through the Application launcher on the standard toolbar.*

**12.** After Corel CONNECT is launched, in the search panel, type in the word fashion and click the magnifying glass to start the search. After the search has completed, look through the results and find some images that may

speak to the idea that you have in mind. Drag these images to the tray across the bottom of the screen. As you can see in Figure 9.14, there are a few that I am considering. I particularly like the image of the woman in the evening gown. Once you are done, you can close Corel CONNECT.

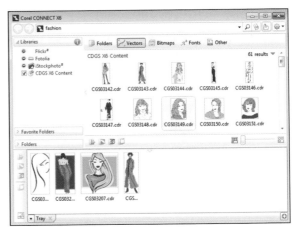

**Figure 9.14**
*After searching for fashion, the results show a few promising images that I could use.*

**13.** Back in CorelDRAW, from the Windows Docker menu, select Tray. As there is no need to search for images, we do not need CorelCONNECT, only the Tray.

**14.** Add a new page to the document and use this as a working space. I'm going to use the image of the woman in the blue evening gown (CGS03208). Drag this image (or the image you've chosen) onto the page.

**15.** These next few steps are specifically for CorelDRAW X6. From the Windows menu, select Dockers and Color Styles. Drag this image to the Color Styles Docker to create a color harmony. When you do this, you will be asked to create some color harmonies. For this image, I have created two harmonies.

16. Adjust the harmonies as you see fit (see Figure 9.15). Try clicking on the folder icon that has the first row of colors with it and drag the colors around on the color wheel below until the colors are as you like. Click on the folder icon for the second row of colors and drag the colors on the color wheel as you see fit. You can also click on a single color on the color wheel and move it independently. If you want to move all the colors again, simply click on the folder icon and it will select all the colors in the harmony once again.

If you are using an earlier version of CorelDRAW, ungroup the image and select the individual colors and change them by selecting the various colors in the Color palette. As there are very few colors in this design (or objects), you could also hold down the Ctrl key to select objects (without having to ungroup it).

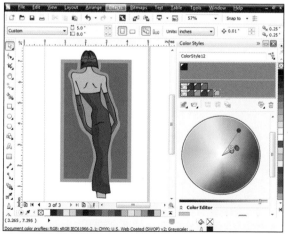

**Figure 9.15**
*By adjusting the color harmonies, you can get a completely different look from what the original was.*

17. Now that I have the colors the way that I want them, there is only one more bit of editing that I need to do on this piece of content. I want to remove what looks like a "tab"

where shoes should be. Select the woman and from the Arrange menu, select Ungroup. Select the Pick tool and click on the light brown object; then press the Delete key. Select the Shape tool and marquis-select the lower half of the "tab" to select the nodes and press the Delete key once again to remove these nodes (see Figure 9.16).

18. Select one of the nodes along the bottom and using the Node control handles, reshape the curve to contour the bottom of the dress (see Figure 9.17).

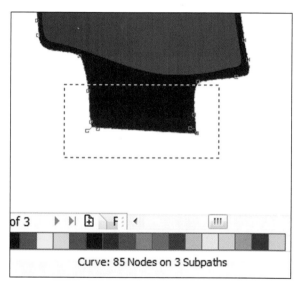

**Figures 9.16 and 9.17**
*Node editing is a very powerful tool and the precision it offers is one of the main benefits of vector artwork.*

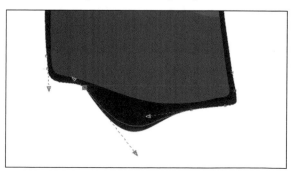

# Working with Nodes

Vector graphic objects are created with nodes and either curves or line segments. These together are called curves in CorelDRAW or paths in some other applications. Each curve has a start and an end node, and it can have nodes in between. In order to control the shape of the curve, a control handle on the node is manipulated. There are four types of nodes, and they vary depending on how the control handles move in order to manipulate them. They are the following:

▶ **Cusp:** Cusp nodes let you create sharp corners between curves, such as points, in a curved object. Moving the control handles in a Cusp node will allow you to independently change the lines on either side of the node and either make the appearance more pointed or smooth.

▶ **Smooth:** With a Smooth node, you can change the angle as it passes thorough the node to create a smooth transition. The control handles are always directly opposite one another, but the length of the handle on either side of the node may vary.

▶ **Symmetrical:** These are like Smooth nodes, because they create a smooth even path between line segments. The control handles on both sides move in unison.

▶ **Line:** These nodes allow you to shape an object by having perfectly straight lines within it.

Manipulating nodes and understanding exactly how they act and react can take a bit of time, but with practice, you would be amazed what you can do with nodes (see Figure 9.18).

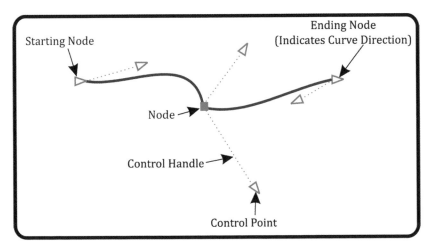

**Figure 9.18**
*Learn about nodes, as they are especially useful.*

19. Now that the image is ready to incorporate, select the entire image and group it; then drag it off the page onto the desktop of CorelDRAW.

20. Go to page two, select the image that we just created, and on the Interactive property bar, ensure that the Lock ratio is closed. In the vertical Object size, enter a value of 1.25" and press Enter. Now position this image in the upper-left corner of the card.

21. Using the Text tool, click on the page, type in Charlotte's Fashion House, and set the font to Bodini BT 24 pt.; then center justify the text.

22. Using the Eyedropper tool, click on the darker purple in the dress and now, if you are using CorelDRAW X5 or 6, click on the Text tool to color the text. If you are using CorelDRAW X4, hold the Shift key down and then click on the text. If you are by chance using CorelDRAW X3, upgrade!

23. Now that the company text is properly colored and formatted, type in the address 280-6227 Eros. St, Concord, ON Z6Q 8D2, and on the second line type (613) 728-0826 Email: charlotte@cfh.com.

24. Double-click the Pick tool, which is a quick way to select all objects on the page, and then go to the Arrange menu and select Group. Your postcard should look like Figure 9.19.

Now it is time to output this postcard. Because it is a mail-out to a select group of customers, we should be using a database of customer addresses to send it out, and since we are also going to be awarding a $1,000 gift certificate to one lucky attendee, we will need to have these cards sequentially numbered. In this next tutorial, we will look at Print Merge and how to apply the addresses of an external database to a project.

**Figure 9.19**
*If you have been following along, the back of your postcard should look like this.*

# Print Merge

The Print Merge feature has been around for the past couple of decades in applications such as word processors, although you might not have known that a graphics application also had the capability to use that feature. In CorelDRAW, you have been able to use it for at least the past 15 years.

Print Merge allows you to take a database of information (usually names and addresses) and merge them with your design. But before we see how it's done, we need to make an assumption, and that is that you have a customer database that can be exported as a .csv file, or you are prepared to type in the customer information. We will look at both options.

To start this exercise, we will ensure that the last project is still open. From the File menu, select Create > Load Merge Fields to open the Print Merge Wizard. Here you have two options. For this project, we will be using the Import Text file option, but before you get to that, I want to show you the Create New Text option. Using this feature instead will help you better understand the formatting that is required when creating a text document that can be used with Print Merge.

**To use Print Merge:**

1. Select the option to Create new text and click Next.

2. Type the name of the first text field (Name) and click Add.

3. Type the name of the second field (Address 1) and click Add.

4. Repeat until all fields have been entered; they should include City, State, and Zip code. Click on the Next button.

5. Here you have the option to enter the actual data. We are going to go ahead with that, but only enter two or three records. The objective with this exercise is not to complete the entire database, but more importantly to see how the application formats the information.

The information that we will enter is as follows:

Angela Dixon, 1042 Leo. St., Chico, Alaska, 10896

Helen Maldonado, P.O. Box 882 9094 Lorem St., Meriden, SC, 22724

Cassidy Hansen, Apt #711-2852 Aliquam Street, Columbus, MA, 38490

6. Click in the Name field and enter the first name, Angela Dixon; in the second field, enter the address, followed by the city and Zip code. Repeat this for three more records and click Next.

7. On the next screen, select the check box that says "Save data settings as" and click the Browse button to dictate where you want this file to be saved. Give it a file name and click Save.

8. Click Finish. This will bring the Print Merge toolbar on the screen, as shown in Figure 9.20.

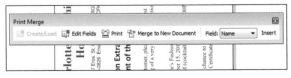

**Figure 9.20**
*The Print Merge toolbar provides access to the various tools required to perform a print merge.*

9. From this point, you can cancel this out and go back to your text document.

10. Now, let's perform the merge with your database, as a comma separated file (.csv) I have already exported my database and in WordPerfect (my word processor of choice), I have formatted the document properly. From the File menu, select Print Merge and then select Create/Load Merge Fields.

11. Select "Import text from a file or an ODBC data source" and browse to your file that contains your contacts. Once it is selected, click Next to import the text file.

## Additional Features of Print Merge

The Print Merge Wizard not only has the ability to allow for data to be merged with a document, but you can also add sequential numbering and specify the numeric format starting number as well as ending value.

12. In the Numeric field, type the word Number and click add. Now scroll down through the list of field names and select the field "Number" that you just added. This will cause the fields on the bottom half of the dialog box to become active.

13. As this design is being sent to a very small group, we only need about 50 tickets. Set the Numeric format to 00X. Continually increment the numeric field and set a Starting value of 100. Click Next, click Next a second time, and then click Finish (see Figure 9.21).

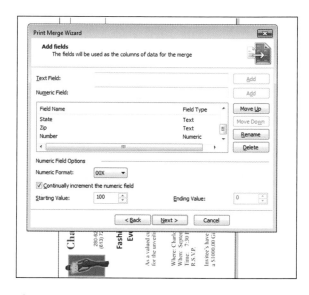

**Figure 9.21**
*A whole realm of possibilities for design opens up with the ability to use sequential numbering on tickets.*

14. It is now time to add the fields to the document, which is fairly easy, but unless you follow a certain process, it can be a bit more difficult than it needs to be. On the right end of the toolbar, you will see a Field drop-down and an Insert option. Click the Insert option to put the Name field on the document. Move it somewhere else, because at this moment, it does not matter where you move it.

15. On the Field drop-down, select Address 1 and click Insert. See why we moved the name? Now move Address 1, click the Field drop-down, select City, and click Insert. Go ahead and bring the other fields in by using the same method.

16. Now that you have all of the fields in, marquis-select them and change the font to 12 point Arial.

17. Position the Name, Address 1, City, State, and Zip on the right-hand side of the card in the position where an address would typically go. Place the number field at the top of the card just above the name and then duplicate it. Ensure that all of the elements are aligned and spaced.

18. Move the duplicate number fields just below the text on the left side of the card. This way, it can also act as a ticket number for the drawing.

19. It is now time to merge the data with the graphic, so from the Print Merge toolbar, select Merge to New Document. This will create a multipage document. From this point, save your file to the Desktop. The final postcard is shown in Figure 9.22.

**Figure 9.22**
*Our completed postcard is ready to print once the fields have been added and the data merged.*

Now that you have gone through the exercise of creating the front and back of the card, as well as merging the data, there are a couple of options available that are open to you.

▶ If you have access to a color laser printer, print the file yourself.

▶ Save this file and take it to a print shop that uses CorelDRAW.

▶ From the File menu, Publish to PDF so that a copy center can print the file for you in the event that they do not have CorelDRAW.

This type of file is best printed on card stock. There are a number of different manufacturers and different finishes available. My recommendation for this particular type of collateral would be 100 lb or 14 pt gloss card stock.

Once this job is printed, drop it in the mailbox and sit back and watch the number of invitees that will respond.

**Did You Know?**

## Pounds Versus Points

OK, what's that about? Points or pounds? Card stock or cover stock—which is thicker? Pound weight is the weight of 500 sheets of $20 \times 26$ paper. In the United States, the term "points" is used where a point is equivalent to a thousandth of an inch. For example, a 12 pt card is 0.012".

# Creating a Desktop Background

CREATING DESKTOP WALLPAPER is very easy in CorelDRAW, and it can be fun just to play with the tools to see what CorelDRAW is capable of. This particular section will be a bit difficult to give step-by-step instructions, so what I will do is just steer you to some of the tools and features in CorelDRAW and then let you discover them on your own. I will create my own design, but feel free to follow along or just use some of the same tools that I am using—perhaps changing the colors and positioning of objects.

## The Setup

I just got through telling you that there were no step-by-step instructions, but there has to be some order to this, so here are just a few. We will be using one of the document presets called Web. The Web preset not only can be used for creating a Web layout, you would also use similar settings if you were creating an image to be used as wallpaper or creating a background for a presentation slide deck. This preset includes the following items:

▶ Units of measure set to pixels (px)

▶ Primary Color mode set to RGB

▶ Rendering resolution set to 96 dpi.

Using a preset can save you time during the setup process and make it easier to start designing projects.

Within the presets under Size, there are a number of Web banner sizes. We will not be using one of those, so just select Full screen. This will default to 1024 × 768, which is a pretty standard size for wallpaper, as well as a slide deck background. If you want to go with a different resolution, determine what resolution your monitor is and use those settings. To do this, right-click on the Windows desktop and select Screen resolution. The value will be displayed in the resolution drop-down.

**To create a desktop wallpaper:**

1. Start by creating a new document by going to the File menu and selecting New (Ctrl+N).

2. From the Preset destination drop-down, select Web. Ensure that the Width is set to 1024px and the height is 768px and click OK.

3. Right-click on the grayed out Eyedropper at the top of the RGB Color palette. This will bring up a context sensitive menu that will allow you to change some parameters. Select row 3. This will cause the Color palette to display in three rows.

4. You now have a blank page. Start by double-clicking on the Rectangle tool to add a page frame.

5. I'm going to click on the Forest Green. Hold down the Shift key while clicking on a color.

6. I'm going to use the Mesh Fill tool. It is the fill flyout in the bottom of the toolbox, so click and hold on the Fill bucket to find it. You can also press the M key. This will put the start of a mesh grid on the page with four "cells."

7. Double-click in the center of the lower-right cell to add two more divisions. Do the same for the upper-left cell. Your document should now have 16 cells on it.

8. Click and hold on the Forest Green color swatch in the Color palette. This will open a flyout of swatches based on hue and lightness of this color. Hue runs top to bottom, and lightness is left to right.

9. Select the first color swatch you like and drag it to the second grid from the bottom and drop it in the center. You will notice that it fills the area with that color and also creates a smooth blend outward from there.

10. Now remember, we are just playing here. Nothing is wrong with having a bit of fun, right? Using the Freehand drawing tool (the fifth from the top), draw two freehand lines on the page. It does not matter where you draw them, or the shape, just have them cross each other at some point (see Figure 9.23).

11. Select each line individually and change the line width to 2 pixels.

12. With one of the lines selected, right-click on a color swatch in the Color palette. Now select the second line and right-click on a contrasting color.

13. In the Interactive tool flyout (15th tool down in the toolbox), grab the first tool, the Blend tool, and apply a blend from one line to the next. Remember, if you are not sure how to use a tool, open the Hints Docker. (It can be found under Help > Hints.) By default, it will blend in 25 steps. Increase the number of steps to 150 in the Interactive property bar (see Figure 9.24).

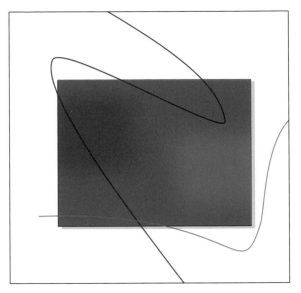

**Figure 9.23**
*Feel free to draw your lines any size, shape, or position on the page.*

**Figure 9.24**
*The Interactive property bar allows you to adjust the blend in a specific number of steps, in a straight line or along a path, as well as modify the progression of colors through the color spectrum. Here I have set mine to 150 steps.*

14. Once you have the blend created, double-clicking on the Pick tool will select everything on the page. Now group them by going to the Arrange menu and selecting Group (Ctrl+G).

15. Move the grouped elements off the page and double-click the Rectangle tool to create a page frame.

16. Right-click and drag the grouped elements onto the rectangle and let go of the mouse button. A pop-up menu will appear that allows you a few different options, such as Move Here, Copy Here, and PowerClip Inside. Select PowerClip Inside. Remember that by right-clicking on the PowerClip (or Ctrl+click), you can edit the PowerClip. Then position the contents where you want them.

17. I'm going to finish this off by adding one more element. With the Ellipse tool selected (that's Canadian for circle), hold down the Ctrl key and draw an ellipse about 15px in diameter. (Remember the property bar will read out the size as you are drawing the ellipse.)

18. With the Ellipse still selected, click on the Eyedropper tool in the toolbox, click on the green background, and then fill the ellipse. Now right-click on the X in the Color palette to remove the outline.

19. Select the last tool in the toolbox, the Interactive Fill tool, and drag it across the ellipse. On the Interactive property bar, change the fill type from Linear to Radial.

20. Still on the Interactive property bar, select the drop-down for the Last Fill color and click on a lighter green.

21. Position the start and end handles with the darker in the center and the lighter toward the outer edge, as shown in Figure 9.25.

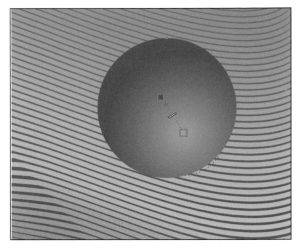

**Figure 9.25**
*Adjusting the start and end handles can help to add dimension to a fountain fill and depending on the colors, give the illusion of a light source striking the surface.*

22. To add one more element of depth to this object, from the Interactive tool flyout, select the Drop Shadow tool and on the Interactive property bar, select the Preset drop-down and click on Small Glow.

23. Also on the Interactive property bar, change the Shadow color to a light green. Feel free to play with the other settings here like Drop Shadow Opacity and Shadow Feathering. OK, it's time to put this file into use.

## Finishing It Off

The final step for our newly created wallpaper image is to export the file. From the File menu, select Export. You'll see four Exports:

▶ **Export:** This option will allow you to export or "save out" a file or portion of a file in one of almost 60 file formats, some with multiple variations.

▶ **Export for Office:** This option allows for more compatibility when exporting for Microsoft Word or WordPerfect.

▶ **Export for Web:** When exporting for the Web, you'll want to have the smallest file size while still maintaining a quality looking image. Export for Web provides up to four panels to preview not only what the image will look like in various Web-compatible formats but also to predict the file size and estimated download time.

▶ **Export HTML:** This feature allows you to actually create HTML code from the document and create basic Web pages. Some of the features that Export HTML support include generating Java, CSS file image maps, roll-overs, and FTP upload.

**To export the file:**

1. From the File menu, select Export, and in the Export dialog box, indicate where you want the file saved.

2. In the Save as type drop-down, select JPG – JPEG Bitmaps and click Export (see Figure 9.26).

3. Change the Quality drop-down to Highest (100%) and click OK. You can now make use of the file (see Figure 9.27).

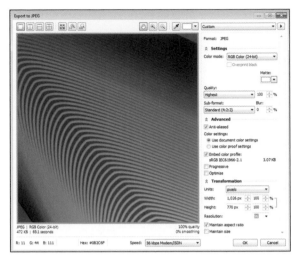

**Figure 9.26**
*The Export to JPG dialog box provides access to all of the options required to export the best quality image for quick upload.*

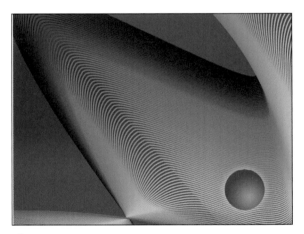

**Figure 9.27**
*The final wallpaper or background image is ready to install into Windows.*

Creating a wallpaper for your system or any system for that matter can be as simple as importing a photo, or group of photos, and then exporting it as a .jpg file. Don't be afraid to experiment and have fun with the program. After all, if you do not like what you created, just delete it.

# Backgrounds for Presentation Software

CREATING A TEMPLATE for Microsoft PowerPoint or a background for Corel Presentations is just as easy as creating a wallpaper image for your desktop; however, there are a couple of tips to consider.

- ▶ Focus on white space and do not make the background too cluttered.

- ▶ Make a few different variations, so they can be used for title slides and content slides.

- ▶ Create pleasing color schemes that do not take away or distract from the message being delivered. If you use darker colors in a template, the viewer will focus on the content.

- ▶ Look at other designs, not to copy, but to determine what you like about them and try to incorporate some of those ideas into your own design.

We are going to create a template for a slide deck that will be used by a plant nursery that wants to conduct weekly seminars for its customers. Be sure to download the content from www.courseptr.com/downloads.

**To create a template:**

1. Create a new document by going to the File menu and selecting New (Ctrl+N).

2. From the Preset destination drop-down, select Web. Ensure that the width is set to 1024px and the height is 768px and click OK.

3. We will start by creating the design for the Master layer. By using a Master layer, it will allow us to create a design that will be used for all pages (or slides) in a presentation. From the File menu, select Import and browse to a photograph that you want to use as a background. This image will appear as a watermark or faded image on all the slides.

4. Size this photograph to fit the page (1024 × 768). Select the Interactive Transparency tool from the Interactive tool flyout. From the Transparency type drop-down, select Uniform and then use the slider to set the transparency level to 40.

5. Select the Rectangle tool and create a rectangle the same size as the page. Left-click on the white from the Color palette. From the Interactive tool flyout, select the Interactive Transparency tool and then on the Interactive property bar, under Transparency type, select Square and set the Transparency midpoint to 50.

6. Create a rectangle that is 1024 × 80 and give it a fill of Dull Green (R:153 G:204 B:102). Position this rectangle at the top of the page and then duplicate it. Move the duplicate of this rectangle to the bottom of the page.

7. Create a rectangle that is 260px wide by 200px in height.

8. With the rectangle still selected, on the Interactive property bar, you will see an area where you can adjust the Corner Radius. Set the lower-right corner radius to 100.

9. With this object still selected, select the horizontal 80 × 1024 rectangle that you created and then press the letters T and L to align these objects to the top-left corner.

10. From the Arrange menu, select Shaping and Weld.

11. Because you selected the filled rectangle last, once welded together, the two objects will take on the fill of that object.

12. Next, we are going to apply a Drop Shadow to this object to give it some depth. With it still selected, click on the Drop Shadow tool and then click the center of the Title Bar object and drag straight down about 200px. (Use the ruler as a guide.)

13. Press the spacebar to return to the Pick tool and then press Ctrl+C to copy this to the clipboard, as you will use it shortly.

14. The next step is to import the logo into the design and place it in the upper-left corner. For this exercise, use your own logo.

15. Select the Text tool, click in the banner at the top, and type your company name. This slide is complete and will become the main slide for the content of your presentation.

16. Now to create the main title slide, right-click on the Page 1 tab in the bottom-left corner of the Navigation area and select Duplicate Page. This will open a dialog with some options.

17. Select the Radial button beside Before Selected Page Copy Layer(s) and their contents. Click OK.

18. Go to the new Page 1, hold the Crtl key down, and press the V key. This will paste the object that was copied previously.

19. With this object still selected, on the Interactive property bar, change the angle of rotation from 0.0 to 180 and press Enter on the keyboard.

20. Select the Text tool, click in the banner at the bottom, type your address in the lower-right corner, and save the file as a CDR. We will be using it for the next tutorial.

21. Select File > Export and export the two pages as PNG files or another suitable format based on the slide presentation tool that you use.

Whether you are using Microsoft PowerPoint, Corel Presentations, or another presentation program, follow the Help file instructions for using your own graphics as backgrounds in that application.

With a bit of preplanning, you can quickly and easily create a presentation background that will captivate and keep your audience's attention through the show, as shown in Figure 9.28.

**Figure 9.28**
*The finished slide background.*

# CorelDRAW as a Presentation Tool

ALTHOUGH CORELDRAW is not a true presentation software, it certainly has the capability to be a basic tool in conveying your message to small or large audiences alike. Although it's not as flexible when it comes to transitions and animations, you can still create graphics with rich content, have bulleted text appear on the screen, and use the "slide sorter view."

**To create a simple bulleted slide presentation:**

1. Open the file in CorelDRAW that you saved from the previous project. Ensure that the Object Manager is open.

2. To create a Master layer, in the Object Manager, click the Option button (the small right-pointing triangle in the top-right corner of the Docker) and select New Master Layer. In CorelDRAW X6, it will say New Master Layer (all pages).

3. Drag the New Layer onto the Master page below the Document Grid.

4. Starting on page (slide) one, select the Text tool and click on the page. Type "Preparing Your Garden for Spring". Set the font to Arial Black 72 pt and center justify it. This will become the title slide (see Figure 9.29).

We are going to switch to page 2 and format the text frame. Although we could use Artistic Text here, by using Paragraph Text, it is much easier to create bullet points for our slide.

**Figure 9.29**
*The title slide of any slide deck should clearly state the topic of the discussion and be easily read from a distance when projected on a screen.*

5. Switch to page 2 to set up some properties for the text format. In CorelDRAW X6, from the Text menu, select Text Properties. (Prior to CorelDRAW X6, it was referred to as Character Formatting.)

6. With nothing selected on the page, from the font drop-down, ensure that the font is set to Arial. When you select a font, you will see the Change Document Defaults dialog box open that will indicate that text properties are about to be set as the default (see Figure 9.30). Ensure that Paragraph Text is selected and click OK. Repeat these steps to change the font size to 25 pt and line spacing to 150%. Note, for line spacing in CorelDRAW X5, you will need to go to the Text menu and select Paragraph Formatting and change it there.

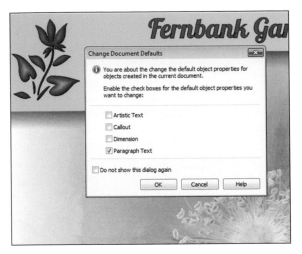

**Figure 9.30**
*Change Document Defaults will allow you to create text quickly with the formatting that you need.*

7. To simulate bulleted text coming on the slides one at a time, create as many pages as you do bullets by clicking on the + just to the left of the Page1 tab in the Navigation area.

8. Create a Paragraph Text frame and then either type your bullet points in or copy and paste them from a text document. Alternatively, you could also import them if there is a fair amount of text or tables.

9. With the text still selected, click the Bulleted list icon on the Interactive property bar (Ctrl+M).

10. Select the Paragraph Text frame with the Pick tool and copy it to the clipboard (Ctrl+C).

11. Go to each page and paste in a copy (Ctrl+V). Once you are done, go back to the first page with that frame on it. Select all the text except the first bullet point and delete it.

12. Go to the second page and select all the text except the first two bullets and delete it. Now on to the third page, bet you know what we are going to do here, eh? Delete all but the first three bullets. Continue to the last bullet point remains (see Figure 9.31).

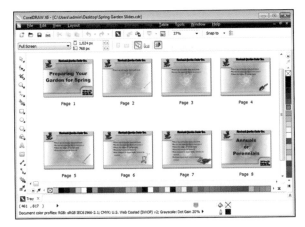

**Figure 9.31**
*Here you can see a Page Sorter view of the completed slide deck.*

Where do we go from here? We could get a bit fancier by changing the color of the previous bullets that were reviewed to a lighter gray so that only the main talking point was in black.

We could also import graphic images or photos to help communicate the concept being discussed. Color is an option and, of course, when it comes to editing graphics in a slide deck, nothing is better than CorelDRAW.

# Web Tools

EARLIER WE LOOKED AT CREATING desktop wallpaper and backgrounds for slideshows. What they have in common is that they are both measured in pixels. When working with HTML, pixels are also used. As both CorelDRAW X5 and CorelDRAW X6 ship with Website Creator, I have opted not to include any website tutorials specific to CorelDRAW; however, we will look at some of the tools and features that are included with CorelDRAW that aid in the creation of Web graphics and basic HTML pages.

## Pixel View in CorelDRAW

As you have already seen, there are a number of views available in CorelDRAW. When CorelDRAW X5 was launched, it introduced a new view that

made it much easier to design Web graphics. The Pixel view in CorelDRAW lets you create drawings in actual pixel units, providing a much more accurate representation of how a design will appear.

First, create a new Web document and draw an ellipse. Give it a red fill and then zoom in to 800%. Looks like what you would expect for a vector object, right? Now from the View menu, select Pixels, as shown in Figure 9.32.

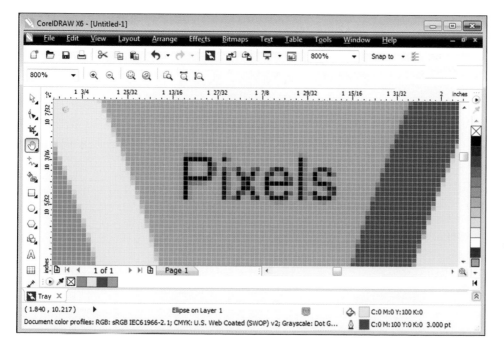

**Figure 9.32**
*With Pixel view selected, when zoomed into 800%, you can actually work at the "pixel level." Here the status bar indicates that it is actually an ellipse that is selected.*

# Export for Web

The Export for Web dialog box provides a single access point for common export controls, eliminating the need to open additional dialog boxes when preparing a file for export. It also lets you compare the results of various filter settings before you commit to an output format, making it easier to achieve the best results (see Figure 9.33).

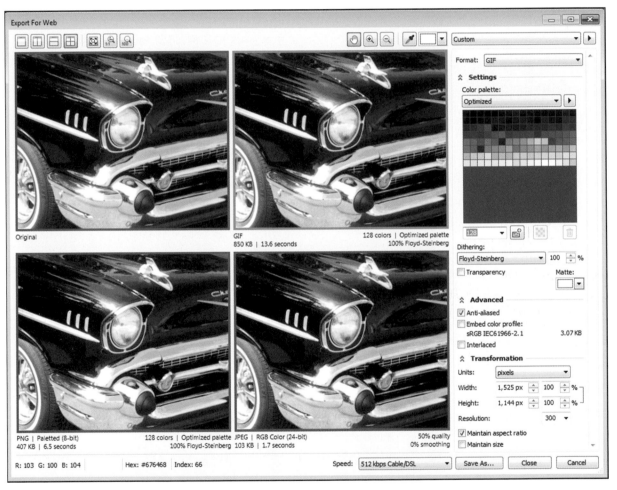

**Figure 9.33**

*You can select parameters for various Web suitable formats, and feedback provides the anticipated file size and projected download time based on the transfer rate that you dictate.*

# What File Format Is Best

CorelDRAW allows you to export to the three common file formats used in Web design. Determining which format is best for a design that you may be working on would greatly depend on the requirements for the file. Here is a brief explanation of each file type.

- ▶ **GIF:** GIF images are best used for line drawings, text, images with few colors, or images with sharp edges, such as scanned black-and-white images or logos. GIF offers several advanced graphic options, including setting a single color to be shown as transparent, interlaced images, and animation. It also lets you create custom palettes for the image.

- ▶ **PNG:** PNG files are best for various image types, including photos and line drawings. The PNG file format (unlike the GIF and JPEG formats) supports the alpha channel or soft transparency. This allows you to save transparent images with soft edges and high quality.

- ▶ **JPEG:** Photos and scanned images are best exported as JPEG files. JPEG files use file compression to store an approximation of an image, which results in some loss of image data, but does not compromise the quality of most photographs. You can choose the image quality when you save an image—the higher the image quality, the larger the file size.

## Options for Exporting a JPG

From the Export for Web dialog box, choose JPEG from the Format list box. There are a number of options available to you: Control Color Mode, Quality, Subformat, and the ability to blur the transition between adjacent pixels of different colors.

There is also the ability to overprint blacks when exporting to CMYK and apply a matte color to the object's background to help blend the edges of anti-aliased objects.

To load the JPEG file gradually in certain Web browsers so that it displays only portions of the image before it finishes loading, enable the Progressive check box. Use the optimal encoding method to produce the smallest JPEG file size and apply the document color settings. You can also use the color-proof settings.

## Palette-based Bitmaps

From the Export for Web dialog box, choose GIF or PNG from the Format list box. You will have the option to choose a Color palette, specify a Dithering setting, and you can also sample a color and add it to a Color palette by clicking on the Eyedropper tool. This is especially helpful if you have reduced the number of colors in an image (to reduce file size) and realize that a specific color is missing that you would like to add. One other feature here is that you can double-click on any of the visible colors and modify them.

## 3D Buttons and Roll-overs

Let's take a look at a couple of quick little exercises for creating buttons and roll-overs.

**To create a 3D looking button and use it for a roll-over:**

1. Create a new document with the preset Destination set to Web and click OK.

2. While holding down the Ctrl key, draw an ellipse about 75px in diameter and give it a Fountain fill from lime green to black; then remove the outline.

**3.** Duplicate this ellipse and resize it to 60px; then on the Interactive property bar, set the Angle of rotation to 180 and press Enter. You can see the buttons we've created in Figure 9.34

**Figure 9.34**
*Creating buttons for a Web design or a PowerPoint presentation is easily accomplished.*

# Creating a Feature Sheet Template

IN THIS TUTORIAL, we are going to create a feature sheet that can be used for a real estate agent when listing properties. The feature sheet is typically a sales tool that is used to help advertise a property to potential buyers. This type of document is usually a single- or double-sided document that is 8 $1/2$" × 11". We will start by creating the template and then populating it with the content.

When creating a feature sheet, it makes sense to use PowerClip frames because with each new property that is listed, it will be necessary to update the template with an image of the new listing.

In CorelDRAW X6, it is very easy to create PowerClip containers and text boxes and be able to visualize how a project is going to look. For those of you who are using a version of CorelDRAW prior to X6, simply create text frames and rectangles on the page that can be used for PowerClip containers.

## It's the Process That's Important

Note that it is not overly critical if you use the same colors, sizes of objects, or positioning. The idea is to understand how to place the various elements and learn some of the tools while doing it.

**To create a feature sheet template:**

**1.** After launching CorelDRAW, create a new document from the CorelDRAW defaults and have a letter-size page set to Landscape. Set the Primary color mode to RGB and leave the rendering resolution set to 300 dpi. Click OK.

2. I'm going to start by clicking the ruler in the top-left corner where they intersect and drag the cursor to the top-left corner of the page. This will reset the ruler position to the top-left corner of the page.

3. Click on the vertical ruler and drag a guide-line out to the 5 1/2" mark on the horizontal ruler to divide the page in half and create two panels.

4. Using the Text tool, click on the right-hand panel about 3/4" from the top and type in an address, for example "1417 Birchwood Dr, Nepean Ontario" and below this put in a price: $389,900.

5. Format the text using a font that will stand on its own. A suggestion would be to use Bodoni Bk BT and set the point size to 16 pt. Make it red.

6. Next, select the Rectangle tool and create a rectangle that is 4" across by 3". Right-click on the toolbar and select Layout (the Layout toolbar is in X6 only). With the rectangle still selected, click PowerClip from the Layout toolbar. With versions earlier than CorelDRAW X6, it is not possible to have an empty PowerClip frame. Leave the rectangles as they are and then use the menu options to create the PowerClip.

7. Still with the rectangle selected, from the Interactive tool flyout, select the Drop Shadow tool and then on the Interactive property bar under the Presets List drop-down, select Small Glow. Note that you will see no difference in the rectangle until you clip the image into the container.

8. Select the Text tool and create a text frame below the PowerClip rectangle that measures 4.5" × 1.5" and then right-click on it and select Insert Placeholder Text. This is another feature that is new to CorelDRAW X6. To obtain placeholder text for earlier versions, visit http://www.lipsum.com/.

9. From the File menu, select Import and browse to where you have a copy of your logo and click and drag to position it below the text frame.

10. Add your name and contact information. Use Bodoni 12pt and make it red. We are now finished with what will be the front of this Feature sheet.

11. On the left-hand panel, create six rectangles, four that are 1" × 1.5", one that is 1.5" × 2.5", and the final one that is 3" × 4".

12. Select each rectangle and convert it to PowerClip containers and position the first five with the four smaller ones overlapping the corners of the larger one. Then place this grouping on the top half of the panel (remember, CorelDRAW X6 only).

13. Apply the same Drop Shadow to each of these frames that you did in step 7. Select the last one and change the outline to 3pts. Then make it red.

14. With the Artistic Text tool, type the text "Your New Neighborhood" and make it Bodoni Bk BT 24pt and red.

15. Right-click the Page 1 tab and select Duplicate page (without contents). Click OK.

16. On the right panel for side two, create a rectangle that is 4" × 6.75". Give it a 3 pt red outline.

17. Select the Text tool and position the cursor on the inside edge of the rectangle until you see the I beam cursor with a small AB. This is an indication that you are about to create a text frame inside the rectangle. Click the mouse button. Right-click and select Insert Placeholder Text.

18. Using Artistic Text, type the title "Features to Suite." Set the font to Bodoni Bk BT 24 pt and change the color to red.

19. On the left panel, create a rectangle that is 2" × 1.25". With the Rectangle selected, click on the PowerClip Frame icon on the Layout toolbar and then apply a Drop Shadow to it using the same settings as those on the other panels.

20. Duplicate this PowerClip container three more times and position them in the four corners of this panel (see Figure 9.35).

21. Create a rectangle that measures 1.75" × 1", convert it to a PowerClip frame, and apply a Drop Shadow the same way that you have been doing the others. Duplicate this one four more times and position it like you did the frames on the other side.

22. Now that the template is complete, save it by going to the File menu and selecting Save As. In the Save As dialog box, select CDT – CorelDRAW Template from the Save as Type drop-down. If you are not sure what to do next, refer to Chapter 8.

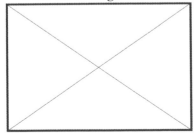

Lorem ipsum dolor sit amet. Consectetuer et clita id nonumy in diam hendrerit. Vero labore in elitr erat accusam invidunt quodvidunt sit nibh exerci ut.

**Your New Neighborhood**

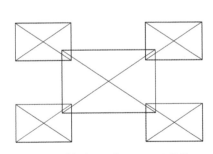

**1417 Birchwood Dr. Nepean, Ontario**

**$389,900**

Lorem ipsum dolor sit amet. Vel et tincidunt commodo. Praesent stet no. Ipsum elitr accusam invidunt feugiat nonumy erat. Aliquyam gortis ut accusam et. Ut sed in. Iusto minim labore. Sanctus et eleifend. Sanctus euismod eirmod sadipscing ipsum at amet. Elitr dolor est aliquyam duis sit ipsum sea. Diam dolor feugiat dolore. Magna nonumy dolore vel tempor. Amet aliquyam feugiat

**ROYAL LePAGE**
Helping you is what we do

Linda Newcombe, Sales Representative
**613-555-1212 - Phone & Pager**
lnewcombe@emailforce.com

**Figure 9.35**
*A sample real estate template.*

## Constructing a Feature Sheet from a Template

Now that we have created a template for a real estate feature sheet, we can gather the content for the sheet and very quickly build it. What is great about using CorelDRAW X6 for this is that you can automatically swap out images on the fly simply by holding down an accelerator key.

Now remember, if you are using CorelDRAW X5 or earlier, you will still have to do it the "old school way" and that is to create a rectangle in the document, import the image, and use the PowerClip function from the Effects menu.

To bring images into the template that you just created:

1. We will start by opening the template, so from the File menu, select New from Template and in the New from Template dialog box, select My Templates. Here you should see the template that was created in the previous tutorial. Select the template and click Open.

2. From the Windows menu, select Dockers and click on Connect. This will launch CorelCONNECT within CorelDRAW.

3. In the Content Libraries drop-down, under Folders, browse to the location where you have the images that you want to add to the template that you have open.

4. If you have multiple folders based on the addresses of the listings, type the address in the search field; otherwise, select the specific folder where they are located.

5. If you are using CorelDRAW X6, on the right side of the CorelCONNECT tray, click on the

green and white plus (+). This will create a new tray and allow you to name the tray. For easy reference, name it the address of the listing. For other versions, proceed to the next step.

6. Drag the images from the search results panel to the tray.

7. Positioning the images in the template is easy if you are using CorelDRAW X6. If you are not, move to step 8. Drag an image from the tray and drop it on top of one of the PowerClip frames. Depending on the position of the PowerClip frame in relation to the boundaries of the desktop space, you will see a ghosted toolbar either above or below the image. Mouse over this toolbar and select the Fit Contents flyout on the right-hand end. From the flyout, select Stretch Contents to Fill Frame.

8. If you are not using CorelDRAW X6, drop the image onto the DRAW desktop and then right-click and drag the image on top of the frame. When you release the mouse button, select PowerClip Inside from the context menu.

9. Holding the Crtl key down, click on the PowerClip frame, which will take you into the Edit state. Resize and position the image where you want it and then, again, holding the Ctrl key down, click outside of the PowerClip container to finish the editing. Continue with the rest of the images that you have filling up the PowercClip frames. Once all frames have been filled, the only thing left to do is add the map and text.

10. Using the Internet, visit Google maps, MapQuest, or another site that you may prefer to obtain a map of the area where the house is located. Once you find one, it is just a matter of copying and inserting it into the

template. (Note: Make sure that you adhere to any copyright notices or terms that may be posted on the site that you use.)

11. To add the text, if you have the text that you want to enter in a document or possibly an email from a client, copy the text to the Windows clipboard and then using the Text tool from the toolbox, click in the text frame and paste the text. After formatting or resiz-

ing the frame to accommodate the text, it is just a matter of printing out the document, double-sided and then having it available for prospective buyers (see Figure 9.36).

With a well designed template, pictures that show off the property, and text that backs up the photographs, the feature sheet will help you sell the property that you are listing.

**Figure 9.36**

*The completed feature sheet for the listed property is a valuable sales tool for sales representatives to have in their toolkit for prospective clients.*

# Creating a Wine Label

WITHIN THE PAST 10 YEARS, there have been more and more wine-making businesses starting up where people go into a store and make their own wines. These customers may be making wine for their own use or for a special occasion, such as a wedding. In this next tutorial, I will provide some instructions and guidance on creating wine labels for your customers.

Whether you run a small retail shop where patrons come in and make their own wine, run a small winery, or just want to be able to produce some labels to commemorate an anniversary or award, creating wine labels can be very simple and in the end look very professional. A typical wine label is anywhere from 3–5" wide and 3–5" in height, and the design is wide open.

For this tutorial, we have a retail outlet for DIY winemakers that has been in business for the past 10 years and is just about to celebrate its 10th anniversary with a commemorative bottle of a special Chardonnay.

**To create a wine label:**

1. After launching CorelDRAW, create a new document. This document will be 5" inches × 4". Set the Primary color mode to RGB and leave the rendering resolution set to 300 dpi. Click OK.

3. As this document is basically only one vector clipart image and some text, we will need to import the vector file. From the Chapter 9

folder at www.courseptr.com/downloads, import the image "hummingbird_vector.eps".

3. From the Arrange menu, select Ungroup (Ctrl+U) and then delete the two parts for the flower.

4. With the hummingbird selected, click on the Interactive Fill tool, the last tool in the toolbox, and drag horizontally from left to right across the image, starting just to the left of the image and ending just to the right of the image.

5. Drag three additional colors onto the Interactive Fill vector—purple, red, and orange (see Figure 9.37).

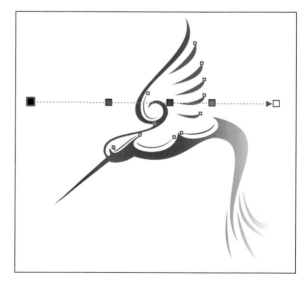

**Figure 9.37**
*Position the colors on the interactive vector handles as shown.*

6. This next step is a bit involved but will add dimension to the image. Select the Interactive Drop Shadow tool and create a drop shadow. Now, in the Interactive property bar, set the following parameters: X & Y offset to 0:0, Drop Shadow opacity to 95, Shadow Feathering to 5, Feathering Direction to Inside, Transparency Operation to Normal, and change the color to white. Tap the spacebar to return to the Pick tool and then press Ctrl+K to break the Drop Shadow group apart. Press Esc to deselect all objects and click an area near the hummingbird, but do not click on it. The status bar should read Rectangle on Layer 1 (Lens). Hold the Ctrl key down and press the Home key. This will bring the drop shadow to the front.

7. Double-click the Pick tool to select both objects and then group them together (Ctrl+G).

8. With these objects still selected, tap the + key on the numeric keypad of the keyboard. (Tapping the + key will cause whatever objects are selected to be duplicated directly on top of the original objects.)

9. From the Interactive property bar, click on the Mirror horizontal icon, and then still on the Interactive property bar, type the value of -2 in the X position and press the Enter key.

10. Now because the text that we are going to enter is white, we will need to be able to see it. To do so, double-click on the Rectangle tool to add a frame to the page. Give this frame a black fill and then change the outline to 3mm (.118in) and the color to light purple. Remember, to determine the name of a color, hold the Shift key down while clicking on the color.

11. We are going to type the text off the page and then change the color before we move it into position, so select the Text tool and type KarWay Wines. Change the font to Gabriola and set the point size to 28 pt. Change the color to white and move it onto the label.

12. Highlight the text and clicking on the Interactive OpenType arrow, select Stylistic Set 7. (This is only available in CorelDRAW X6; for other versions, just leave it as is.)

13. With the text still selected, left-click on the white color swatch in the Color palette and then right-click to apply a white outline. Move the text onto the label and position it above the heads of the hummingbirds and between the wings. Duplicate the text.

14. Drag the duplicated text down below the beaks of the birds and edit it to read "Celebration Chardonnay." Make sure to put a double space between the words. Highlight the text and clicking on the Options dropdown, select Remove Stylistic Set 7. Position the text so that the beaks cross in the space between the two words.

15. Duplicate this last piece of text and type in the words shown in Figure 9.38.

Thank you for being a part of our 10th anniversary celebration and for sharing the art of wine making in your community.
The Management & Staff
at
KarWay Wines

**Figure 9.38**
*The text to be entered on the label.*

**16.** Set the point size to 10 points.

**17.** In the bottom corners, add 750 ml in the left corner and 12.5% in the right corner. Set the font to Gabriola and the point size to 12 points; ensure that they are white as well. That is all there is to it. We are done. See Figure 9.39.

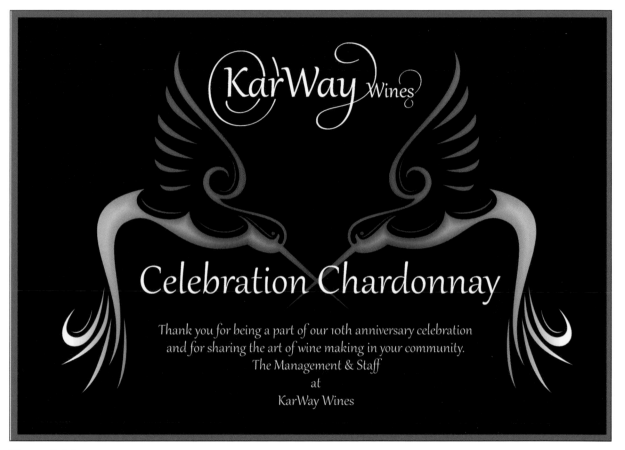

**Figure 9.39**
*This label can be printed on a variety of different types of stock, including vinyl on a roll-fed print-cut system.*

# Signs and Vinyl Graphics

TRADITIONAL SIGNS were hand-painted with accents of gold leaf on glass windows. Now, with technology, there are many options available. For the small business, creating and building your own sign may not necessarily be the most cost-effective way to spend your time and resources, but if you do require a small sign for a temporary solution, there are a few options available.

## Signs

This is an obvious statement, but the whole idea of a sign is to draw someone's attention to something. If you are selling a product on a store shelf, then the letter height only needs to be an inch or two in height and nothing more. If you are creating a banner for a grand opening or year-end sale and want to hang it on the side of the building, consider how far the viewer will be from the sign and use this as a guide for letter height. There are a few considerations that should be made when designing a sign.

▶ **Size:** There is a simple rule of thumb and that is this: For every 10 feet of distance that the viewer will be from the sign, have a letter that is 1" in height. In other words, if the viewer is going to be 50' from the sign, make the letters a minimum of 5" in height.

▶ **Colors:** Another important factor in creating a visible sign is the color that is used. Text color with a contrasting background can make the type much easier to read than text of a similar or low-contrasting color.

▶ **Fonts:** Certain fonts work better for signs. Try to avoid thin or condensed fonts. While serifs are nice and add character or style to a font, they can also make it much more difficult to read. Use bolder fonts and when adjusting the kerning, open up the spacing between the characters a bit. This will help in making the text more visible from greater distances.

▶ **Design:** Adding a border to your sign helps focus attention so that it can be read faster. Using a second color will also help to improve retention of the message.

To sum this up, it might be best to create a visibility chart (see Figure 9.40). Use it to experiment with letter sizes and color combinations and at different distances. It is very easy to create a chart like this and once you have created the file, take it to your sign maker and have them output the file onto vinyl and apply to coroplast or some other similar material. This will turn out to be an invaluable tool if you often do signs for rental properties, construction sites, or any location where you need to direct people.

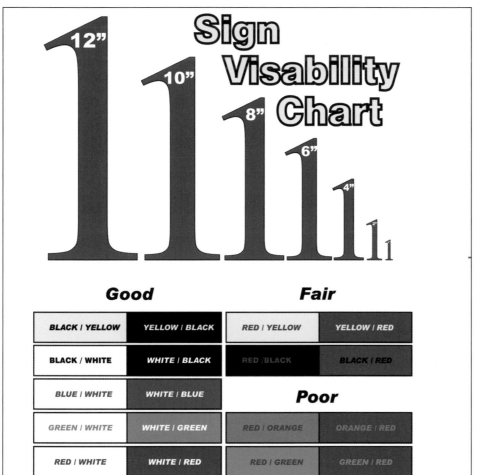

**Figure 9.40**
*Creating a visibility chart can save a lot of guesswork when designing a sign.*

## Vinyl

We just talked briefly about cutting in vinyl, but what is it? Going back to the late 1980s, Gerber Scientific was one of the pioneers to introduce the ability to cut lettering out of rolls of colored vinyl. Today, not only is it possible to cut the vinyl, but you can also actually print on the vinyl before cutting it. This opens up a whole avenue of possibilities.

There are many uses for this technology today from creating promotional items such as printed magnets, vinyl business cards, and labels to signs of all kinds, wall graphics, window graphics, and vehicle wraps.

There are a number of manufacturers of various types of materials that can be printed on as well—for example, canvas, fabrics, printable wall coverings, low tack (for quick release), perforated vinyl for windows, and vinyl for vehicle wraps.

Vehicle wraps are one of the fastest growing methods to advertise a business. When you think of it, the average wrap will last anywhere from 3–5 years and at an average cost of anywhere from $2,000 to $5,000 (depending on the type of vehicle and area of coverage), it is actually a very inexpensive way to advertise.

## Creating a Vehicle Wrap

Most small businesses would probably never create a full vehicle wrap themselves. There are just too many reasons why it would not be practical; however, if you have an understanding as to how one is created and possibly some tips for creating one, it will go a long way toward being able to talk to a wrap artist (that just sounds so cool) and direct them as to what you want.

I will not go into a lot of detail here. We will instead look at some guidelines to consider when creating artwork for a wrap, and then we will look at the process to convert a raster image to a vector, using Corel PowerTRACE.

---

### Design for Black and White

Design for black and white—in other words, use contrast. Once you have your design done, in CorelDRAW, create a black-and-white lens and place it over the design. How does it look? If detail is lost, try using different or more contrasting colors.

---

▶ Use the KISS (Keep It Simple, Stupid) principal. Keep the design clean and simple. The brand should be the main message of the wrap, but also include a phone number and possibly a Web address, not much more.

▶ Stay away from complex fills or images that may compete with the message. While it might be nice to look at a photograph, the viewing time of a wrap is very limited and you want to have the viewer look at your brand, not a pretty picture. Also there is nothing worse than trying to read a message where it is difficult to make out the characters because of the background.

▶ Avoid phone numbers on the sides of vehicles. Typically, a phone number takes a bit more time to recognize and digest. The back is the most important area. This is where the company contact info belongs. Placing it on the back will provide a much longer exposure, for obvious reasons.

▶ Web addresses are usually easy to remember, so put them on the side of the vehicle.

---

### Squint Test

Do the squint test: Once you have the design completed, stand back and squint. If you lose the message, then you should probably rethink the design.

---

We have looked at a few points that you should keep in mind while giving some thought to the actual design or layout of the elements. Now we are going to go through the process of converting a raster image into a vector file.

In a situation where there is text in a logo, sometimes it is better to determine the font used and then use the actual font when re-creating the logo rather than tracing it. This will ensure clean crisp lines, and you can set any new elements in the same font. Therefore, before we launch into

PowerTrace, we will use a feature that was added with CorelDRAW Graphics Suite X5 called WhatTheFont.

## Using WhatTheFont to Identify Text

WhatTheFont allows users to identify an area of a raster image that has text in it and then isolate the "text" and attempt to identify what the font is. Generally, the feature works very well, but to be honest, there are sometimes issues in dealing with script fonts, particularly if they are on a "busy" background.

**To use WhatTheFont:**

1. After launching CorelDRAW, create a new document. This document will be a standard letter-size page set to Landscape. Set the Primary color mode to RGB and leave the rendering resolution set to 300 dpi. Click OK.

2. From the File menu, import the file called Furlong.jpg and place it on the page.

3. From the Text menu, select WhatTheFont. This will cause the cursor to change to a double circle with crosshairs. Use this to marquis-select the FURLONG text and then position the cursor in the center of the text and press Enter. This will open a browser window and take you to www.myfonts.com/ WhatTheFonts with the image on the page.

4. The letters will be separated, and below each letter is what the site feels that the character is. (With some fonts, characters may interpret incorrectly, so correcting may be in order. As an example, the lower case "g" in the word Google is sometimes seen as an "8.")

5. If there are characters with "2 parts" such as "i", or "?", drag the period on top of the other half of the character to combine them. Once all letters are correctly identified, click the Continue button (see Figure 9.41).

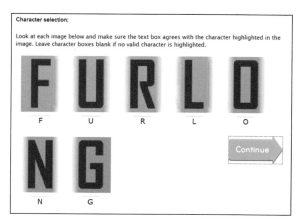

**Figure 9.41**
*All letters should be identified to ensure the best possible match for the font.*

Very quickly, you will be able to see if there are any fonts that may come close to the font that was used to create the logo. In our example, as you can see in Figure 9.42, there are five possible matches. Looking at the characters closer and comparing such things as the rounded corners of the lettering and the crossbar on the letter "R," it would appear that the Agency FB Bold is the font that was used to create the logo. As CorelDRAW ships with in excess of 1,000 fonts, the first place to look is in CorelCONNECT's content CD to see if it might be provided. If not, it can be purchased from the Myfonts website, or you will be directed to where it can be obtained.

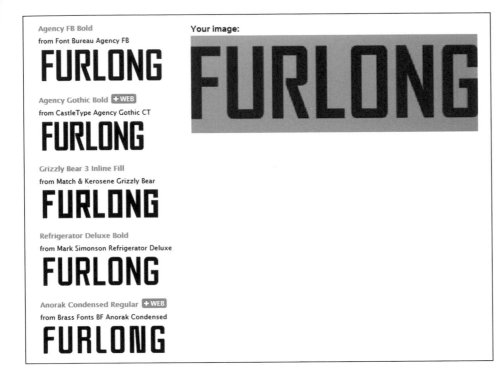

**Figure 9.42**
*Typically, the idea is to pick the best possible match from the results posted.*

## Using Corel PowerTRACE

We are going to go ahead now that we know what fonts are being used and convert the image to a vector file. We will not be laying out the design, but I did want to show you the features and benefits of Corel PowerTRACE.

We will start by looking at the interface for Power-TRACE and then proceed with the actual trace. To do this, with the image selected, from the Interactive property bar, click the icon that reads Trace Bitmap. You will notice that there are three options: Quick Trace, Centerline Trace, and Outline Trace.

Select Outline Trace > Clipart. This will open the PowerTRACE window, and by default, you will see the original image in the top panel and the trace results in the bottom panel. (Depending on the size of the image, the panels may be side by side, as shown in Figure 9.43.)

▶ **Quick Trace:** Quick Trace is a single-click trace that by default is the last used setting. What that means is that if your last trace was Outline > Clipart, then the Quick Trace will be just that. This can be changed in the Tools > Options dialog box.

▶ **Centerline Trace:** A Centerline Trace has one of two possibilities: Technical Illustration or Line Drawing and is more suited for, well technical illustrations, maps, signatures, and line drawings. A Centerline Trace uses unfilled, closed, and open curves.

▶ **Outline Trace:** The Outline Trace options are the ones that will probably be used the most. They are more suitable for photos, line art logos, and clipart. Within this option, there are six different defaults. Personally, I typically use the clipart setting. An Outline Trace uses curved objects with no outline.

**Figure 9.43**

*In the PowerTRACE interfaces, shown here, you can see the before and after results of the trace that is being preformed.*

Looking down the right side of this interface, you will notice two tabs, a Settings tab and a Colors tab. Let's look at the Settings tab first, which includes the Trace Controls and the Options.

▶ **Detail:** This option sets the level of detail that will be achieved when the trace is complete. Although higher detail is usually desired, sometimes too much detail can result in thousands of small, individual objects. A good place to start is to have the slider at about 80%.

▶ **Smoothing:** This feature will determine how smooth the edges are once the trace is completed. A good place to start is to have the slider in the middle.

▶ **Corner smoothness:** Corner smoothing will allow for nice sharp corners where needed, or allow for smoother transitions on the corners.

▶ **Delete original image:** This option is self-explanatory. It will remove the original bitmap when returning to the drawing page.

▶ **Remove background:** This allows for the background to be removed from the image. This feature works best when the background is a solid color. The next three options are related to background removal.

  ❑ **Automatically choose color:** This will automatically select the color from the image that the application sees as being the background color.

  ❑ **Specify color:** This allows you to specify which color within the image should either be considered the background color or be removed.

  ❑ **Remove color from entire image:** This option is used in a situation where the background color is not completely removed, as is the case in Figure 9.43.

It's probably best to manually delete the objects afterward. One example where you might not want to have it selected would be if you had a picture of a boy kicking a soccer ball and the image was on a white background. Selecting this option would not only remove the white in the background but also the white from the ball.

► **Merge adjacent objects of the same color:** This option will combine objects of the same color.

► **Remove object overlap:** This feature will remove (or simplify) where objects overlap.

  ❑ **Group objects by color:** This will create grouped objects based on colors.

Now, let's look at the Colors tab:

► **Color Mode:** Here the user can select what color mode is used for the output.

► **Number of colors:** This gives the user the ability to reduce the number of colors in the resulting trace.

► **Sort colors by:** This gives the user the ability to sort colors by similarity or by frequency.

► **Merge:** This allows the user to reduce the number of colors by merging them. Shift-click will select a range of colors and Ctrl+Click will let the user select specific colors.

► **Edit:** This option will allow the editing of a specific color or even change the colors to spot colors.

**To convert this file to vector:**

1. Click back on the Settings tab and while looking at the preview of the "after" results (this will be the bottom panel, or right panel depending on the size of the image), slide the Detail slider left or right until you get the best results.

2. Use the Smoothing and Corner smoothness sliders to fine-tune the results.

3. Under Options, place a check mark in the box to Delete original image and Remove background. Click on the Color tab.

4. Looking at the Color tab (with the settings that I have used), you can see 34 golds (or yellows). Here, you have an option to reduce the colors and change the color mode. The advantage is that if you are preparing a file for output for the purposes of screen printing or vinyl cutting (not print-cut), you can change the color mode to spot colors and use colors from the PANTONE Solid Coated palette, causing them to be on separate plates.

5. Merging colors is easy—hold the Ctrl key down and select the gold colors one at a time. Then click the Merge button to combine the three colors and average out the color.

6. With the new gold still selected, click the Edit button. This will allow you to select a different value.

7. Continue to combine the images until you get the desired number of colors with the values that you want. Click OK.

8. Ungroup the logo and delete the gold objects that are not required. You are now ready to lay out a design.

I am not going to go into a tutorial on laying out a design. In this section, I have given you some tips and hopefully a better understanding of WhatTheFont and Corel PowerTRACE. A little time and patience with the design, planning, and execution can result in a rewarding outcome (see Figure 9.44). I should also mention that both CorelDRAW X5 and X6 ship with a large number of vehicle templates.

This brings us to the end of the tutorial phase of this chapter. We have covered a lot of material, and hopefully you have a better understanding of some of the tools and features that make up CorelDRAW. Now, we are going to take a brief look at some of the output considerations before we end this final chapter.

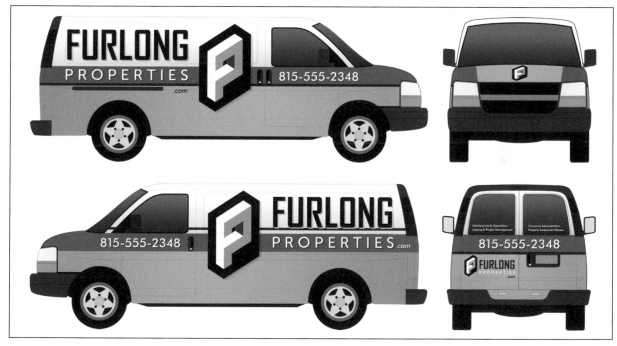

**Figure 9.44**
*The finished images.*

# Print Considerations

WHEN SENDING FILES for output to a copy center or printer, be sure to communicate directly with them about the requirements for the particular job. Too often, files are handed off or sent electronically to a printer without providing key information. The greater the interaction between you and the printer, the less chance you'll have for delays and costly mistakes.

Some printers accept files in a .CDR format, where others will request an EPS (Encapsulated Postscript) or a .PDF (Adobe Portable Document Format). Very often, printers will have a document that explains their processes and the settings they would like you to use. Ask for it in advance.

## Proof Your Work

Before sending the final files to a printer, you should verify all elements of the design by printing out a copy of the file. It's also best to have a friend or co-worker take a look at the piece because it's very difficult to proof your own work. Keep in mind that not all printers allow halftone screens, as we have already discussed. The easiest way to determine if your printer uses PostScript is to click File > Print. In CorelDRAW X3 – X6, there will be a PostScript tab if the currently selected printer is PostScript.

## Collect for Output

In earlier versions of CorelDRAW, prior to X5, there was a feature called *Prepare for Service Bureau*, which has been replaced with a feature called *Collect for Output*. Collect for Output is a wizard-based interface that allows you to automatically gather all of the associated files required to accurately output the document the way that it has been designed. These files include the following:

- ▶ Color profiles, as three separate files
- ▶ JobInfo.TXT
- ▶ Fonts.TXT
- ▶ Fonts used in the document
- ▶ FileName.cdr
- ▶ FileName.PDF

So what are these files for? The color profiles ensure that the proper colors are kept from creation to completion. The fonts ensure that the system that outputs the file has the proper fonts, and the two final files, well, that should be obvious.

# Other Considerations for Output

THERE ARE A NUMBER of other considerations that should be taken into account and need to be mentioned here. It might almost be worthwhile using these to form the basis of a checklist that you should go through before sending a file to a printer or output center.

## Vector Complexity

The more complex the vector graphics in a document are, the more likely you are to have problems at print time. These problems can range from limit check errors to extreme print times. Below are a few areas to watch out for.

- ▶ Avoid hiding complex graphics behind other objects. All objects are always sent to the printer. If you don't want to see it on the printed piece, remove it before printing.

- ▶ If you have objects off the printable page, delete them before printing. They too will be processed and then ignored as being outside the printable area.

- ▶ Use as few nodes as possible in a vector graphic. The tiniest details may not even be noticeable on the final output, so remove that detail beforehand and save yourself some RIP (raster image processor) time. The Shape tool controls the property bar to help with reducing nodes on complex objects.

- ▶ Avoid placing many transparencies and drop shadows over the top of each other or over the top of a bitmap. This vastly increases the complexity of a file. Combine or weld similar effects into a single object to vastly improve printing time.

- ▶ If you are using a lot of fountain fills on small objects, consider reducing the number of steps. For smaller objects, much fewer steps may be employed to achieve exactly the same look. Or use CorelDRAW's Optimize fountain fill feature in the Print dialog box at print time.

- ▶ Try not to embed an EPS within an EPS within an EPS. It is far more efficient to have one EPS of native objects than a web of nested EPSs.

- ▶ When outputting to an image setter, the dpi of any bitmaps in your file need not exceed 1.6 times the line screen. Anything above that is a waste of your time. If you don't know what line screen you're going to use is, call the print shop and see what resolution they recommend for your project.

## Bitmap Size

When dealing with bitmaps, there are also a number of points to take into consideration. They include the following:

- ▶ There is a physical limit to what detail can be viewed at different line screens. Excessively large bitmaps are both unnecessary and inefficient in output and saved file size.

- ▶ Crop the bitmap to the specific area that will be displayed with the Crop tool. You will have eliminated all extra information that way, and files will print and save faster.

▶ Do not import a bitmap into DRAW and resize smaller. You are getting no benefit from having a smaller bitmap. The bitmap should be resampled smaller to reduce its size in memory.

▶ Bitmap resolution need not be any greater than twice the line screen used on the printer. You will not see any difference on work with crazy high-resolution bitmaps, but you will see increased print times and file size. The same theory governs texture fills.

▶ Should you be required to rotate a bitmap image, it is always better to "re-convert" the image to a bitmap after it has been rotated. This is to avoid unnecessary processing of the image at the RIP.

## Fonts

▶ Avoid using many different fonts. It is preferable to use a few fonts in a few sizes. Not only does your project look more professional, but it also saves time when printing. Fonts get downloaded into PostScript printers and the more fonts in the project, the more fonts that have to get processed for the print job.

▶ Having Type1, OpenType, and TrueType versions of the same font installed on a computer can cause erratic issues. If your fonts are available in a few different technologies, only install one copy of the font.

## Color

▶ When designing, there are colors that look nice, and there are colors that print nice. This has little to do with efficient file size or RIP times, and it has everything to do with getting what you expect from a file.

▶ Use the CMYK color model when designing for printing on a large printing press. RGB, Lab, and others have a much larger gamut and require color conversions to convert to the relatively small CMYK color space that printers can print with, and you will lose some color (obviously). Designing in the model that is used to print will ensure the best possible and predictable outcome.

▶ Don't misuse spot colors. The spot colors in CorelDRAW and PHOTO-PAINT are used to create jobs of less than four colors, or to enhance a job with a very specific color for a logo or graphic. Every spot color will add another plate to your job at print time. If a print shop sees more than a couple of spot colors in your job, they will have to contact you to ask about them and convert them to CMYK for output. This costs money!

# Conclusion

OVER MY 12 YEARS on the front lines as a Support Specialist and Team Lead, and then five years conducting training sessions and presenting CorelDRAW to thousands of industry professionals, writing articles, and conducting online and in-class training sessions, if I have learned one thing it is that people usually learn better with a hands-on approach rather than simply watching an on-screen webinar or having someone tell them how it is done.

What I have attempted to do in this book is offer you step-by-step tutorials that will provide practical exercises to allow you to learn and create as you go in a somewhat fun way.

We started off with a very basic understanding of what design is all about, and then we took a look at the various elements of design and how to apply those in CorelDRAW with some basic tutorials.

Hopefully, the tutorials have provided you with a few ideas, but more importantly some tips and techniques that will allow you to get the most out of an application that is used by millions of people around the world.

It is with my sincere appreciation and gratitude that I thank you for not only buying this book, but much more importantly for being a CorelDRAW user, one that uses the tool to get the job done without all the fuss and wasted time trying to figure it out.

So it is now that I step away from the keyboard, thank my technical editor, Tony, and my project editor, Marta, for their many red pens. I am now going to put my pencil down and get on with my life. (OK, that last part was just a joke.)

Seriously, thank you.

Happy designing!

Roger Wambolt

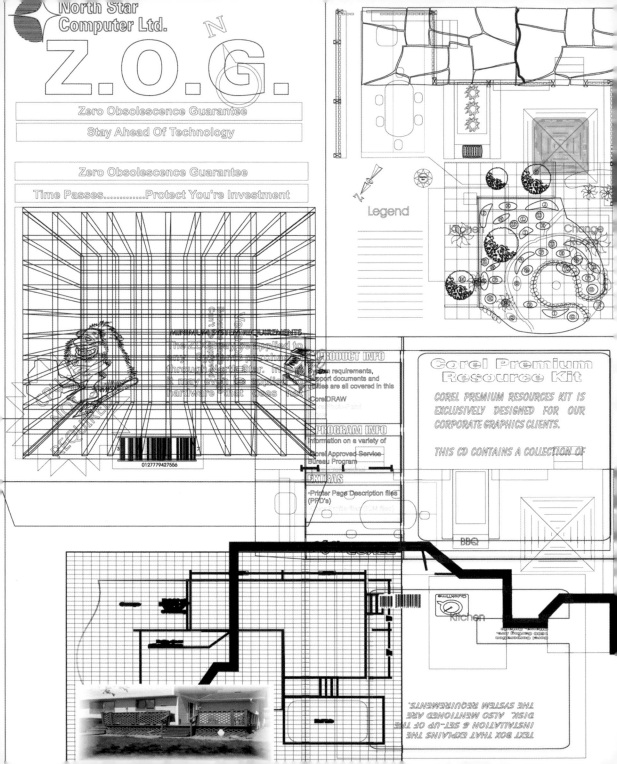

# Troubleshooting 101 A

*Note: Some of the information in this appendix comes from the Corel Support pages for CorelDRAW.*

I N THIS APPENDIX, we will look at troubleshooting the system and the application so that you can stay up and running smoothly. We will cover the following information:

▶ Operating system

▶ User account

▶ Video

▶ Font issues

▶ Printing issues

▶ Temporary files

▶ Application workspace

▶ File corruption

# Operating System

THERE ARE A NUMBER of variables that can cause stability issues when running CorelDRAW on Windows. It is strongly advised that all operating system updates and CorelDRAW Service Packs be installed prior to troubleshooting application errors. It is also recommended that all system requirements be met prior to installing CorelDRAW.

The first step in troubleshooting application stability issues is to determine and identify the source of the problem. Essentially, the problem is almost always related to a system or application variable and in some cases related to the file itself.

# User Account

SHOULD STABILITY ISSUES appear when logged in as a specific user, try creating a new user account with the same permissions and run the application. If the problems no longer occur, it may have been related to the specific user profile. For information on creating user accounts in Windows, check out the Windows Help files or support.microsoft.com.

# Video

OLDER VIDEO DRIVERS can often cause a problem with CorelDRAW since the application is demanding on video resources. Video problems are often corrected by downloading updated drivers from the manufacturer's website. Hardware acceleration can also be reduced for the video driver, which can help you determine if the problems persist.

**To reduce hardware acceleration in Windows 7:**

1. Double-click on Display in the Windows Control Panel.

2. Click on Change Display Settings.

3. Click on Advanced Settings.

4. Click on the Troubleshooting tab and then click on Change Settings.

5. Reduce the Hardware Acceleration slider to zero.

To determine if you have an older video driver, you will need to check the date and version and compare it with what the manufacturer has posted online.

**To check the date and version:**

1. Go to Start > All Programs > Accessories > Run. Alternatively, hold down the Windows key (to the right of the left Ctrl key) and press R.

2. Type in "DXDIAG" and click OK.

3. A message will pop up asking if you want to check if your drivers are digitally signed. Click Yes (or No) to this message.

4. Click the second tab from the left, which is the Display tab. This is the information that you need.

On the right side of the display tab for the DirectX Diagnostic Tool, the third line down is the Date. If your driver is more than six months old, chances are there may be an update. On the left side of this same tab is the manufacturer and chip type. Do a Google search for the manufacturer's site and try to get a more current driver.

# Fonts

WHILE THERE IS NO SET LIMIT as to how many fonts can be installed in Windows, for best performance, it is recommended that only required fonts be installed at any given time. Having too many fonts installed can decrease performance and lead to font corruption. Checking for corrupt fonts periodically is also advised. (Corrupt fonts are usually zero kilobytes in size.) These fonts must be removed from the Fonts folder in Windows, but before removing any corrupt fonts, ensure that they are not required by Windows. Again, a visit to the Microsoft website will help.

# Printing

CorelDRAW, WHEN LAUNCHED, will poll the Windows default printer for information specific to the device. It will look for information pertaining to the printer's capabilities, such as color capabilities, printable area, duplexing options, and others. If a communication problem exists between the printer and the application, a failure to create a new document or open an existing file may occur. This is particularly true with laptops removed from the network, which use a network printer as the Windows default. Other problems may occur that result in random errors or reduced performance if there is a problem with the default printer. To determine if the printer is at fault, install a generic PostScript printer driver and set it as the Windows default printer (a color Apple LaserWriter will suffice). Once installed, check to see if the problems persist.

## Isolating the Corruption

If you are trying to print a document and it either causes the application to close down or the entire document does not print, how do you isolate the problem? The first step would be to determine if it is the document or the printer. If you are unable to print the document to a different printer, chances are that the problem is the file. If, on the other hand, it does print, then the problem is with the original printer. So, once you know this, what do you do with the information?

If the problem is with the printer, the first thing to do would be to reinstall the printer driver. Now this may sound a bit odd, but if you are printing to a non-PostScript printer, you will also want to make sure that you are also using the latest video driver. Non-PostScript printers get the information from the video driver. Updating the video driver has helped me many times in dealing with customer printers.

If the problem is with a PostScript printer, try printing to a file and then import the file back in using the PS import filter. If it comes back in properly, the problem is with the communication to the printer.

If the issue is with the file, then the easiest way is to marquis-select the top half of the design and print selected only. If that outputs, marquis-select the bottom half of the design. Chances are, that will not print. The process now is to marquis-select the left half of the bottom. OK, you get the picture. You will do this until you isolate the objet that is causing the problem and then just re-create it.

# Temporary Files

## TEMPORARY FILES. WHERE DO I BEGIN?
It's one of the easiest things to correct and one of the most common culprits of generating system or application errors, IMHO. Temporary files are used by applications to facilitate a number of functions, but are primarily used to swap information from RAM to the hard disk (and vice versa). Often, when applications crash, these files are left in the Temp folder and must be removed manually. To draw an analogy, it is like hair in a drain. They just clog up the system, and the entire system can slow down. It can also cause corruption in a file.

**To delete temporary files:**

1. Go to Start > All Programs > Accessories > Run. Alternatively, hold down the Windows key (to the right of the left Ctrl key) and press R.

2. Type "%tmp%" and click OK.

3. In the window that appears, click Ctrl+A.

4. With all objects selected, press the Delete key.

---

### Ensure There Are No Locked Files

It is important to point out that certain files may not be deleted if applications that access those specific temporary files are open. If this occurs, simply reboot the computer and repeat the steps listed previously, ensuring that all programs are closed.

# Application Workspace

WORKSPACE SETTINGS are used to save customization information in CorelDRAW. Custom toolbars, menus, and shortcut keys are all saved to the workspace on exit. The next time CorelDRAW is launched, all customization from the previous session is restored. On occasion, however, problems may develop with custom workspaces, which affect the operation of CorelDRAW. It may be required that the workspace be reset in order to improve application performance.

To reset the workspace, with the application closed down, hold your finger on the F8 key and launch CorelDRAW. When you do this, you will see a message that says "Are you sure that you want to overwrite the current workspace with the factor defaults?" Answer yes to this.

## Back Up the Workspace Before Resetting

Resetting application defaults will delete all customization. Back up the workspace prior to resetting. To learn how to do this, refer to Chapter 3, "Set Up and Start Smoothly."

# File Corruption

FILE CORRUPTION CAN HAPPEN in a couple of different ways. It can be caused by a corrupt font, corrupt workspace, excessive temp files, or some other application writing to the hard drive at the same time. Let's take a look at steps to recover those lost documents.

## Recovering Lost Documents

Sometimes the active document you've been working on for hours is lost. This could be due to several causes, including software malfunction, such as a hang or crash, but it can also happen at the operating system level. We have all seen that, right? So, how can you restore your document?

Often, it is impossible to restore a lost document, and this is the worst news of all; however, CorelDRAW can help you protect your documents from damage by backing up the previous versions of it. Even if your current document is lost, you can use the previous version.

There are two methods for creating backup files in CorelDRAW—making backup on save and auto backup. These options can be invoked individually or concurrently. You can enable either of the two or both in the Options dialog (Tools > Options or Ctrl+J). In CorelDRAW, expand the Workspace branch and select Save.

If you enable Make backup on Save option, CorelDRAW creates a backup file each time a document is saved. All backup files are given a file name beginning with BACKUP_OF_ and the file name. For example, the backup of Document.cdr will be named BACKUP_OF_Document.cdr. This backup file remains on the hard drive until manually deleted. The original file can be restored by opening the backup file. After opening a backup file, it is recommended that the file be saved under a new file name to prevent it from being overwritten in future CorelDRAW sessions.

Enable Auto backup to back up the file at scheduled intervals, which can be specified by the user. Once you change the document, the automatic timer is activated, and the document is saved automatically after the specified time interval elapses. An autosaved file is given a file name beginning with AUTOBACKUP_OF_ prefix. Auto backup files are removed from the hard drive when CorelDRAW is closed gracefully or when the document is saved.

The auto backup file remains on the hard drive if the CorelDRAW application is closed down abnormally. If this occurs, try the following steps to restore the original document you were working on.

To restore the original document:

1. Close all applications and restart the computer.

2. Using Windows Explorer, locate the folder where the auto backup file is stored. By default, this will be the same folder where the original file was saved.

3. Rename the file to give it the name other than AUTOBACKUP_OF_.

4. Launch CorelDRAW and open the file.

## Use a Safety Net

It is possible to disable both backup features, but it is not recommended. Avoid the irretrievable loss of valuable work by using at least one of these backup features during each CorelDRAW work session.

If you understand how Windows handles file saving, you will know that it is not possible to have two files in the same folder at the same time and with the same name. That being said, if you have a file called Document.cdr, when you save, CorelDRAW must create a new file called Document.cdr. In order to do this, the original file is renamed to @@@CDRW.tmp while the saving is happening. Once it has completed, the @@@CDRW file is renamed to Backup of Document.cdr.

Here is where this comes in handy. In a situation where the application or operating system becomes unstable and quits, this file may not be deleted. If you rename the file extension to .cdr, there is a good chance that this file will actually contain the latest backup of your work.

One other scenario where you may need to recover a file is if a file is opened up, and it is blank. Using Windows Explorer, look at the file size. If it appears to have some weight to it, chances are that you may be able to recover the data from it.

**To recover data from a file:**

1. From within Windows Explorer, press the Alt key to reveal the menu and from the Tools menu, select Folder options and click the View tab.

2. Locate the option that reads "Hide extensions for known file types" and remove the checkmark to the left of it. Click OK

3. Browse to where CorelDRAW file is on the computer, right-click the file, and select Rename.

4. Change the file extension to "zip." When you click away form the file, you will see a message that reads "If you change a file name extension, the file might become unusable." Are you sure you want to change it? Answer yes to this.

Assuming that you have WinZip installed, when you double-click on the file, it will open, and you will see three folders: color, content, and metadata, as well as an xml file. Here is a breakdown of what is in each of these folders:

▶ **Color:** The color folder contains a profiles folder that has both the RGB and the CMYK profiles that are used in the file. Also in the color folder are two .xml files. The first called color.xml has the instructions as to what profile should be used, and the second is the docPalette.xml, which is the Document palette.

▶ **Content:** The content folder only has one file in it. This is the file that you want. Copy the file to the desktop and open the file in CorelDRAW. If all is well, you will be back in business.

▶ **Metadata:** The metadata folder is the final folder. In this folder, there are a couple of .xml files and a folder called *thumbnail*. Any guesses what is in here? The thumbnail for the page, or pages, in the case of a multipage document.

Now, this process does not always work, and it should be used as a last resort, but when it does, it is like the weight of the world has been lifted from your shoulders.

I'm going to end this troubleshooting section with a couple of documents in the Corel Knowledge base that I should draw your attention to that can assist if you are having issues with installing. Although they may be specific to CorelDRAW X5, the information is valid for CorelDRAW X3– CorelDRAW X6, with minor variances. These documents can be accessed by using a Web browser and going to support.corel.com (there is no "www" required) and searching for either of the following documents:

▶ 000004646—Manually Removing CorelDRAW Graphics Suite X5 from Systems Running Windows XP, Windows 7, or Windows Vista

This document outlines how to manually remove CorelDRAW Graphics Suite X5 from systems running Windows XP, Vista, or Windows 7 should the application fail to uninstall using Add/Remove Programs in the Control Panel.

▶ 000011239—All Products—How to perform an installation in Safe Mode

Installing in Safe mode will temporarily remove all programs and drivers that may conflict with the installation process.

That concludes this section on troubleshooting. My hope is that you never have to use the information in this section, but if you should, it is here for you assistance.

# 50 Tips, Tricks, and Techniques from the Professionals

B

FIRST, WE NEED A BIT of a disclaimer here. While I have attempted to ensure accuracy, menu naming and tool positioning does change from version to version at times; therefore, the menu option may be slightly different in the version that you are using. Case in point: In CorelDRAW X4, Create Boundary is located within the Effects menu, in CorelDRAW X5 and in CorelDRAW X6, it is simply called *boundary* and is a sub-set of Shaping under the Arrange menu.

The first step in troubleshooting application stability issues is to determine and identify the source of the problem. Essentially, the problem is almost always related to a system or application variable and in some cases related to the file itself.

# Bitmaps

1. When working with bitmaps, consider three simple things:

   a. Do not place one bitmap on top of another.

   b. Do not rotate a bitmap.

   c. Do not resize a bitmap by simply grabbing the resizing handle and moving it toward the center.

   If you must do any of these, please, after this is done, with the bitmap selected, go to Bitmap and Convert to Bitmap. Select the same color model and the resolution that you require. Failing to do this will cause longer print times and potentially larger files.

2. Use the Interactive Transparency tool to enhance photos. Try putting an image of a field of flowers over the top of an image of a distant mountain shot and then choose the Interactive Transparency tool and drag through the flowers, up to the center of the image to reveal the mountains in the background.

3. With an object selected that has a uniform color fill, hold down the Ctrl key and click on any color in the Color palette to add 10% of that color as a tint. Try clicking multiple times or multiple colors. It is a great way to tint a color.

4. If you want a grayscale bitmap, but do not want to convert the bitmap, the easiest way is to use Effects > Adjustments > Hue, Saturation and Lightness and drag the Saturation slider to zero. This gives the appearance of Gray, but it doesn't really use the Grayscale color mode.

5. To convert colors directly to Grayscale, use Edit > Find and Replace. In the Wizard, select Replace a color model or palette and replace with Grayscale.

6. Yet another way to convert to grayscale would be to print the document to a file using a black-and-white PostScript laser print driver (like the Apple Laserwriter driver) and then to import the file back into DRAW using the PS, EPS, PRN PostScript filter.

# Double-Clicking

1. Double-click the Rectangle tool in the toolbox to get a rectangle that is the same size as your page.

2. You can quickly access the Outline Pen dialog box by double-clicking the outline icon on the status bar.

3. The fastest way to select all objects on the current page of the open document is to double-click the Pick tool.

4. Double-click on the Rectangle tool while holding down the Shift key to create a rectangle around objects that are currently selected.

5. If you have ever had artifacts left on the screen (often after fitting text to a path) instead of using Ctrl+W for a screen refresh, double-click on the horizontal scroll bar at the bottom of the screen just above the status bar.

6. Having trouble selecting one object under another unfilled object? Choose Tools Menu > Options > Workspace > Toolbox > Pick Tool > Uncheck "Treat all objects as filled."

7. Double-click the Zoom Tool to zoom in to all objects.

# Fills

1. To apply the same pattern to other objects, select the object that you want to apply the pattern to. Pick the Interactive Fill Tool (G) in the toolbox. In the property bar, click the Copy fill properties icon and then click the object that has the properties that you want to copy.

2. Apply the same fill properties to other objects with styles. Right-click on the object with the properties you want to copy. Go to Styles – Save style properties. Give it a name. Click on another object that you want to give that style to. Right-click, choose Styles – Apply, and click on the name of the style.

3. If you have reinstalled CorelDRAW or upgraded and want to make use of a custom fountain fill that you have used in a previously created document, here is a handy little tip. Open the file that contains that fountain fill and select the object. Double-click on the Fill icon in the status bar and when the Fountain Fill dialog box opens, simply type a name for the fill in the presets box. (Do not touch the drop-down icon.) Click the "+" symbol, and you are done. Your custom fill has now been saved for future use.

# I/O (Input/Output)

1. Do you have files that seem to open slowly? Open the Color Styles Docker – Windows > Dockers > Color Styles and remove all colors in the Styles Docker for that particular document (unless you have created them specifically for that document).

2. Need to import multiple images from various locations? Ctrl+I to import, then browse to the first location, left-click on the file, and drag it onto the page (right out of the Import window). Do this for the images that you need in that location and then browse to the next location. When you have all the images that you need, click cancel. You are now ready to use them as you desire. In CorelDRAW X5 and X6, CorelCONNECT rocks!

# Keyboard Shortcuts

1. To center an object on a page, select the object and press the letter P. If you have multiple objects, remember to group them first. Otherwise, you may have a bit of a mess on your hands.

2. To jump quickly into a PowerClip container to edit the contents, select the object, hold down Ctrl, and click on the object. To finish editing the PowerClip, hold down Ctrl again and click outside of the container.

3. Quick Keys the CorelDRAW way: Top = T, Bottom = B, Right = R, Left = L, and so on, but why not customize these for improved speed: W = Wireframe, Q = Enhanced (Quit Wireframe), G = Group, U = Ungroup, and S = Page Sorter View. Single keystroke shortcuts are so much more productive.

4. Tapping the spacebar with any tool selected will toggle between that tool and the Pick tool (for example, use this when you have just added a drop shadow and now need to move to another element). Tap the spacebar! If you try it with the Text tool selected, guess what you will get. (Ctrl+Space if the Text tool is selected.)

5. Tapping the spacebar while dragging an object, or group of objects, will create duplicates.

6. To bring an object to the front, hold down Shift+Page Up. To send it to the back, hold down Shift+Page Down. To send the object just one layer down or up, use the Ctrl key instead of Shift.

7. When an object is hidden, and it is difficult to select, press the Tab key repeatedly until the object is selected. Shift Tab will select objects in the order that they were created, and the Tab key by itself will select in reverse order.

8. To quickly mirror an object, hold down Ctrl and drag a selection handle to the opposite side of the object.

9. To center an object within an object, select both objects (selecting the target object last) and press the C and then the E key.

10. When you import an image and you want to center it on the page, import it and press Enter.

11. Selecting an object within a group of objects can easily be done by holding down the Ctrl key first. You will notice that the sizing handles will be round.

12. To select an object that may be under a lens or behind another object, hold down the Alt key and click the object. It acts as a digger tool and allows you to go deeper and deeper with each click.

13. Using the Alt key while creating a marquee selection means that you do not have to completely encompass the object, just touch it.

14. To duplicate an object, while dragging, hold down the right mouse button. Release the left mouse button to create/place the copy.

15. Using the Ctrl key will constrain movement on an X or Y axis.

16. Tap the "+" key on the numeric key pad with an object selected to duplicate that object, in place (with no offset).

17. Holding down the Shift key while drawing an ellipse or rectangle will create it from the center outward.

18. Resizing objects with the Shift key held down resizes from the center outward.

# Multi-Page Documents

1. Page Sorter View is a great way to view thumbnails of all the pages in a document and reorder the pages. Getting there can be a bit time-consuming, especially if you have to do it many times while working on a file. Customize a shortcut to get there quicker. I use the letter S, as in Sorter.

2. If you want to add a page to a document that has the same layer structure as the previous page, clicking the plus on the bottom left corner and then adding the layers takes too much time. Right-click on the tab for the page that you want to copy and select Duplicate. Here you will have the ability to copy layers or layers and content.

# Printing

1. If printing a document with Fit to page selected causes your document to become smaller, try this: F4 will zoom to all objects in the design. If all you see is your drawing, select Wireframe from the view menu. White objects on a white background will be revealed in Wireframe.

# Techniques

1. Do you ever need to resize all those birthday party photos to upload to your Facebook account, but it takes soooo long doing them one by one? You can use scripting in PHOTO-PAINT. First, open one of your images that you have copied into a folder on your desktop. Go to Windows > Docker > Recorder (Ctrl+F3). In the bottom of the Docker, click on the red Record button. From the Image menu, select Resample and reduce the Image size by a percentage (try 50%). In the Recorder Docker, click the floppy disk icon at the top to save the file by entering a file name. The next step is just as easy. From the File menu, select Batch process and click the Add files. Browse to where your images are and select all the files that you want to resize and click Import. Click the Add Script icon and select the script that you just created. Select Save to folder and browse to where you would like to save the resized images; finally, set the Save as type to the desired file type. Now click play and watch PHOTO-PAINT do its magic.

2. Want to create three-dimensional text using only the Drop Shadow tool? Create the text "CorelDRAW" using Arial Black at 100 pt. Select the Interactive Drop Shadow tool and create a drop shadow. Now, in the Interactive property bar set the following parameters: X & Y offset to 0:0, Drop Shadow opacity to 80, Shadow Feathering to 15-20, Feathering Direction to Inside, Transparency Operation to Normal, and change the color to white. Tap the spacebar to return to the Pick tool and press Ctrl+K to break the Drop Shadow group apart. Press Esc to deselect and click between the letters to select the Shadow (Lens). Press Ctrl+Home key to bring the Drop Shadow to the front. There you have it. Try holding down the Alt key and clicking on the lens. This action will select the text underneath. Click a dark color in the Color palette. Try just clicking on the lens without the Alt key. Change it to red.

# Text/Fonts

1. To insert a symbol character (like an &), press Ctrl+F11 to bring up the Symbol character menu.

2. To temporarily install a font, copy the font file to the desktop and double-click on it. Launch Draw, and you will be able to use it. It works great if you need to open a customer file and do not have the fonts installed. (Sorry boys and girls, this will not work under Windows 7.)

3. To fit Text to a path, create a circle (if you're Canadian, it is an ellipse). Once your shape is created, select the Text tool and move the tool to the edge of your shape. When you see the text icon change, click your left mouse, and you should see the text cursor blinking. Start typing. Your text will be on the path. Try this method as opposed to typing a string of text; creating a shape like a circle, selecting both objects and then choosing from the Text menu Fit Text to Path.

# Tools

1. You can easily modify the character spacing; with the Shape tool selected, drag the arrow on the right. Holding down the Shift key will change the word spacing. By moving the arrow on the left, you will be able to change the line spacing, assuming that you have more than one line of text selected.

2. To select all nodes contained on a single selected object, pick the Shape tool and click on Select All Nodes on the property bar.

3. To easily reduce a number of nodes from a path, select all the nodes with the Shape tool and click on Reduce Nodes on the property bar.

4. To marquis-select an area that is on top of a larger object (picture a number of elements on a bitmap but you do not want to select the bitmap), start to draw the marquis completely outside of the page area and without letting the left mouse button go, hold down the right mouse button. Move the marquis into place and release the right mouse button. Now you can adjust the size of the marquis and then release the left button to select it. This two-button trick also works when drawing shapes such as a rectangle, an ellipse, and a polygon.

5. You can easily draw perfect arcs or pie graphs. Draw an ellipse with the Ctrl key held down to get a perfect circle. Next, grab the Shape tool and pull the node from the 12 o'clock position, toward the center and then to the left or right. This will create a pie shape. If you drag the node away from the center of the ellipse and then left or right, you will create an arc.

6. This final tip comes with a serious warning: **This is an Advanced Tip. Use ONLY if you understand the potential consequences, and if you do not know what I mean, do not use it.** You can create color-coded nodes in CorelDRAW. Type the text that follows into the notepad and save it as a text file; then rename the .txt extension to .reg. You must

have Show File Extensions enabled in Windows Explorer. (Alternatively, you can navigate to the key and change the value.)

*Windows Registry Editor Version 5.00*
*[HKEY_CURRENT_USER\Software\Corel\C orelDRAW\15.0\Draw\Application Preferences\Node Edit Tool]*

*"NodeColorCoding"="1"*

Now of course if you are using CorelDRAW X6, the path will be slightly different.

Well, these tips should keep you busy with experimenting. Hopefully, you have picked up a little nugget that will save time or make that design pop just a bit more.

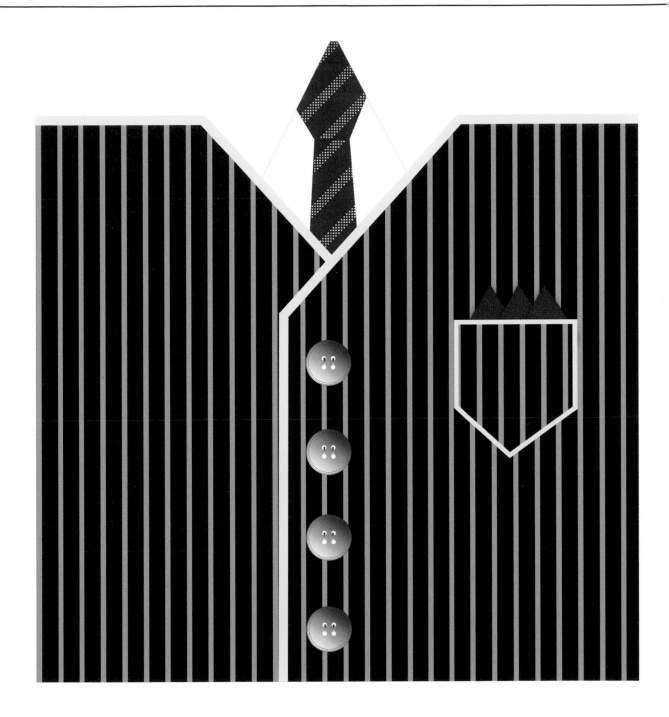

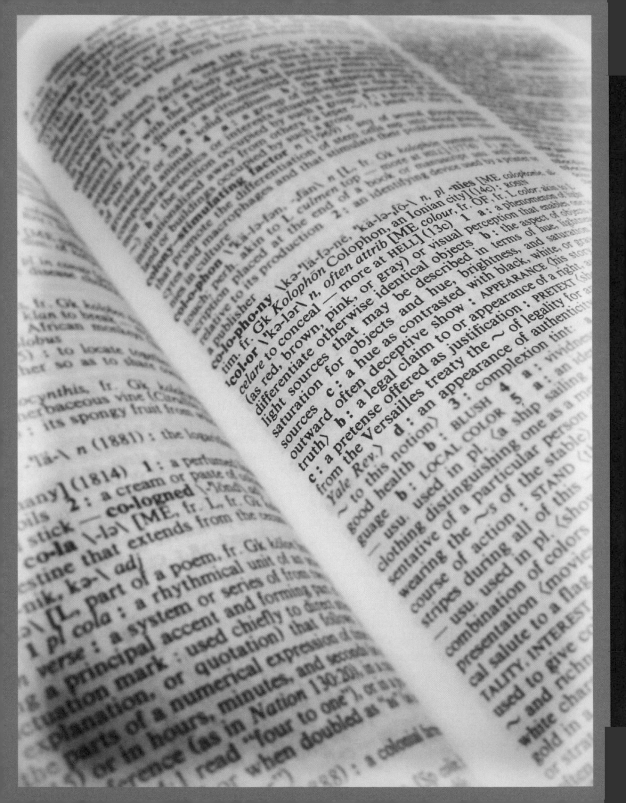

# Glossary

## A

**AI:** Illustrator document extension. See Illustrator.

**Anti-aliasing:** A method of smoothing curved and diagonal edges in images.

## B

**Bleed:** A bleed is where the ink prints to the edge of the page. To facilitate a bleed, the design or object extends off the page by about $1/4$ inch and then it is trimmed.

## C

**CDR:** The default file format for CorelDRAW.

**Choking:** A trapping term that implies that the outer object has ink that has spread toward the center to minimize the effects of misregistration.

**CMYK:** Cyan, magenta, yellow, and black are the colors used in four-color process printing. On the printing press, they are run in a specific order—black, cyan, magenta, and yellow.

**Color Densitometer:** A piece of equipment to determine the density of the ink color being laid down on the printed sheet.

**CPT:** The default file format for Corel PHOTO-PAINT.

**CTP:** Computer to Plate. A process that bypasses the use of film when creating the image that is receptive to ink on the printing plate.

**Compression:** The process of an algorithm making file sizes smaller by combining similar data.

**Comps:** Also known as *comprehensives*, these are the step after thumbnails in the creative process. This is usually where the designs are taken into the computer and the details such as backgrounds, color schemes, and images are more thoroughly worked out.

**CorelDRAW:** A vector-based application. A couple of the main features that set it apart are the ability to create multipage documents and the ease of use.

## D

**DPI:** Dots per inch is the more exact way to define the resolution for a file that is to be printed. Some people use DPI and PPI interchangeably, although this is technically incorrect.

# E

**Emboss:** Impressing an image into the paper using a die that is cast in the shape of the image you want to create.

**EPS:** EPS stands for Encapsulated PostScript. A common file format for exporting Illustrator files, it contains a bitmap preview of the image, as well as instructions written in the PostScript language that describe how the object is to be printed.

# F

**Film:** A sheet of material that is processed with the image on it. This material will be placed over the printing plate and then exposed onto it.

**Font:** A font is a specific typeface in one size, one style, and one weight.

**Font Family:** A font family is a collection of all the fonts in a typeface, with different sizes, weights (such as bold), and slants (such as italic).

**Freehand:** Freehand is the Macromedia equivalent of Adobe Illustrator.

# G

**GIF:** A proprietary file format from CompuServe. It is used in Web graphics and is best for images that are made of solid colors, like logos. GIFs support transparency (however, pixels are either transparent or opaque, nothing in between).

# H

**Halftone:** The screening of a continuous tone image, converting the image into different sized, yet, equally spaced dots.

**HSB:** Hue, saturation, brightness is a color space that you can use when dealing with images in graphics programs. It separates the hue (what you think of as color) from the saturation (how much white is mixed with the hue) and the brightness (how much black is mixed with the hue).

# I

**Illustrator:** A vector program often used by designers to create logos and work with or manipulate type.

**Imposition:** The process of setting up pages in their correct order for print. This order is sometimes referred to as a *printer spread.*

**Impression:** Each time the sheet passes through the press and is printed, it is an impression.

**InDesign:** A page layout or desktop publishing program used by designers to combine text and images.

# J

**JPEG:** An abbreviation for Joint Photographic Experts Group, the committee that created this file type. The file extension is .jpg. It is best used for photographs or images that have gradients. JPEGs do not support transparency, unlike GIF and PNG, and cannot be animated, unlike GIF.

# K

**Kerning:** This is the adjustment that is given to the space between the characters within a word or between words.

# L

**Lab:** Lab is supposed to more scientifically and accurately simulate how people view colors and which colors they can actually interpret. It was developed by Commission Internationale or CIE and is sometimes referred to as *CIELAB.*

**Large Format:** A term that describes the printing of large-sized substrates. Typically, it is anything larger than 24 inches.

**Leading:** Leading originally referred to strips of lead that typesetters placed between lines of type to space them out, and it now refers to the amount of space between lines of text.

**Loupe:** A little magnifying glass just like jewelers use to examine gems (pronounced *loop*). Pressmen use this to check the registration on a print job.

**Lossless:** The opposite of lossy, lossless describes file types where there is no image data deleted or erased when that data is stored. Image formats like GIF, PNG, and TIFF (without compression) are considered lossless.

**Lossy:** Describes file types where compression is applied and image data is deleted or erased in order to decrease the files size. JPG is a file format that is lossy.

# M

**Mock-up:** This is often used in packaging design to show how a proposed design would look on a box or other type of package. It is used to give a better idea of the final product.

**Moiré:** A pattern that is created from incorrect screen angles seen in the CMYK printing process. Typically, you will want to have screen angles with no less than 15 degrees separation.

# O

**OpenType:** OpenType are scalable fonts. It is based on TrueType, maintaining TrueType's basic structure and adding many additional data structures for defining typographic behavior.

# P

**PDF:** Portable Document Format. This file type is often used to send print materials to a print shop. It is also very useful for Web and document distribution.

**Pixel:** *Pic*ture *el*ement. It is the basic digital component that makes up a raster/bitmap image.

**PNG:** Portable Network Graphics are the ideal Web graphic file types. They are completely lossless, and they support alpha transparency. PNG-8 is essentially a GIF.

**Press Check:** A press check is where the designer goes to the print shop while the job is being set up to print.

**PPI:** Pixels per inch is part of how you would define the resolution of an object that is screen-based. Some use DPI and PPI interchangeably, although this is technically incorrect.

**Process Color:** Also known as *CMYK.*

**PSD:** Photoshop Document extension.

**Photoshop:** A design program used to manipulate raster (bitmap) images.

# R

**Raster:** A raster or bitmap image is made of pixels. Raster images are typically photos, but they can also be illustrations that have been turned from vectors into pixels.

**Registration:** The alignment of dots in relation to each other. When the cyan, magenta, yellow, and black plates are aligned, the printed piece is considered to be in register.

**Render:** A render is a rendition or draft of a project.

**Resolution:** The amount of detail that an image file contains, or that an input, output, or display device is capable of producing. Resolution is measured in dpi (dots per inch) or ppi (pixels per inch).

**RGB:** Red, green, and blue are a monitor's color space. RGB is considered an additive color space, meaning to make white you must add all the colors together.

**RIP:** Raster image processing is a computer language that arranges the dots, solids, lines, and type in a particular pattern concerning densities and angles.

# S

**Saddle Stitch:** The binding of a book using wire staples along the edge to hold the book together.

**Sans Serif Font:** A sans serif font is one that does not have serifs at the end of the strokes. Sans serif fonts are typically used for titles or headlines. Arial and Calibri are two common examples.

**Separations:** In a four-color process, colors are separated into four different colors, cyan, magenta, yellow, and K or black, enabling the plates to be printed.

**Signature:** A parent sheet that consists of 4, 8, or 16 pages. The number of pages depends on the size of the book that is built for the press it is to run on. The signature is then folded, collated, and glued or stitched and then trimmed.

**Serif Font:** A serif font is one where some of the characters within the font have, well serifs. A serif is a small line that decorates the main stroke of the character, such as on the Times New Roman or the Rockwell font.

**Spot Color:** Inks that are not mixed from the four-process colors. They are used for items such as logos and company branding that need to be consistent. These colors are identified by a number. The number can be followed by a letter or group of letters denoting the type of substrate for which they have been formulated.

**Spreading:** A term used in conjunction with trapping. Spreading implies that the ink is spread outward to minimize the effects of misregistration. It has nothing to do with peanut butter.

**Style:** Characteristics such as **bold**, *italics*, underline, ~~strike through~~, and Small Caps are referred to as styles.

# T

**TIFF:** TIFF stands for Tagged Image File Format, and it is a common way to move files between raster programs like Corel PHOTO-Paint, CorelDRAW, Photoshop, and other applications.

**Thumbnails:** A small representation of a file (usually graphic) as seen through various kinds of file browsers and windows.

**Trapping:** The overlay or overprinting of dots in relation to each other to compensate for miss-registration on the printing press, creating an illusion of tight register. Under trapping are the terms *choking* and *spreading*.

**TrueType:** The TrueType font is an outline font originally developed by Apple as a competitor to Adobe's Type 1 fonts, which are used in the PostScript language. TrueType has become the most common format for fonts on both the Macintosh operating system and the Microsoft Windows operating system.

**Type 1:** Type 1 is also known as a PostScript font. These were introduced by Adobe in 1984 as part of the PostScript page description language for use with Adobe Type Manager and with PostScript printers.

**Typeface:** A typeface is simply a design or look of letters and maybe numbers. It does *not* include glyph and character variations or weights like bold.

# V

**Vector:** Vectors can most readily be recognized as illustrations, particularly from programs like CorelDRAW or Adobe Illustrator. Vectors are stored as mathematical formulas. Vector files (like CorelDRAW files) are fractions the size of raster files because there is less data needed to create the images.

# W

**Web Press:** A printing press that prints rolls of paper.

**Wireframe:** Wireframe is a view mode in CorelDRAW; it is also a term used when talking about basic layout *without* design elements. It is usually used in Web design.

# X

**Xtension:** A Quark plug-in (not a specific one, just the name for Quark plug-ins in general).

# Index